ALICE MEYNELL

ALICE MEYNELL

from an etching by Tristram Ellis
after a water-colour drawing by Adrian Stokes, 1877

ALICE MEYNELL
A Memoir

by

VIOLA MEYNELL

JONATHAN CAPE
THIRTY BEDFORD SQUARE
LONDON

FIRST PUBLISHED SEPTEMBER 1929
SECOND IMPRESSION NOVEMBER 1929
REISSUED IN
THE LIFE AND LETTERS SERIES
1933
REISSUED IN THIS EDITION 1947

PRINTED IN GREAT BRITAIN
BY J. AND J. GRAY, EDINBURGH
BOUND BY A. W. BAIN AND CO. LTD., LONDON

CONTENTS

TO
MY FATHER

A DICKENS FRIENDSHIP

CHRISTIANA WELLER and Thomas James Thompson, the
future mother and father of Alice Meynell, had an early
friendship with Charles Dickens, who even presided over
their destinies.

"I cannot joke about Miss Weller, for she is too good;
and interest in her (spiritual young creature that she is,
and destined to an early death, I fear) has become a
sentiment with me. Good God, what a madman I
should seem if the incredible feeling I have conceived
for that girl could be made plain to anyone!" Thus
did Dickens in 1844 unburden himself to his friend
Thompson after their joint meeting with Christiana
Weller. The two friends, Dickens and Thompson, had
gone together to Liverpool, where Dickens was to speak
at the opening of a new Mechanics' Institute, and there it
was that the pianist of the evening, young and beautiful
and a brilliant player, so affected Dickens. The next day,
after calling, still with Mr. Thompson, at her home, he
wrote:

"My dear Miss Weller, – Riding out to you to-day
– the horse's name is not Pegasus – I conceived
the idea of putting this piece of doggerel in your

album. But you do nothing like anybody else and therefore did not produce one. So I send it now. Faithfully yours ever, CHARLES DICKENS."

LINES FOR MISS C. WELLER'S ALBUM

I put in a book once by hook and by crook
  The whole race (as I thought) of a 'feller'
Who happily pleased the town's taste much diseas'd,
  And the name of this person was Weller.

I find to my cost that *one* Weller I lost, –
  Cruel destiny so to arrange it!
I love her dear name which has won me some fame,
  But, Great Heaven, how gladly I'd change it.

So the "joke about Miss Weller" he had said he could not make was made; – but the touch of the sentimental was duly restored. As soon as he reached London again, two Tennyson volumes were sent to her, and this letter to her father:

1st March, 1844   *1 Devonshire Terrace, Regent's Park*

"My dear Sir, – Finding that your daughter had not read the volumes which I send her in the enclosed parcel (from one of which I quoted a few words last Monday night); and knowing that they could not but prove most acceptable to such a mind as hers, I obtained her permission to send them – and made a promise which it gives me real pleasure and delight to fulfil.

"Will you tell her that I have marked with a pencil,

in the index to each, those pieces which I would like her to read first – as being calculated to give her a good impression of the Poet's genius? And will you say that I have sent her a copy which is not quite new, in preference to a new one: hoping she might like it none the worse for having been my companion often, and for having been given to me by Tennyson himself?

"I scarcely know whether I do right or wrong in not closing my note to you here. But I cannot help saying to you that your daughter's great gifts and uncommon character have inspired me with an interest which I should labour in vain to express to you, though I set myself to it as to a task. I see many people, as you may suppose; and many whom Nature has endowed with talents of one kind or another. The figures which come and go before me are so numerous, and change so constantly, that however bright they may be I am not accustomed to care much for them, or to feel any great degree of concern in their proceedings. But I read such high and such unusual matter in every look and gesture of the spiritual creature who is naturally the delight of your heart and very dear to you, that she started out alone from the whole crowd the instant I saw her, and will remain there always in my sight.

"Your affection will not be displeased to hear this, I know. And therefore I disregard the singularity of the impression or lose it in the singularity of the cause – and tell you the honest truth. With cordial remembrances to Mrs. Weller and all your family, believe me always faithfully yours, CHARLES DICKENS."

3

Other letters from Dickens concerning Christiana show a generous and romantic urgency for her happiness, while at the same time they discover the Author, gladly dealing with emotions. Dickens left his friend Thompson behind in Liverpool, from whom came surprising news. Dickens replied:

"My dear Thompson, – I swear to you that when I opened and read your letter this morning (I laid down my pen to break the seal, being just shut up in my own room) I felt the blood go from my face to I don't know where, and my lips turn white. I never in my life was so surprised, or had the whole current of my life so stopped for the instant, as when I felt, at a glance, what your letter said. Which I did, correctly. For when I came to read it attentively, and several times over, I found nothing new in it.

"This was not because it contained a word to astonish *me*, but because I had never imagined you remaining in Liverpool; or seriously admiring her. Forgive me when I say that I did not think it lay in your temper or habit to do so unless it had become a thing of pretty long custom. I supposed you had returned to Yorkshire – I expected you in town any day – and have often wondered within myself whether you would still have an interest in recalling, with me, her uncommon character and wonderful endowments. I know that in many points I am an excitable and headstrong man, and ride, oh God, what prancing hobbies! And although I knew that the impression she had made on me was a true, deep, honest, pure-spirited thing, I thought my nature might have been

4

prepared to receive it, and to exaggerate it uncon-
sciously, and to keep it green long after such a fancy,
as I deemed it probable you might have conceived,
had withered. So much for my injustice, which I must
release myself of, in the first instance.

"You ask me to write, and I think you want me to
write freely. I will tell you what I would do myself, if
I were in your case. And I will tell you without the
least reserve. If I had all your independent means,
and twenty times my own reputation and fame – and
felt as irresistibly impelled towards her as I should if
I were in your place, and as you do – I would not
hesitate or do slight to the resolution of my own heart
which hesitation would imply, but would win her if
I could, by God. I would answer it to myself, if any
world's breath whispered me I had known her but a
few days, that hours of hers are years in the lives of
common women. That it is in such a face and such a
spirit, as a part of its high nature, to do at once what
less ethereal creatures must be long in doing. That as
no man ever saw a soul or caught it in its flight, no
man can measure it by rule or rod. And that it has a
right in such lofty development, to pitch all forms
laid down by bodies to the Devil – the only Being, as
far as I know, who was never in love himself, or inspired it in others.

"And to the father I *would* point out, in very tenderness and sorrow for this gentle creature, who otherwise is lost to this sad world, which needs another,
Heaven knows, to set it right – lost in her Youth, as
surely as she lives – that the course to which he is

5

devoting her, should not be called her Life, but Death; for its speedy end is certain. I saw an Angel's message in her face that day, that smote me to the heart. He may not know this, being always with her; it is very likely he does not; and I would tell it him. Repose, change, a mind at rest, a foreign climate, would be, in a spring time like hers, the dawning of a new existence. I believe, I do believe and hope, that this would save her; and that many happy years hence, she would be strong and hardy. But at the worst: contemplating the chance, the distant chance in such a case, of what is so dreadful: I could say in solemn and religious earnestness, that I could bear better her passing from my arms to Heaven, than I could endure the thought of coldly turning off into the world again to see her no more; to have my very name forgotten in her ears; to lose the recollection of her myself, but at odd times and in remorseful glances backward; and only to have the old thought stirred up at last by some indifferent person saying 'You recollect her? Ah! She's dead.' As I live, I write the Truth, and feel it.

"So many ideas spring up within me, of the quiet happiness we might enjoy abroad, all of us together, in some delicious nook, where we should make merry over all this, that I don't know whether to be glad or sorry at my own hopefulness. Such Italian castles, bright in sunny days and pale in moonlight nights, as I am building in the air! –

"But time is precious, and Dick is (to a certain extent) a prosing Donkey if you give him the rein. . . .

I will go on with my building after I have despatched this. I never was more in earnest, my dear Thompson, in my life. Always faithfully your friend, CHARLES DICKENS."

Christiana's playing had been brought to concert-pitch when she was eight years old. Now, at nineteen, she was preparing for a début in London – equipped, by the way, with good health, the fears entertained by Dickens for her life if she should follow this career being only the imputation of that charm of delicate health which was dear to the period.

Thomas James Thompson was then a widower and was, like Dickens, in the early thirties. He had been at Trinity College, Cambridge, and in accordance with the Will of his grandfather he had followed no profession.* He had contested unsuccessfully two expensive elections for Parliament as a Free-trader; otherwise want of ambition left him at liberty for his friendships, his club-life, reading and travel. He was one of the George Henry Lewes, John Leech, Douglas Jerrold, Forster group of friends who belonged to Dickens's company of amateur

* The income on which he lived had been derived from property in the West Indies and in Lancashire, by the Will of this grandfather who died when his heir, an orphan, was only six years of age. This grandfather's Will curiously links the families of Thompson and Barrett, for the money settled on his grandchildren is to pass, failing them, to "his friend Edward Moulton Barrett, of Mount Royal, Jamaica," and to his heirs, – thus making Mrs. Browning a possible legatee of money that came eventually to Thompson's children. The Will does not mention any relationship between the two families, but Browning appeared to think there was one, for he said: "Our wives are kinswomen, I believe," when he and Wilfrid Meynell first met in 1882.

actors.* As Christiana's suitor he was not welcomed by
her parents, to whom it seemed that a great career would
be spoilt by marriage. Each vicissitude of the courtship is
enthusiastically reflected in Dickens's letters:

"At the father, I snap my fingers. I would leap over the
head of the tallest father in Europe, if his daughter's
heart lay on the other side, and were worth having. As
to my chance of having it – well – I think I could make
a guess about that (tesselating a great many little things
together) which should not be very wide of the
mark."

But Dickens wished his friend to leave Liverpool so that
they might visit Italy together:

Sunday, March 24th   *Devonshire Terrace*
   "My dear Thompson . . . What are you doing?
When are you coming away? Why are you stopping
there? Do enlighten me, for I think of you constantly, and have a true and real interest in your
proceedings. D'Orsay, who knows Italy very well indeed, strenuously insists that there is no such place
for headquarters as Pisa. Lady Blessington says so,
also: What do you say? On the first of July, the first
of July, Dick turns his head towards the orange
groves. . . . Every morning I proclaim 'At home to
Mr. Thompson.' Every evening I ejaculate with
Monsieur Jacques – 'But he *weel* come. I know he

* One of their tours was made for the benefit of Leigh Hunt;
another for Miss Kelly, the actress to whom Lamb proposed.

weel!' After which I look vacantly at the boxes; put my hands to my grey wig, as if to make quite sure that it is still on my head, all safe; and go off, 1st entrance O.P. to soft music. Give her my love, and don't appropriate it by the way. Always Faithfully your friend, CHARLES DICKENS."

At a favourable turn of events he writes on the 29th March, 1844: "I congratulate you, with all my heart and soul, a million of times. It is a noble prize you have won. And I am sure you have won it in a noble spirit. A hearty God bless you! Good Heaven what a Dream it appears! Shall we ever forget that night when she came up to *the* Piano – that morning when Dick, the energetic Dick, devised the visit! Shall we ever cease to have a huge and infinite delight in talking about the whole romance from end to end – in dwelling upon it, exaggerating it, recalling it in every possible way, form, shape, and kaleidoscopic variety! Ask her to save the dress – the dress with the fur upon it. Let it be laid up in lavender. Let it never grow old, fade, shrink, or undergo millinerial alteration, but be a household God, Immortally Young and Perpetually Green. . . ."

But many words were to flow from Dickens's pen before he could resign his charge of the affair. From Malton Abbey, Yorkshire (Eighth April, 1844), he wrote to Miss Weller: "To my amazement, I have found one friend of mine very much the worse for a visit to your town. – Something comes over the paper like the light of a blush from you; I don't know what is the cause of the effect, but it is very red. He went to Liverpool, and fell desperately, madly, irretrievably, in Love there, which was so perfectly natural (the circumstances of his case being quite uncommon and his provocation enormous) that I could not find it in my heart to remonstrate with him for his folly. Indeed I rather encouraged him in it than otherwise; for I had that amount of sympathy with his condition, which, but that I am beyond the reach – the lawful reach – of the Wings that fanned *his* fire, would have rendered it the greatest happiness and pleasure of my life, to have run him through the body in no poetical or tender sense, I assure you, but with good sharp steel. He fell in love, this man, and after divers misgivings and hesitations and deliberations, and all that, mentioned the fact – first to the winds, and to the gentle airs that blow in Mr. Radley's bedchambers; and afterwards to – to Her. Well. He thought he was getting on hopefully, gently, reasonably smoothly, and wrote as much to me in London. I immediately threw up a small cap (sky blue) which I keep on a peg in my study for such joyful occasions as very seldom happen; and remained for some days perpetually casting it into the air and catching it again, in a transport of delight. In the midst of this enthusiasm I was summoned down here (he visits hereabouts) to attend a funeral; and at this funeral I found him, to my great amazement, acting as chief mourner to his own hopes, and attending them to an early grave with the longest hatband and the usefullest pocket handkerchief I ever saw in my life. At this I was very much surprised & very sorry, as you will believe; and the sky-blue cap (still in the air) fell down upon my head with the weight and velocity of a Cannon Ball."

Meanwhile, the grave, affectionate and somewhat admonishing lover was writing to his Christie:

"My own darling darling love, – That ever we should be otherwise than *d'accord* on all points and at all times seems the strangest thing in the world when I am absent from you. Let me impress upon you, my own dearest love, the necessity of being altogether open and unreserved with me. You who are generally so impulsive ought to be particularly so towards me. If ever I do anything you don't like, remark upon it on the instant. Trust me if you persuade me you are right I shall never prove obstinate or unreasonable – and it will always be a source of pride to find you in the right, even in opposition to myself."

And again in their adversity:

"My darling Christie, – I have not written to your Papa, nor can I write in such a tone as you have suggested after receiving from him such cruel treatment as I consider and have proclaimed his to be. Dickens however has opened the way to a communication between us in the course of which I promise you that I will cheerfully make all reasonable concession. Of that be assured. Your conduct on Monday evening was, I hear, glorious – and has done you much good in D's estimation, and I must acknowledge also in mine. To find you displaying such firmness under such circumstances is the most gratifying thing I could have heard of you. I had instructed D. to watch you closely and to tell me candidly if he discovered any infirmity of purpose – but he rejoined me full of admiration of your bearing, than which nothing, he said, could be better: I thank you for it, darling, and believe me I shall not soon forget it.

"That we shall come together eventually if it please God to spare the lives of us both I have no doubt – I am very patient and determined – and I have no fear whatever of your truth and constancy. Your ever attached and devoted lover, T. J. THOMPSON."

Another indication of his feeling is contained in a book he presented to her called *The White Lady and Undine*, and inscribed thus: "To her who, in these lovely fictions, may see her own character reflected, – good and gentle as the White Phantom, spiritual as Undine, I offer this little volume. – I have written this lightly in pencil that you may readily expunge it should I ever prove unworthy of you, or should you ever wish to forget the name of him who wrote it."

They were married in 1845, when Christiana was twenty years old, and they had two children: Elizabeth and Alice, born in 1846 and 1847.

The "greatly gifted" mother had talents in music and painting, rather than any grave intellectual heritage to bestow on her two children. Her brilliance was of feeling. Her simple exuberant nature shows itself in her journal, parts of which shall serve to give an idea of her influence on her children's early life. That life was a nomadic one; they halted nowhere for much longer than one would pitch a tent. The father's choice took them wandering about Italy; and the mother's attachments brought them back to various impermanent homes in the neighbourhood of her family in England. The little girls' education was the care of their father, sometimes carried on in the loggia of an Italian villa, sometimes in English towns and villages, and greatly in the journeys and halting-places that lay between.

II

CHRISTIANA THOMPSON'S JOURNAL

Mrs. Thompson's journal was not intended to convey ideas to other people – witness this extract: "Tom bought me a splendid present, a brooch of exquisite workmanship – but I trust it will never be lost, so it is unnecessary to describe it." No art is used upon the flying impressions. They telegraph themselves on to the page as if they were recorded in the actual hurry of their happening, instead of in the quiet pause afterwards. Her entries have the rush of travel, as well as its incident: "Off to station alone in wind and dust. Dreadful fright. Lost Tom's dressing-case. Nowhere. Tom and porter back to hotel. No. At last I bethought me I had fixed window open with it behind curtain. Off Tom rushed again and got it." It is a journal full of events, but only because the character of each day was an event, the weather, each different kind of weather, an ecstasy to her. Painting had become since her marriage another occupation. Her paintings are called in the journal her "arts":

"August 17th, 1852. Arrived at Villa dei Franchi (Sori, near Genoa) in a resplendent afternoon. On entering we all wildly rushed up and down the balcony, until Agostino (the cook) pulled me up by mundane grievances – imperfect state of the kitchen – nothing to eat – &c. &c.

"Morning noon and night too divine. Tom and I cannot contain ourselves. . . . Little angels and I bathed in the blessed moonlight.

"To Recco to see grand illumination and fireworks for *festa*, Nativity of the Virgin. Town densely crowded, Sweet Ones shouting with rapture as we approached. Beautiful effect of coloured lanterns on each side of river-bed, far into the distance. . . . Oh the ecstacy of the Babes. *'Oh maman, c'est trop beau!'* – with shouts and clapping of hands. Home in pitch dark – road lined with people – carriages coming along distractedly – precipice on the other side – a nightmare.

"All the morning tried to read – hopeless, scene too lovely. Angels exquisitely lovely in the sunshine playing at the water's brink. Sea all colours and calm as a lake, and emerald coloured stones at bottom visible at a great depth. Home to dine, and then again down to blessed shore, and into little boat for the first time, and round as far as Guoco's Palazzo. Under an old tower a magnificent grotto which we entered and penetrated some distance – Babes half charmed, half frightened. Exquisite row back after sun-down, water like an opal, in breadths of blue and rose. Getting dark as we landed, superb effect of orange, lemon, rose, & blue sky, and evening star, and black masses of rock. Up our wilderness of olives and orange trees and vines as usual.

"We to Nervi to dine. . . . A youth who raved whilst I played – he writhed and clasped his hands and appealed distractedly to the General. Very amusing to me coming from England.

"Sweet Babe's (Alice's) fifth birthday. She and Mimi

(Elizabeth) as gay as larks. Spent the afternoon on our rocks. Tom read us Arabian Nights. Agostino, bringing down dessert, slipped on the dangerous path near the bottom and it all went adrift, apples hopping into the sea. . . . Went to take down an art in the blessed moonlight near the ruined tower.

"Magical morn! No white paint – despair.

"Little Babe beginning the Beethoven air (Fanchi). Dear angel, it is a marvel of patience and sweetness. . . . Babes are drawing heads by the hundred, and learning history.

"Into Genoa and to Exhibition for the first time. Saw my arts, and was proud, on a screen all to themselves. Let me not forget blessed cherry-tree in olive wood in our villa with sun streaming through its blossoms."

"Nov. 23, 1856. After dinner we went to new house Palazzo Bagnarello, Albaro – alias Pink Jail, sweet and grand place. Babes' room with sweet elaborately vaulted ceiling painted with stars, yellow satin hangings, vaulted ceiling to staircase, broad marble balustrade and marble pillar. Exquisite Italian combination of sunshine, campanile, pine, cypress, hill and palazzo."

Dickens had stayed in this Palazzo and had named it Pink Jail, a name explained in later life by Lady Butler (the Mimi of the Journal). "It was rose-coloured, and its lower windows were barred with iron as all Genoese houses are. Dickens therefore named it well, according to his unfamiliar English view of things Italian." Dickens made frequent visits to Italy, and the Journal has such entries as: "To Gibbs' to dine. Dickens very cordial and gay. I sat next him. He is brilliant as ever, his face most intense, and has the vitality of twenty ordinary men. Afterwards played at games, Dickens taught us two new ones – *Buz* and *What advice would you have given him?* Great laughter and merriment. Afterwards I played some Mendelssohn, and *Carnaval*."

But in one of Dickens's letters to his wife there is to be found a somewhat shocked account of the unconventionalities of the Thompson family in Italy. "Then I went on to the T(hompson)s," he says, writing from Genoa, "and found them living in a beautiful situation in a ruinous Albaro-like palace. Coming upon them unawares, I found T(hompson), with a pointed beard, smoking a great German pipe, in a pair of slippers; the two little girls very pale and faint from the climate, in a singularly untidy state – one (heaven knows why!) without stockings, and both with their little short hair cropped in a manner never before beheld, and a little bright bow stuck on the top of it. C(hristiana) said she had invented this headgear as a picturesque thing, adding that perhaps it was – and perhaps it was not. She looked very well, and seems to be greatly liked here. We had disturbed her at her painting in oils, and I have rather received an impression that, what with that, and what with music, the household affairs went a little to the wall. T(hompson) was teaching the two little girls the multiplication table in a disorderly old billiard-room, with all manner of maps in it." This particular visit had taken place in 1853, when the children were six and seven years old.

From the Journal again: "May 5, 1860. Party in eve. Put on Bondian muslin with green stripes, and in hair white and red carnations. Babes in white. . . . At eight,

Sala lighted and soon the company came. . . . We opened windows after supper to gaze at glorious moon, and saw three or four boats put off from shore, filled with men cheering – Garibaldi's men!"

Suffering from the drastic hygiene of the time, Mrs. Thompson complains, when she had a cough: "Just commencing tints for a sunset art when Mr. Cook came and I was dragged away and bled. Saw my art fading thro' the window while I was obliged to stay on the bed." Of Alice, a January entry: "Babe had toothache in the night and Amélie put it into a cold bath, poor soul, which cured it." Italian hygiene was used on Alice; owing to some fears as to her chest she was largely fed on snail broth and snail jelly. A cough was met by lozenges derived chiefly from snails. She liked to think, in later life, that she had not been compelled to eat actual snails, – only their supposed virtue, conveyed in stewings and boilings!

Of visits to the Genoese dentist, who had a big tooth hanging outside the door for a sign, there are dreadful records. This is of Alice: ". . . He said she had better have chloroform – he gave it to her. I held its blessed head – he pulled three times – then she screamed violently and fell off the chair. He gave her some more and then pulled out another tooth. When it was over the angel lay quite insensible and white and cold like a seraph. I saw the dentist look anxious and his hand trembled. Oh the horror and agony of that morning. We laid it on the sofa and she opened her eyes in about ten minutes. We then carried her into his room and laid her on the bed. Soon she came to, but was drowsy and sick. He told me there had been danger. Ah what I went through! Seeing the angel quiet I went off and bought it a lovely dolly, with wax head, – brought it to the angel – she enchanted & consoled." Of Mimi it is recorded that she was taken, "but would not go up." Another time, however, "she behaved like a heroine. She did not know she was going, poor soul – began to weep on the fatal staircase but when in the chair placed her hands before her and said she would say nothing and would be good. So she was. Two great tugs – a firm tooth."

But there were compensations – visits to Romanengo's, the confectioners – purchases of toys – and sometimes the Opera. Here, the first time, the little children were entranced by the object that first met their eyes – the chandelier; and ever after remembered the shame of finding they had done wrong to applaud it.

Many were the distresses of Mrs. Thompson at the ways of certain Italians with animals and birds: "Dreadful misery one day at Signor Vinzoni's. He took me to see his poor blind birds shut up in a dark closet, where they are kept until he wants them to entrap others by their singing. I was dreadfully affected and of course cried bitterly, and appealed to him as well as I could in Italian – the first time perhaps in his life the idea of cruelty and wrong had been suggested to him. As far as I saw, *no* effect was produced." But there was one bird in a cage she did not weep for, but instead she leaned out of her window at Levanto to sing "with an exquisite blackbird in a cage high up in a huge ruin of a house across the narrow street." She was constantly making efforts to influence the muleteers, who flogged and kicked their beasts up the hilly roads. One occasion used to be re-membered afterwards by her two grown-up children, when the muleteer smilingly retorted to her abuse *"E voi siete bella!"* To every accusation made by their exas-perated mamma, – *"voi siete un cattivo, voi siete un birbante, voi siete uno scelerato,"* – from a distance and to the end his voice still replied *"E voi siete bella!"*

In Italy the children grew up chiefly to the use of the Genoese dialect; later they acquired the more beautiful Tuscan. Sometimes, with childhood's love of convention-ality, they suffered in realising that their upbringing was unusual. All the misery that a child can feel about dress, they might feel if they were not themselves wearing the modish *petit jupon bouffant* when correct little Parisians accosted them in the gardens of the Tuileries with *veux-tu venir jouer avec moi?* Doubting the merits of being brought up internationally, and distrusting the unconventionality of the liberty they yet so much enjoyed in their games with all kinds of playmates and in many dialects, eagerness to be more like "other people" became almost a passion with them; and Alice recalls later how this longing to be other than she was cost her some years of her simplicity.

Rapture and distress are in startling proximity in the mother's accounts of their journeys between England and Italy. They were certainly no luxurious affairs.

The first journey to Italy, for instance, with the little girls was done partly by boat through France. These are two days in the Journal: "Nov. 12, 1851. Lyons to Valence. Down to the boat, cold miserable morning. Sat on deck some time, then obliged to go down, cold could not be borne. Poor Babes obliged to lie down in little stifling cabin. I up again in order to recognise my dear old places, but oh how drear and different! Latter part of journey, beauty increased – villages getting wonderfully Southern, with Campaniles, and open window-frames with shutters outside. . . . Hideous flurry and even demoniac confusion getting off the boat in the dark, mingled with the smell of garlic. I and little Mimi wandered away and were blinded by the steam, and I thought we should inevitably tumble into the river. In fiacre, up the town to Hotel de la Poste. Got a suite of glorious clean large rooms where we were quite wild with delight for some time.

"*Nov. 13th.* Up at five – Babes highly excited. In fiacre down the hilly town to the river. – Again into filthy boat. . . . At last to Avignon. Great uproar of tongues. – No trucks or carts for luggage which had all to be carried some distance to Hotel du Palais National. Sweet court-yard, and at porch a canopy of vines with bunches of purple grapes. Our room exquisite – muslin curtains inside beds, chintz over. Flowered paper. Dined sump-tuously – splendid dessert. Sun shone sweetly and three large trees on the opposite side of *Place* made waving shadows on the walls. . . . Mistral blew down all the smoke of our fires. – I had to put them out with water. Stayed up late watching the smoke slowly abating in poor Babes' room. Got much excited about Petrarch and Laura and could not go to sleep for a long time. Expected to see the shade of Petrarch."

Mrs. Thompson sometimes returned to England alone, to see the parents and sisters she loved. Of one of many such visits and journeys she writes:

"July, 1851. . . . Sat with my Anna under a blessed oak-tree in a lovely meadow. Oh the sweetness and English delight – felt a rapture of love for it. . . . In eve had one of the sweetest and most blissful walks in the world, through corn fields and sweet meads, and through an avenue of chestnuts the branches of which would make trunks at Ruta. It poured as we made our start, but soon the sweet shower passed us and left a golden eve behind it to West – our direction. Through the dear little English town of Dorking and on to my lovely Betsey's. Raced down the path joyfully. . . . She was habited in a green gown with flounces worked in rose colour and looked lovely. . . . Alas! all alone after so much blessedness with all kind angels."

"The children's great amusement," their father reported during this absence, "is writing History – the history of their respective Islands. Mimi illustrates hers with portraits of the sovereigns, not without variety and character."

The children's infantile letters are written in a style often influenced by their mother's. "My dear Rose of a Mamma," one begins; and another: "My dear Mamma, I hope you and little Papa will come very soon, my little sweet elves." "My angel little mamma, I send you and dearest angel papa a thousand loves and kisses. We went on a beautiful road on the top of Shakespear's Clif. Exquse this short letter." And from Elizabeth: "O dear I am weting for you and dearest papa so impetionitly. Alice is improving a little in drawing eies, for I give her lessons. I send you some drawings of botes, there are such a quantity on the sea. Exques this short letter." "We went on a high mountain amongst the clouds and we saw such rugged rocks and heath upon them, at Carrara we saw the marble mountains and we plucked some wight ma."

Literary compositions were sometimes enclosed in their letters, and here the honours, as was proper to her year longer in the world, seem to have been with Elizabeth, who at seven wrote, out of her imagination:

> In the north of Asia I sat,
> Not knowing what to do
> And thinking of great Cæsar,
>   But his time is past.
> O Brutus and Cassius, why did you kill great Cæsar?

while Alice was writing about knights and ladies with no idea that was not borrowed from Scott or Whyte Melville. "On the rural bank I sat," writes Elizabeth once more, in what must have seemed to her the most excellent way of beginning, "to lisston at the rolling waves, and watching at the setting sun. The soft wind coming oer the wide sea changed my idears into joy; the gloomy Spirit took his flite, and all the joyful Spirits came to nesstle arownd me."

Other *diligence* journeys were made with the children: "September 10th, 1859. . . . Got out at Lanzlebourg, in the midst of horses – the change for three diligences. – Chaos and darkness, save moonlight. Upstairs to a savage w ld room, curtain dividing us from a man in bed. Babes and Tom set out to walk, but I could not attempt it, and slept a little. They walked in moonlight and dew, in darkness of rocks and light of moon, for about two h ours,

poor doves. . . . Off again and stopped in pitch darkness, 4.30, at Susa. The going at a fast trot down the zigzags when you are lying down with your back to horses
is horrible, and the swing round corners. Poor Babes
made a point of not sleeping. Descended at the dirty café
– no room to go into and be quiet . . . could bear it no
longer – out at dawn to walk about Susa."

"18th April, 1861. All night in diligence, and the usual
bitter weariness. . . . Smoke, alas, clouding Marseilles
and blotting out distant hills – Marseilles was formerly as
sharp in light and shade as Rome. To hotel. We had
breakfast in my room. Mimi then as before got out her
book to draw but fell asleep with her head on the table."

"24th. . . . Hideous appalling London. We took a
carriage to Fulham, thro' the most distressing squalor,
meanness, dirt and vulgarity."

But English resting-places were more often in the
country than at Fulham. At Hastings, when Alice was
ten, the joy of riding began for both the girls; and again
there, at thirteen and fourteen, they are described on
horseback by their mother "in green shirts with little
white collar turned over and white wristbands, black
skirts and Spanish black hats with feather and pompom –
pictures against blue sky."

Mrs. Thompson's violent distresses never do more than
keep her blessings just at bay. She may write with youthful despair: "Mr. Fothergill with a few Daguerrotypes.
In one I look without any exaggeration 50 and a most
melancholy and worn wretched woman. Can't express
the gloom it inspired me with. All the unhappiness I have
ever felt, bad nights and other miseries, seemed therein

set down. Bah! I cried. Tom stern and severe." Or
another time: "I saw a lark in a cage. Thomas refused to
let me buy it to let it go. I hope I shall get some money
some day by my arts." But generally she is running to
meet her blisses and finding them under countless "enchanting Italian skies," or in innumerable "divine misty
English eves." The normal thing holds much enchantment for her. The lodgings at St. Leonards are "sweet
and gay and pleasant. Sun always shining in. Bands
playing. Nice little sofa by fire. Tom after dinner reading
Quentin Durward aloud. . . . I write many letters and
practise. We indulge in cakes, etc."

The Journal shall end with one of the happy English
days: "July 15, 1861. I thirty-six years old to-day! In the
morn it rained heavily. Down, and saw table all covered
with flowers, and my present from the Babes sweetly laid
out. I wore my white gown and the little flowery muslin
mantle. – Dear Papa had stopt to spend this day here. –
After breakfast the lovely sun came gradually out and a
divine radiant day succeeded. Soon came, first, the
Piano! – Men brought it in through drawing-room
window thro' sunshine and glistening raindrops. – Cloth
laid down for the mud. – Then my Betsy and Lucy (her
sisters) came, just as I was beginning to play. Pretty B.
looked very sweet and young and beautiful. – Dinner,
fowls, ham, stewed beef. – Currant and raspberry pie –
Babe picked the raspberries from garden. – Glorious sun
whilst at dinner – wonderful blue and white clouds.
After to drawing-room and I played, and Betsy played
some sweet Mendelssohn while I lay on ground before
window with sofa pillows under my head and looking at

two divine birches in sun and shade and waving in summer wind. – Into sweet garden and to foot of hill and looked at exquisite newly-come harebells. – Soon to tea and plum-cake – and then all of us for blessed walk to Dorking. – Exquisite walk home by dark and divine western sky. – All hay gone and meadows emerald again. – Coming up our hill a lovely glow-worm in bank, – Home – dark – and alas my dear birthday over – past and gone – for evermore."

III

A CHILD AND HER FATHER

THEIR father taught the two little girls all that he would
have taught them had they been sons. He was perhaps
a stern task-master. Alice's memories of first reading
lessons were memories of despair, and in a later year
Mimi, the inferior speller, would often be saved by Alice's
aid from the displeasure they dreaded. His scholarly love
of precision may have reached the point of a little
pedantry. Once when, long after he was dead, his
younger daughter happened to read in the paper the
name Ekbatana, she paused upon it, knowing that some
important and even unique event was associated with it.
And the memory, when it was found, was of her father
pronouncing the word in the course of his history-reading
to his two little girls, of a sudden conviction of error
coming over him, and of his emphatic correction of the
only false quantity they had ever heard him make.

He was something of a collector. "Ah my poor
pictures!" he exclaims in a letter in the early years of
their travels, "my poor bronzes! my poor books! When
shall I see them all together and enjoy them? It won't
bear thinking of." Even with a fixed and ample income,
he found that difficulties occasionally made the economies
of Italy necessary when England would have been pre-

ferred. "Are you by way of gaining any information respecting Antwerp or Bruges or Malines or any of the Belgian towns as places of residence?" he writes once to his wife. "Or Caen? Or any old French town with Norman architecture and pleasant surroundings? Or what of Heidelburg, or Nuremberg with their picturesqueness, their cheapness, their accessibility (comparative) from England, their German for the children?" From those children he had an absence while he watched by the sick-bed of his grown-up daughter by his first wife; but from afar he still pulls the strings of the little girls' work and play. "Singing of course they will practise without my injunction," he concludes. "Above all, keep well. There is a young lady here who plays magnificently. She is now playing your Carnaval. I wish she wouldn't."

It was the Italian years that were the most memorable of the children's youth. It was not the way of the grown-up Alice to talk of her own life; but the rare reminiscence of childhood was always of this time, and Italy invades her essays on childhood: "The Mediterranean under the first perceptible touch of the moon, the calm southern sea in the full blossom of summer, the early spring everywhere, in the showery streets, in the fields, or at sea, left old childish memories with you which you try to evoke now when you see these places again. But the cloudy dusk behind poplars on the plains of France, the flying landscape from the train, willows, and the last of the light, were more mournful to you than you care to remember now. So were the black crosses on the graves of the French village; so were cypresses, though greatly beloved. . . . You had shocks of delight from Swiss woods full of lilies-of-the-valley, and from English fields full of cowslips. You had disquieting dreams of landscape and sun, and of many of these you cannot now tell which were visions of travel and which visions of slumber. Your strong sense of place made you love some places too keenly for peace." "That is a fortunate child who has tasted country life in places far apart, who has followed the wheat to the threshing-floor of a Swiss village, stumbled after a plough of Virgil's shape in remoter Tuscan hills, and gleaned after a vintage. You cannot suggest pleasanter memories than those of the vintage, for the day when the wine will be old." And again: "One of the privileges of a child is that he is very near the earth; he knows moss and the scudding creatures near it. When Oliver Wendell Holmes found the scent of a little box hedge to be suggestive of eternity, it was no doubt merely suggestive of time – the incalculable remote time of childhood, which stands very fairly for eternity – because he had smelt it when he was on the level of its fresh leaves." "The feet also ought to have communication with the fields; they have their own sensations of flowers . . . but to have had their tenderness touched by nothing save dead sand at the seaside is a little loss that one wishes the civilised child had not to undergo." There is a journalistic essay on Agostino, the cook, who awaits them on the pier at Genoa amid the confusions dear to childhood, "the brown porters, the apple women screaming, the ships and chaos of the port"; it was he who would go to town with the doll whose head, but not personality, was to be renewed, and who would "match the type of beauty, grave and intent, without condescension."

ALICE MEYNELL

Writing of sundials she says: "The garden of my childhood faced a blue sea, across olives and oleanders, and
the sundial bore an inscription which, translated,
threatened the generation: 'Thou seest the hour and
knowest not the hour.' . . . There are tunes composed
for bells, and like their brief music is this brief literature
of sundials, restricted to the means and the opportunity.
. . . The phrase, the melody, have both their home on
the happy Ligurian coast." Over that garden at night
their mother's music would also be heard by the little
girls: "Often when we were in bed," wrote Mimi, grown
up, "I cried my heart out when through the open windows I could hear my mother's light soprano drowned
by the strong tenor of some Italian friend in a duet . . .
it seemed typical of her extinction and I felt a rage against
that tenor. Our nurse, Amélie, would come to me with
lemonade; and mamma, when apprised of the state of
things, would also come, her face, still bright from the
singing, becoming sad." And Alice, in a poem written
late in life, remembered the same night-thought:

INTIMATIONS OF MORTALITY: FROM
RECOLLECTIONS OF EARLY CHILDHOOD

A simple child
That lightly draws its breath
And feels its life in every limb,
What should it know of Death?
Wordsworth.

It knows but will not tell.
   Awake, alone, it counts its father's years –
How few are left – its mother's. Ah, how well
   It knows of death, in tears.

If any of the three –
  Parents and child – believe they have prevailed
To keep the secret of mortality,
  I know that two have failed.

The third, the lonely, keeps
  One secret – a child's knowledge. When they come
At night to ask wherefore the sweet one weeps,
  Those hidden lips are dumb.

Her father was accused of a *dilettante* existence, and
must have given an impression of power to be reproached,
even in his learning and industry, for making but a
languid use of life. "He never grasped at happiness, and
many of the things he had held slipped from his disin-
terested hands," wrote Alice, years after his death. And
yet he loved life. "How should he not have loved a life
that his living made honourable? How should he not have
loved all arts, in which his choice was delicate, liberal,
instructed, studious, docile, austere?" It is in a short
essay called *A Remembrance* that she records what her
childhood and youth had taught her of her father:

"When the memories of two or three persons now
upon earth shall be rolled up and sealed with their
records within them, there will be no remembrance
left open, except this, of a man whose silence seems
better worth interpreting than the speech of many
another. Of himself he has left no vestiges. It was a
common reproach against him that he never ac-
knowledged the obligation to any kind of restlessness.
. . . The delicate, the abstinent, the reticent graces

were his in the heroic degree. Where shall I find a pen
fastidious enough to define and limit and enforce so
many significant negatives? Words seem to offend by
too much assertion, and to check the suggestions of
his reserve. The reserve was life-long. Loving literature, he never lifted a pen except to write a letter.
He was not inarticulate, he was only silent. He had
an exquisite style from which to refrain. The things
he abstained from were all exquisite. They were
brought from far to undergo his judgment, if haply he
might have selected them. Things ignoble never approached near enough for his refusal; they had not
with him so much as that negative connexion. If I had
to equip an author I should ask no better than to arm
him and invest him with precisely the riches that were
renounced by the man whose intellect, by integrity,
had become a presence-chamber.

"It was by holding session among so many implicit
safeguards that he taught, rather than by precepts.
Few were these in his speech, but his personality
made laws for me. It was a subtle education, for it
persuaded insensibly to a conception of my own. How
if he would not define, could I know what things
were and what were not worthy of his gentle and implacable judgment? I must needs judge them for myself, yet he constrained me in the judging. Within
that constraint and under that stimulus, which seemed
to touch the ultimate springs of thoughts before they
sprang, I began to discern all things in literature and
in life – in the chastity of letters and in the honour
of life – that I was bound to love. Not the things

of one character only, but excellent things of every character . . .

"He had always prayed temperate prayers and harboured probable wishes. His sensibility was extreme, but his thought was generalised. When he had joy he tempered it not in the common way by meditation upon the general sorrow but by a recollection of the general pleasure. It was his finest distinction to desire no differences, no remembrance, but loss among the innumerable forgotten. And when he suffered, it was with so quick a nerve and yet so wide an apprehension that the race seemed to suffer in him. . . ."

It was typical of her that all her life she had no more personal details to utter concerning even one so close as he. Or only once for a moment in after life did something escape from her habitual reserve, when she was found by one of her children weeping in contrition for what?—a day long ago when her father had wanted her company for a walk and she had refused him.

With a mother adored for her beauty and tenderness, the two children had also this special obligation in regard to their father – that, being daughters and not sons, they should yet be able to make his qualities their own. "Thy father was transfused into thy blood," wrote Dryden to Anne Killigrew; and one at least of these daughters was conscious all her life of her direct inheritance from her father, not diverted by her difference of sex. When towards the end of her life the war robbed men of their sons, she then pressed home her thought of how completely those fathers might still pass into their daughters:

ALICE MEYNELL

A FATHER OF WOMEN

Ad sororem Elizabeth Butler

Our father works in us,
The daughters of his manhood. Not undone
Is he, not wasted, though transmuted thus,
   And though he left no son.

Therefore on him I cry
To arm me: "For my delicate mind a casque,
A breastplate for my heart, courage to die,
   Of thee, captain, I ask.

"Nor strengthen only; press
A finger on this violent blood and pale.
Over this rash will let thy tenderness
   A while pause, and prevail.

"And, shepherd father, thou
Whose staff folded my thoughts before my birth,
Control them now I am of earth, and now
   Thou art no more of earth.

"O liberal, constant, dear!
Crush in my nature the ungenerous art
Of the inferior; set me high, and here,
   Here garner up thy heart."

Like to him now are they,
The million living fathers of the War –
Mourning the crippled world, the bitter day –
   Whose striplings are no more.

The crippled world! Come then,
Fathers of women with your honour in trust;
Approve, accept, know them daughters of men,
   Now that your sons are dust.

IV

GIRLHOOD

In 1864 and 1865 the Thompsons had a house at Bon-church in the Isle of Wight in which, with furniture of their own, they settled more permanently than was usual with them. There the girls found a life of neighbours, croquet parties, concerts, dancing and riding, which supplied much that the heart of seventeen hankers for and is unfulfilled by. There is an account from Mrs. Thompson of their gaieties:

"My precious sweet Dickon," she wrote to Alice who was absent, "Bless thy sweet heart! I wish thee a happy New Year, and I wish we were all together this Day. . . . The H.'s ball was splendid – a profusion of pink wax lights, a flow of champagne, – but poor me! about 12 I was so utterly exhausted I had to go up into the bedroom and there lie covered up till 2.30 in a torpor. I seemed to be listening for a week to hideous galops, waltzes, etc., drumming up thro' the floor – all of which Mimi pro-nounced delicious. – Also every now and then poor Miss Johnson was brought up to be sick by her mama. I wore my grey dove with tulle and red camelias – pretty when viewed at home but bald and poverty-stricken when con-trasted with the furbelows of society. Really, what lavish absurdity to the tired looker-on the whole thing is. I am

35

sure I should not think the same if the dances were such as peasants dance in the glorious Southern lands. At 12 Miss F. would introduce me to her papa although I told her I was too done up to open my lips – and he began a conversation upon Pre-Raphaelitism and Turner which put the finishing touch to me – and I then retired. Lovely bedroom and fire blazing and Mrs. H. so kind."

And then Alice's diary on another occasion: "Mama and I went to a ball at Mrs. Hambrough's, Steep Hill Castle. I wore a ravishing yellow tarlatan of the palest possible tint by night, made exquisitely, with a plaid écharpe over one shoulder, a red rose with its leaves in my hair and one at my waist. Off at 9.15. In time for the first quadrille. Glorious fun. Captain Sewell many times watched me going round and told Douglas how well I danced (who told me). I had no regular flirtation, and no particular compliments, save that truest of all, that the men quarrelled to dance with me. I would willingly have given a certain Mr. Bury a dance had I been free as he very much desired it. To this dance there were *no* drawbacks."

But the age that discovers these delights discovers also the first wild melancholy of young girlhood, which lies in wait in the dusk, in journeys, partings, in the earliest loves that come to afflict it. Nothing can be more real than this horror, though it comes at an age when expression has not yet learnt the quiet note of reality. Alice writes in her diary: "We have had a great disappointment to-day in the matter of money affairs – some mistake of the lawyers. So instead of having a jolly fortnight in London and then going to Germany, we must retire into some cheap country place. To-day I have shed more tears I think than I have before in all my life. I went round the garden and into every nook, and watered the grass with my tears. Tears to me are most poignant agony, a mark of the utmost extremity of pain. They do not come in torrents, but by twos and threes, and each one seems to break my heart. Now it seems to me that I must live on memories, that the sun of my life set behind the down which hid Bonchurch from my aching eyes. The sorrow in my soul is beyond words, beyond all expression, beyond the comprehension of happy spirits. That my life will ever be happy again, I cannot believe." She describes the despairing journey to Henley-on-Thames, and perhaps the key is given to that particular fit of young despair when she says: "On the way we passed Fareham where *he* lives."

At Henley, at the age of eighteen, she writes: "Mama and Mimi have found beautiful things to paint, and are therefore contented. I, on the other hand, have no interest here. . . . How unhealthy it is to depend as I do so much on my own thoughts and moods and feelings for employment, for excitement. A young man, occupied with study or business or laborious pleasures has no time to watch and ponder on every half-shade of thought and feeling that flits over his heart, and if the subtle perceptions of his soul are kept in abeyance, the more material mind, as it were, grows strong, grand and healthy. A girl, on the other hand, thrills through every nerve and fibre of her self-consciousness at the touch of the slightest joy or pain. If these nerves are tolerably in tune with one another she becomes a great woman – a writer, say, famous for laying bare the melancholy secrets of the female heart to the curious gaze of man; if the chords jar, she dwindles into a miserably self-conscious melancholy which feeds upon itself. Of all the crying evils in this depraved earth, ay, of all the sins of which the cry must surely come to Heaven, the greatest, judged by all the laws of God and humanity, is the miserable selfishness of men that keeps women from work – work, the salvation of the world, the winner of the dreamless sleep, and the dreamless thought too, the strengthener of mind and body. As to the soul, let that lie fallow. What happiness did excess of feeling ever bring man? By work I mean work of the mind as well as of the body.

"O my dream, my dream! When will you be realised to gladden my soul, to redeem my trampled and polluted sex? O my sisters, are you content to make bricks so long, sitting by your flesh-pots? Come and eat manna in the wilderness with me, and the justice of our cause will be a pillar of fire by night and a pillar of cloud by day to us, and what if we die in the wilderness – we die with the shackles off our wrists at last. O my Shelley, if you were alive you would help me to fulfil my golden dreams!

"Downpour of rain all day, only in the evening it stopt and we went out in the melancholy damp twilight. Oh these overcast spring evenings in the country are very awful. If I look inward I find tears; if outward, rain. My mature life should needs be sunny to compensate for such a youth of sorrow. Shall I confess that I have nothing to do? It is disgraceful, I know, but really what is there to occupy me, but going out, and practising. I must try to cultivate that rhyming faculty which I used to have, if it is not quite gone from me. But whatever I write will be melancholy and self-conscious, as are all women's poems."

There may have been many reasons for her sadness. Although she did not cease to have a certain amount of study with her father (there are many pages of analysis of Aristotle in a notebook of this time), she did in fact lack occupation; the cultivation of the art she leaned to was an indulgence of her melancholy; and, with a wandering life, she had few friends. Her religious ideals, and perhaps her father's standards, also made her morbidly self-accusing. Her journal at seventeen says: "I climbed into a field where I picked cowslips and tried to think myself an innocent little girl again with no love-affairs. But alas, my long womanly gown caught in every bramble, and I was obliged to keep my parasol up in pity to my complexion, and altogether I felt myself but a faint copy of that innocent child."

The sojourn at Henley, though so heavy, was brief; a pleasant tour of Germany followed, then life in the Isle of Wight again. There was one question raised by the girls at any move: "So there's a High-looking church?" writes Alice, at eighteen, when considering a projected stay at Hastings. "How High, I wonder; for there is none mentioned in the *Church Times* as having daily services." "I can't say, pretty babe," replies her mother, "if the clergyman of the new church at H. has yet arrived at the very last stage of development (according to Lucy – a cope), but the church appeared arranged in the High Church style, and certainly very beautiful."

Elizabeth's talent for drawing was by now being trained at the South Kensington School of Art, where her drawings vied with Kate Greenaway's for first place in the school competitions. Study in Florence followed and then in Rome; she was equipping herself for the extraordinary success of her battle paintings, which befell her swiftly with the *Roll Call* at the Academy of 1874. That picture was a commission from a Manchester manufacturer for a hundred pounds; the Prince of Wales tried in vain to purchase it; the Queen had it abstracted for a few hours from its place on the Academy walls to dwell on it undisturbed, and at last prevailed on the owner to cede its purchase to her; a policeman had to control the crowds that streamed before it. It was suggested that she should be made the first woman academician. *Punch* had its Academy banquet with the President remarking: "Shall we join the lady?" The young painter had £1,200 for the sale of the copyright to the engravers, and commissions poured in upon her.

It is pleasant to think of her father and mother looking on. None of their journeys can have shown them anything more spectacular than Elizabeth's career now. The only blemish was that Mrs. Thompson's hatred of war made her daughter's choice of subject, even though it were to expose its evils, painful to her; – though it was the very incongruity of a girl's spirited painting of battle-scenes that delighted public opinion. " *L'Angleterre n'a guère qu'un peintre militaire, c'est une femme,*" said a French writer.

In the meantime the beginnings of the other daughter had been as hidden as these were conspicuous. One girl

had an explicit studentship, the other a mere period of
dreaming melancholy. She was writing the mournful
verses she had predicted, with self-revealing qualities
that must be kept secret. In the handwriting of eighteen
is "In Autumn," with its echo from the diary:

> The low winds moan for dead sweet years,
> The birds sing all for pain
> Of a common thing, to weary ears, –
> Only a summer's fate of rain,
> And a woman's fate of tears.
>
> I know his heart has beat to bright
> Sweet loves gone by,
> I know the leaves that die to-night
> Once budded to the sky,
> And I shall die to his delight. . . .
>
> O tell me, tell me ere you die,
> Is it worth the pain?
> You bloomed so fair, you waved so high
> Now that the sad days wane,
> Are you repenting where you lie?
>
> I lie amongst you and I kiss
> Your fragrance mouldering.
> O dead delights, was it such bliss,
> That tuneful Spring?
> Is love so sweet that comes to this?
>
> Kiss me again as I kiss you;
> Kiss me again;
> For all your tuneful nights of dew
> In this your time of rain,
> For all your kisses when Spring was new. . . .

> There is an Autumn yet to fade,
> There are leaves yet to fall,
> Which when I kiss may kiss again,
> And be my bier, and be my pall,
> And love me in mist and rain.

The influences that were all this time at work in Alice are recorded by herself in later years, and the change to which they were to bring her when she was twenty years old: "In quite early childhood I lived upon Wordsworth. I don't know that I particularly enjoyed him, but he was put into my hands, and to me Wordsworth's poetry was the normal poetry *par excellence*. When I was about twelve I fell in love with Tennyson, and cared for nothing else until, at fifteen, I discovered first Keats and then Shelley. With Keats I celebrated a kind of wedding. The influence of Shelley upon me belongs rather to my spiritual than my mental history. I thought the whole world was changed for me thenceforth. It was by no sudden counter-revolution, but slowly and gradually that I returned to the hard old common path of submission and self-discipline which soon brought me to the gates of the Catholic Church."

One cannot know much of a state of mind she was then very silent about; it is later that she was more explicit about her reasons for taking this step. But one letter written at the time may show the kind of correspondence she had with the priest who received her into the Church. "I have been reading Father Newman's reply (to Gladstone's 'Vaticanism') very carefully," she wrote. "I am very much interested by the little he says of the principle of evolution in the teaching of the Church. It seems to me to explain all difficulties with respect to 'novelties.

I had some idea of this in becoming a Catholic. I received the Church so that whatever she could unfold with time she would unfold it there where I had enclosed her, in my heart." And a few entries in an old notebook show also that she lived according to a strict rule of mortification.

But Catholicism did not take her any far flights into the mystical world she always felt herself unable to explore. Already ardently a Christian, in Catholicism she saw the logical administration of the Christian moral law; and as that she adopted it with a deliberate rational choice, and with what earthly judgment she possessed, more than as a key to the unseen. And never surely was so rational a choice as hers more absolutely embraced in its furthest implications. No single act of hers in life or literature was not pledged and bound by her when she chose that law.

The influence this young decision of hers must have on all her life is the theme of a sonnet written then:

> Who knows what days I answer for to-day?
> Giving the bud I give the flower. I bow
> This yet unfaded and a faded brow;
> Bending these knees and feeble knees, I pray.
> Thoughts yet unripe in me I bend one way,
> Give one repose to pain I know not now,
> One leaven to joy that comes, I guess not how.
> Oh rash! (I smile) as one, when Spring is grey,
> Who dedicates a land of hidden wheat.
> I fold to-day at altars far apart
> Hands trembling with what toils? In their retreat
> I sign my love to come, my folded art.
> I light the tapers at my head and feet,
> And lay the crucifix on this silent heart.

Some years earlier Mrs. Thompson had become a Catholic; an entry in her journal records the little ceremony and ends: "Returned home and told no one." A little later she seems to have become involved in a controversy in which she had to call in the help of her husband, for he writes out for her "Some suggestions for a reply to the Revd. Gent.," beginning: "I know I have exposed myself to harsh judgment by the adoption of the Catholic faith," – and supplying her with expressions in which the feeling was hers and the workmanship generously his.

About a year after Alice, Elizabeth also became a Catholic.

In a notebook of Alice's at this time stray lines were written; – one to Shelley: "Thou who art less a singer than a song." And: "The Calvinist god Shelley repudiated was not God." Excusing herself for lack of homage to Newman's poetry, she notes: "Newman can write verse unworthy of himself without a pang because he is a poet fifthly, sixthly, or seventhly, in the order of his high vocations. It is far otherwise with me."

The migration to Genoa and Florence and Rome, in the days of Elizabeth's studentship, was meant also to restore Alice's vitality which had been very low for a long time. Here is a happy glimpse of them in the Florentine summer, from Elizabeth: "A large family inhabited the peasant quarters of our villa and worked the landlord's vineyards. They delighted in my sketches, and in giving me sittings in the intervals of work. I was invited to dine with them one day as they were having a rare repast. Cencio had found two hedgehogs in a hollow olive tree, and the *ragoût* must be tasted by the *signorina*. Through the door of the kitchen where we dined two white oxen were to be seen reposing in the next apartment. After tasting the *spinosa* stew, I begged to be allowed to sketch the whole family at table. Alice was reading Keats in one of the arbours meanwhile."

V

PRELUDES

BACK in England, Alice's verses were being shown to one friend, the priest who had received her into the Church, who now not only encouraged her by his interest in her writing, but urged her to it as a duty. And even that was but part of this influence of his that helped to make her a poet. Their friendship had become precious to both of them; but in keeping with the strict precautionary rules of his priesthood it was considered best that this friendship should end, and that they should see each other no more. At her side he had encouraged her writing of poetry; in separation, the exceedingly great sacrifice of parting made that poetry inevitable:

> Farewell to one, now silenced quite,
> Sent out of hearing, out of sight, –
> My friend of friends, whom I shall miss.
> He is not banished, though, for this, –
> Nor he, nor sadness, nor delight.
>
> Though I shall walk with him no more,
> A low voice sounds upon the shore.
> He must not watch my resting-place,
> But who shall drive a mournful face
> From the sad winds about my door?

I shall not hear his voice complain,
But who shall stop the patient rain?
His tears must not disturb my heart,
But who shall change the years, and part
The world from every thought of pain?

Although my life is left so dim,
The morning crowns the mountain-brim;
Joy is not gone from summer skies,
Nor innocence from children's eyes,
And all these things are part of him.

He is not banished, for the showers
Yet wake this green warm earth of ours.
How can the summer but be sweet?
I shall not have him at my feet,
And yet my feet are on the flowers.

And again she wrote in a sonnet:

We never meet; yet we meet day by day
Upon those hills of life, dim and immense,
The good we love, and sleep, our innocence.
O hills of life, high hills! And higher than they
Our guardian spirits meet at prayer and play.
Beyond pain, joy, and hope, and long suspense,
Above the summits of our souls, far hence,
An angel meets an angel on the way.

Beyond all good I ever believed of thee
Or thou of me, these always love and live.
And though I fail of thy ideal of me,
My angel falls not short; they greet each other;
Who knows, they may exchange the kiss we give,
Thou to thy crucifix, I to my mother.

47

She knew that they would never meet again; and all feeling that usually finds its escape into distant hopes must be driven into this one thing only, the poetry of parting. To write *Renouncement* must surely have brought even an unhappy girl its own happiness of poetic achievement:

> I must not think of thee; and, tired yet strong,
>> I shun the thought that lurks in all delight –
>> The thought of thee—and in the blue Heaven's height,
> And in the sweetest passage of a song.
> Oh, just beyond the fairest thoughts that throng
>> This breast, the thought of thee waits hidden yet bright;
>> But it must never, never come in sight;
> I must stop short of thee the whole day long.
>
> But when sleep comes to close each difficult day,
>> When night gives pause to the long watch I keep,
>> And all my bonds I needs must loose apart,
> Must doff my will as raiment laid away –
>> With the first dream that comes with the first sleep
>> I run, I run, I am gathered to thy heart.

Every lifetime accumulates its sadnesses. From this part of her life, her young girlhood at home, soon drawing to a close, two things were to go to that fund of sadness which lies only just aside from the present moment, and which can make silences sad even when speech is lively. Those who loved her were unusually powerless to interfere with her griefs, she was so private, so unapproachable, so convinced. One other thing than this parting hurt her succeeding life, and hurt her where she suffered most, in her too-sensitive conscience. Once when one of her grown-up children, suddenly finding it intolerable to be conscious of sadness in her, asked her what the cause of it could be, she answered – seeming to imply some failure in regard to them on her own part – that no day passed without its memory of her father and mother.

Scattered in notebooks were many such poems, till it was time for that subtle change to take place which would make them seem to their author as much part of an art as part of her private self. Her attempts began to belong more to her intense general interest in writing than to the secrecy of her own feelings.

Elizabeth's successful career necessitated London headquarters for the family; a home was established in South Kensington, and there social intercourse broadened for both girls. Catholic society – a thing rather apart in those days – had Lady Herbert of Lea for one of its hostesses, and at her house Alice met Aubrey de Vere, whose advice, after further meetings elsewhere, she ventured to ask. "I am in great need of friendly guidance in the art I have chosen and loved for years and years," she wrote. "Many things that you said at Lady Georgiana Fullerton's have opened my eyes to my own great ignorance and to the errors of taste and judgment which mar my work." Her poems in manuscript were sent to him; and now that the private audience was possible the public one would soon follow. Aubrey de Vere was already in 1874 encouraging her with words of approval drawn from Tennyson and Sir Henry Taylor when he showed them a poem of hers, and a warmer word from Coventry Patmore. And in 1875 he wrote: "I was very much interested at hearing you had made up your mind on the subject of publication. There is much to be said for and against very early publication. I believe that when we discussed the subject I was rather on the side of waiting a little. But a young poet is somewhat the slave of what he has written so long as it remains in his desk."

Acquaintance with Ruskin, which developed now, had been made some time before, when he had come to spend an evening with them. That first visit is described in Elizabeth's diary: "If I had been disposed to be nervous with him, his cold formal bow and closing of the eyes, his somewhat supercilious underlip and sensitive nostrils would not have put me at my ease. But fortunately I felt quite normal – unlike Mamma and Alice, the latter of whom had reason for quaking." The reason was that a friend had sent to Ruskin one of Alice's earliest poems. "It is very pretty, and may be helpful to many," had been the verdict repeated to the author, who until that moment of disappointment hardly knew that she had hoped for anything. But on this occasion of his visit Alice must have felt placated by his more attentive remarks: he could see that she had been forced to write the poem – but was she always going to write so sadly? In her mother Ruskin found one with whom to exchange expressions of feeling on the modern uglinesses of the day – smoke, factory chimneys, the backs of English houses, etc., such things being personal devastating tragedies in her life. He admired Elizabeth's drawings, listened to Mrs. Thompson's playing and Alice's singing and finally discovered Mrs. Thompson's water-colours – until Mr. Thompson, rather conscious of putting the family

through their paces before their visitor, felt his own like‧
ness to a circus man with a long whip touching up the
horses as they were trotted out. Alice, writing to a friend
after that first visit of Ruskin's, had said: "He is very
solemn and weighed down by the sadness of life. What
strikes me about him is that he has no society manner, and
never says light words: not like one who is not used to be
among men, but like one who has taken life and men
deeply to heart."

But now it was from Ruskin that Alice received real
praise when in 1875 her poems were published under the
name of *Preludes*, illustrated with drawings by her sister.
Ruskin abandoned "pretty" and left "graceful" for the
critics; "three of its poems," he wrote on reading the
book, "the 'Letter from a Girl,' the 'San Lorenzo,' and
the sonnet 'To a Daisy,' have done me more good than I
can well thank you for." And to her mother he wrote a
little later:

"Dear Mrs. Thompson, – How nice your letters
are! and how nice you all are! and how beautiful
Alice's verses are! and – I won't say anything of
Elizabeth. I want her to do perfect things for her
sister's poems. The one to San Lorenzo might be
quite perfect merely by completing it and not scratch-
ing in the flower-pot and oranges in that frantic
manner. Door a little overdone at top, on the right.
(What casts that jag in the shadow on floor?) And
then that perfectly heavenly letter from the girl –
Lete Vedrei – musn't be pinned in its place by those
poky poplars. I really think the last verse of that song

51

and the whole of San Lorenzo and the end of the daisy sonnet the finest things I've seen or felt in modern verse. – But don't tell Alice! What an awful business you must have of it – keeping those girls in order! Sympathizingly and affectionately yours, J. RUSKIN."

Another of his friendly and generous letters says, to Alice: "I cannot tell you how very lovely I think this poem. The great gifts you have, all of you, make me ashamed. They are quite different from the skill of artists generally, which is in great part won by toil – and of which one says to oneself: 'If I had worked as long that way, perhaps I could have done something too.' But that easy rightness of your mother's sketching humiliates me."

In the year following *Preludes* a visit to Tennyson at Aldworth, Blackdown, his remote high-hilled house, was a not altogether easy experience for the two girls. Tennyson's invitation to them came through Aubrey de Vere; and on their arrival they were obliged to inform him which was poet and which was painter. A somewhat gruff demeanour intimidated them until they thought they detected in the poet something rather deliberately awe-inspiring – and immediately they feared no more. His offer to read to them, and Alice's request that it should be *The Passing of Arthur*, relieved the flagging conversation; but though he complied he was not pleased with her choice, which he thought should have fallen on his later work. Afterwards, on easier terms, he walked with them in the garden, giving them roses; but his relenting mood was still uncomfortable to them, for he felt free to mock at their tight fashionable dresses, making Alice stay behind with him while he pointed "the walking-stick of scorn" at Elizabeth's skirt where she walked ahead with his son. Another unsuccessful passage was when, referring to Elizabeth's military drawings, he bantered her on being as much agog for the sight of an officer as any Jane Austen young lady – a pleasantry not really enjoyed by his serious-minded young visitor.

Another interesting literary friend was Sir Edwin Arnold, author of *The Light of Asia*. To the two girls he read aloud one day some of Praed's verses, among them the "Letter of Advice" to Araminta, in which verse after verse describes what a lover must not on any account be. Not suspecting in what a desperate predicament a man may find himself when merely reading light verses to two attentive young women, Edwin Arnold proceeded happily until he came to this verse:

> If he wears a top-boot in his wooing,
>   If he comes to you riding a cob,
> If he talks of his baking or brewing,
>   If he puts up his feet on the hob,
> If he ever drinks port after dinner,
>   If his brow or his breeding is low,
> If he calls himself "Thompson" or "Skinner,"
>   My own Araminta, say "No!"

Edwin Arnold did not read it thus, however, for with quick presence of mind he substituted "Johnson" for "Thompson" – a ruse that ought to have been perfectly successful had not the two smiling girls been familiar with the text.

Before leaving this time of *Preludes* one may pause to note how much had been accomplished in these early poems. Hardly without a feeling of treachery can a member of her family pronounce their achievement already fine, so thorough was her own repudiation of them later, so gladly did she make any convert to her own view. For in maturity she liked in her own work only that which had more compact thought in it; her mind used itself later on harder thoughts in her poetry, as it had always been apt to do in her prose; and to please her in those later years praise had to have a very recent date. "Renouncement," which, however, was not included in *Preludes*, was never specifically banned in my hearing; but I fancy that not one of the other early poems would have been even preserved if she could have had her way. I remember her arguing one day the demerits of "A Letter from a Girl to her Own Old Age" when a request came for permission to reprint it in an anthology. The idea of this poem, she said, was good, the working-out poor; and this her opponent in the argument would not agree with. But to one who chanced to express an opinion the same as hers she turned with relief and gratitude, as if something had been conceded that was of infinite value to her. The almost daily requests for poems for anthologies that arrived in later years were constant reminders of the difference between her and my father on this point – when in making a choice of poems he wished to perpetuate what she thought should be forgotten.

But if she had not thus emphatically cast off her former self, she surely would have made exceptions to this general condemnation even though she had fallen in love with the tenser, more concentrated exercise of her mind. There are the lines called "Song of the Night at Daybreak":

54

All my stars forsake me,
And the dawn-winds shake me.
Where shall I betake me?

Whither shall I run
Till the set of sun,
Till the day be done?

To the mountain-mine,
To the boughs o' the pine,
To the blind man's eyne.

To a brow that is
Bowed upon the knees,
Sick with memories.

One can well imagine how the later ideas for poems
more individual to herself, more the very summit of her
thinking powers, came to her with greater reward. But
since it is all her written words, both early and late, that
this book is to commemorate, it may not be too much to
quote one more of those youthful poems, "To a Daisy":

Slight as thou art, thou art enough to hide,
Like all created things, secrets from me,
And stand a barrier to eternity.
And I, how can I praise thee well and wide
From where I dwell – upon the hither side?
Thou little veil for so great mystery,
When shall I penetrate all things and thee,
And then look back? For this I must abide,
Till thou shalt grow and fold and be unfurled
Literally between me and the world.
Then I shall drink from in beneath a spring,
And from a poet's side shall read his book.
O daisy mine, what will it be to look
From God's side even at such a simple thing?

Later she wished to bring more mature treatment to
bear on that early work, and to change and improve it,
for there is a letter written to her by Francis Thompson
dealing with such an idea – a letter so well expressing a
different point of view from hers that it may be given
here to reach other poets besides the one to whom it was
addressed:

"At the risk of offending you by what you may
think officious interference, I take up my pen to im-
plore you to meddle as little as may be with the text
of *Preludes*. In principle, 1 think the modern foible of
poets for revising in maturity the poems of their youth
to be not only most perilous for the poems tampered
with, but a capital sin against that art which the process is designed to serve, and by which you set such
store. It is fatal to *keeping*, and keeping is surely all in
all to art. You would not re-touch your youthful portrait into the contours of mature womanhood, though
they be absolutely more perfect. And all poetry to a
certain degree, but poetry such as *Preludes in excelsis*,
is a portrait. It is a portrait of your youthful self. By
re-modelling it according to the mind of your maturity,
you will destroy its truthfulness to the thing you were,
without making it truthful to the thing you are. It
will be a hybrid; it will lose the absolute fresh sincerity of girlhood, without gaining the greater and
more reticent sincerity of womanhood. It will, indeed,
be a sin against sincerity. For your poetry was intended
to show yourself; and now you are re-touching the portrait for the public as you would like yourself to have

been. It will lose the value it had for us, and must have had for all men, by reason of its single-minded utterance of your young self; it will not have for us any value as an utterance of your matron-self. In the name of your art, which you are going to betray under the notion of safeguarding; in the name of your poetry, which we loved for what it was, not for what it should or might have been; in the name of the sincerity which you have never before falsified; in the name of your admirers, whose instinct for poetry you have not doubted in the case of others; I conjure Alice Meynell to leave us Alice Thompson, unimproved, unsophisticated, with her weakness and her strength as we saw, accepted, admired, and loved her. . . . Be angry, but hear me."

VI

EARLY YEARS OF MARRIED LIFE

ITALY still came before and after everything; and that same year (1876) the two girls did not miss their vintage in Tuscany, going alone to linger along the Genoese coast – travellers, but at home – until they arrived as overdue guests at the *Villa* of Mrs. Janet Ross, near Florence, where the peaches and other garden-harvests of that abundant place were threatening over-ripeness through being kept back for them. From there Alice wrote to Ruskin some account of the agricultural country she loved, and he replied to her: "Of the farmed country all you say and think is absolutely true. . . . Heaven save at least this old Tuscany! I saw lovely things there in peasant life myself, but it seemed depressed, and declining. . . . I have not half thanked you for your lovely letter – but will, and with yet more thanks if I may put it to service in *Fors* some day, when I get back to Tuscan subjects."

They returned to a London winter which must have been a happy one; for at its close both of them were engaged to be married. A feature of their life at this time was their mother's musical afternoon parties, and to one of these came Wilfrid Meynell.* He was then living with

* He belonged to a family long settled in Yorkshire, the earlier variants of whose name (Mesnil, Maynil and the rest) had been

Father William Lockhart at St. Etheldreda's in Ely Place. He was the seventh child in a family of eight, and received from his father a small allowance, which made it possible for him to try his hand at journalism rather than adopt a less congenial profession. His friend, Father Lockhart, was a man of great charm of mind and person, who devoted his service to the slums then at the back of Holborn; and to Wilfrid Meynell the chance of associating himself with the social and literary work connected with St. Etheldreda's had been just the kind of opportunity he most wished for.

Reading one day in the *Pall Mall Gazette* a review of *Preludes* which quoted the sonnet "My Heart shall by thy Garden," it became his greatest wish to meet its author. Father Lockhart, fortunately a friend of the Thompsons, took him to an afternoon party at their house. Thereafter he came again and again; and he and Alice also corresponded. His verses were criticised by her. In sending some of hers to him, she said: "I know you will not care for them at the first reading. The greatest lover of my work used to say that he was obliged to read a piece of mine nine times. But I should be loth to inflict such a task on everyone." So devoted to their literary interests was their correspondence that anything else contained in it has the sound of an interruption. Once Alice interrupts herself thus to say: "What you tell me about the child's kiss is so beautiful. That is a kiss you will wear all your

modernised into Mennell and Meynell. On his mother's side he was a grandson of Samuel Tuke of York, the friend of William Wilberforce whom he helped in the liberation of slaves. The successful attempts of earlier Tukes to ameliorate the treatment of the insane in England were contemporary with those of Pinel in France.

life, will you not? I should like never to receive any kisses but those I shall never part with."

Their engagement was made on the New Year's Day of 1877. Father Lockhart, on hearing the news, wrote to Alice: "My dear Child, – You have determined to link your lot with one who is chivalrous in honour, tender in piety and love, and who will be faithful to the end and true as steel in weal and woe. For him you have been willing to forgo a more brilliant but not, as I believe, a happier lot. My only anxiety is to know that you have your father's and mother's blessing." Her mother's consent to the engagement was happy and immediate. But her father did not conceal his financial misgivings. After a few days, however, Alice was able to write: "I greet you this morning, my sweet, sweet Wilfrid. My father is calmer; he speaks of you with the esteem which you can never fail to win. Write him one of your own charming letters; let him see something of your heart."

During the brief days of their engagement, their excited hopes centred for a time in the possibility of starting a new magazine. "Collect all the facts you can about the magazine," she wrote, "and I will do the same. I have set my heart on having great names in it; I aspire to Tennyson and to Matthew Arnold. Alfred Austin may write prose but he shall not twang that banjo Browning speaks of in our pages. Mivart shall write for us, not on poetry, nor on love (which he told me last summer was the only subject that really interested him), but on comparative anatomy. Mimi, Mrs. Allingham, and a friend of mine, Wilfrid Lawson, shall illustrate us, as they are all popular and good. It is too delightful and exciting.

And my dear Ruskin? . . . Wilfrid, we will start magnificently." *Pen and Pencil* was rejected as a title: it had
been used before. The *Commonwealth* was approved. Dis-
couragement came in a letter from Ruskin: he would not
write for their review; and thought, perhaps with reason,
that his hatred of reviews might have been guessed at;
he did not want his young friend to be a reviewer herself,
a profession in which he held consistent honesty to be
impossible. He wished her a happy marriage and "a
better trade."

They were married in London in the autumn of 1877
by the Bishop of Nottingham, who, as Father Bagshawe
of the Oratory, had been the bride's friend. Elizabeth's
marriage to Major William Francis Butler took place in
the June of that same year.

Married life began at Inkerman Terrace in Kensington; there Sebastian and Monica were born.

Journalism was the pleasant and constant occupation
of both my parents; at the time of her marriage it committed its act of confiscation for ever of leisure from my
mother's life. In the interests of bread-winning the worker
at will became the worker at every demand – a thing no
writer can deplore who knows how possible it is to sit
down to pot-boiling and to rise from authorship.

A snatch of diary recounts a few things in the early
years of married life, the kind of diary which begins re-
pentantly with: "After five years I resume my journal,"
– and which after a few pages falls on another five years
or so of silence. "Though tiny it is exquisitely arranged,"
she says of this first little house, "with Morris papers and
good colour everywhere. Papa and Mamma are next

door." She mentions a party, when Robert Browning who had been introduced by William Bell Scott, was among her guests – "the life of the afternoon." She relates that when she happens to remark on the sweet expression of the then Chinese Ambassador, Browning smilingly informs her that the sweet-faced Ambassador has been sent on the mission to England in order to check his passion for decapitation in his own country. She speaks of Browning's solicitude for his son's painting career; and of his saying, with how deliberate a disingenuousness it is hard to know: "So much is expected of him because of his clever mother." She speaks of Aubrey de Vere's visits, and of his relating how he had in the past contrived to win from Wordsworth his first reluctant approval of Tennyson by reading to him "Of old sate Freedom on the heights" – the older poet having considered till then that no one who had lived only twenty-one years could write poetry for men to read.

This diary of the young woman, entered formally on her career, is full of a new proprietary pleasure in the trappings of a literary life. Not only literature belongs to her, but, in moments of leisure, literary anecdote. She seems like someone who, having inherited a house, arrives to find that the very pictures on the walls, the china in the cupboard, the flowers in the garden, are hers as well.

In the first year of their married life, during a stay at Bournemouth, my parents met Sir Henry and Lady Taylor. "I hope you will like my young poet friend, Alice Meynell," Aubrey de Vere had written to his cousin, Lady Taylor. "To me she is very interesting, but you will find her shy." This friendship made a new link with literary interests, for Sir Henry Taylor, then famous as the author of *Philip van Artevelde*, had known Tennyson for fifty years, and had been the friend of Wordsworth, Rogers, Carlyle and Mill; and Lady Taylor was a good talker of reminiscence. There was the tale of how Thackeray's impulsive daughter, Annie, driving along a London street, saw a woman ill-treating a child, whereupon she stopped, snatched away the child in her fury and drove off with it; and how, after many a vain effort, in colder blood, to restore the infant to its parents, she finally found herself with the child left on her hands. Noting many such little tidings in her diary, and speaking of other friends of the Taylors, whom she now met, my mother had only one regret: "All these people might have seen Shelley, but unfortunately it seems to be always Rogers whom they saw!" But she was to get near Shelley after all, for his descendants both by Harriet and Mary were to be met at Bournemouth. "Friday, September 12, 1878. Lady Shelley came in the afternoon. She has a refined, thinking, intelligent face. To me it is a memorable thing to be visited by Shelley's daughter-in-law." But what my father, after dining with the Shelleys, could never cease to marvel at was the strange effect of hearing the poet, "the eternal child," referred to by elderly respectability as "my poor father."

The friendship with the Taylors led to more visits to Bournemouth. Writing of Lady Taylor when she died in 1891, my mother said: "Her sprightly consciousness helped her talk there precisely where a duller wit would have thought that scruples might mar it, and malice would mend it. Did an ordinary talker find you matter for a smile in some point a little unkind or a little untrue, Lady Taylor would find you cause for a more sudden laugh by surprising you with a touch of mere justice. She had that rare charm of justice. Enjoying it, you wondered why other people would be content to touch your ordinary, habitual, every-day apprehension by exaggeration, when they might be reaching the recollected sincerity within your heart, as she did, by the reverent touches of truth."

My mother was fortunate to have a friend giving an example of a quality so much according to her taste. Truth instead of exaggeration gave value always to her own conversation; and absurdities were always watched in case they were something else besides absurd. Her son, Everard, among a few notes concerning his memory of his mother in his childhood, found after he died, refers to an essay of hers in *The Rhythm of Life* called "Domus Angusta." This "narrow house" of her essay is the being whose capacity is too small for the fate of life and death, the inadequate, dull, insensitive person, an easy subject for the gay injustice of laughter, from whom such laughter may draw, however, a look of involuntary appeal. And she adds in the essay: "Far from me and from my friends be the misfortune of meeting such looks in reply to pain of our inflicting." My brother comments: "That must indeed have been a rule she lived by, – a hard rule in the midst of a large family much given, as is the way in family circles, groups, communities, colleges, courts and even kingdoms, to ridicule the stranger. To children, linked by a common sense of the ridiculous, some visitors seem irresistibly comic. Just as fear would have seized us unanimously in the presence of a rough intruder, so would we be convulsed together in suppressed laughter at an absurd one. Then later, when we would go over the comic scene to relish it yet again, we would seek to inveigle our mother to be one of us. But in vain. 'Laugh, mother, laugh!' is the refrain that still floats back to one from many a forgotten jest. I imagine we were so insistent that she should join us because we knew that she had our own sense of humour. We knew nothing of a reason not to laugh, and were not told. She left us to discover for ourselves that pain is not amusing. Example was her way, not precept. She never sent us to her essay, which ends: 'To be clever and sensitive and to hurt the foolish and the stolid – wouldst thou do such a deed for all the world? Not I, by this heavenly light.' "

In 1880 *The Pen, a Journal of Literature*, gave my father his first experiment in editorship. Dante Gabriel Rossetti, writing to Frederick Shields in July 1880, says: "I think I told you that a thing called *The Pen* had descanted flatteringly on me, as I heard. I have since seen it, and it is very good (I know not by whom at all), but I regret to find that I have killed off *The Pen*, as its writing days ceased with that number." William Michael Rossetti, in his brother's *Letters and Memoir*, notes: "The article in *The Pen*, as my brother afterwards ascertained, was written by Mrs. Meynell." After only seven weekly appearances (the bound volume makes good reading now) *The Pen* was produced for a few times as a monthly, but no longer in my father's care.

In 1881 my parents moved to Phillimore Place, still in Kensington, where they lived for eight years, and where

Everard, Madeline, Viola, and Vivian, who died in early infancy, were born. My mother's father died in 1881. He was received into the Catholic Church before he died.

In the first year of Phillimore Place, at the request of his friend, Cardinal Manning, began my father's editorship of *The Weekly Register*, a Catholic periodical. For eighteen years the functions of editor, sub-editor, contributor and even office-boy, kept my father a busy man on most days, a harassed man on Thursdays, – so that one of the things the childhood of all the young family was chiefly aware of was the indescribable effort and struggle against time on those Thursdays, with both parents silent and desperate with work. My mother undertook any of the odd jobs that were piled too high upon even so quick a worker as that editor. She wrote leaders, and reviewed books, and read proofs, and translated Papal encyclicals from the Italian. (In a letter written later to Coventry Patmore in which she happened to be recounting the day's doings, she says: "I have just translated for the *Register* the Pope's letter to the Hungarian Bishops – without pranks. Sometimes I make His Holiness quote our poets!")

But apart from the hack work, to contribute to the *Spectator* and the *Saturday Review*, as she had begun to do, at a time when those journals were read with an excitement which is now crowded out of existence, was pleasing enough. Also, by way of encouragement to her more personal and precious authorship, she received from Mr. Hall Caine a request for a published and unpublished sonnet for his Anthology, *Sonnets of Three Centuries*, which appeared in 1882. In making his request Hall Caine said he had been advised by his friend, D. G. Rossetti, who had read *Preludes*. "My Heart shall be thy Garden" was the published sonnet sent, "Renouncement" the unpublished one, which Rossetti learnt by heart.

The house in Phillimore Place, built about 1820, and with its characteristic "dish-clout" stone ornamentation, was to my brother Everard the house of his childhood's memories. "I remember my mother's bedroom, with the windows looking on the High Street, the clatter of market-carts in the dawn, the blear-eyed vendors of bird-seed, the large trunks in which my mother used to pack us in turn to drag us round her room, through a back-bedroom on to the landing, making us guess where we were before the lid was lifted."

He remembers the exquisite confectioner's near Kensington Church, the home of magnificent wedding-cakes, which was always visited for ices after the dentist. "She would sit with us while we dealt with our sponge-cakes which broke into yellow crumbs on our suits and tasted warm between mouthfuls of ice. I see her bright eyes smile at first and then become slightly abstracted as she resigns herself to ten minutes at the little table. There are mirrors in the ceiling near the window, so that passing omnibuses are curiously reflected, the legs and hoofs of their horses plodding noiselessly upside-down above our heads. We understand our mother's abstracted look when she has her pencil and writing-pad; we understand it less when there are no implements of work. Then back along Kensington High Street, past a strange railed-in place, near the Public Library, where the scavengers keep brushes and shovels, but to us a place of mystery and terror. So to our own few yards of railing, our own iron gate and brick wall, bright during certain weeks with jasmine of the most ravishing fragrance, exquisite scented stars among dark bricks that even now after thirty-five years thrill me. Past our windows went the little horse-omnibus to Hammersmith; from there by train to Turnham Green my mother went every week or two to visit her mother."

My father had ideas that needed further activity, and with the hopefulness of a boundless possibility *Merry England*, a monthly magazine, was launched in 1883. Characteristic of one of my father's enthusiasms, the first number had a portrait of Disraeli for frontispiece, and all the ardour of the new magazine was in support of the social revolution of the Young England Movement, the revival of the peasantry, the abolition of the wrongs of the poor, the spread of art and literature. Eventual contributors were Coventry Patmore, Cardinal Manning, Katherine Tynan and Wilfrid Blunt, and it was here that some of the earliest work of W. H. Hudson and Hilaire Belloc and Lionel Johnson appeared. My father, to conceal the variety and extent of his own contributions, had to adopt not one pseudonym but several. My mother also wrote constantly. The magazine appeared for twelve years, and the editorship of it must have been a pleasant and not too burdensome task. I remember that when we children enquired of our parents what they were busy at, if it was *The Weekly Register* it had a desperate sound, if it was *Merry England* it had not.

Merry England can never pass into the oblivion of a lost enterprise because it was the means by which Francis Thompson was discovered. As a medical student in

Manchester he read it from its beginning ("I was my-self virtually his pupil and his wife's long before I knew him," he said of its editor); and when at last his useless studies were abandoned, and in London streets he had reached the last stages of raggedness and destitution, it was into the letter-box of the *Merry England* office in Essex Street that he put a packet of manuscript with a covering letter:

"Feb. 23/87. Dear Sir, – In enclosing the accompanying article for your inspection I must ask pardon for the soiled state of the manuscript. It is due, not to slovenliness, but to the strange places and circumstances in which it has been written. For me, no less than Parolles, the dirty nurse experience has something fouled. I enclose stamped envelope for a reply, since I do not desire the return of the manuscript, regarding your judgment of its worthlessness as quite final. I can hardly expect that where my prose fails my verse will succeed. Nevertheless, on the principle of 'Yet will I try the last,' I have added a few specimens of it, with the off chance that one may be less poor than the rest. Apologising very sincerely for any intrusion on your valuable time, I remain yours with little hope, FRANCIS THOMPSON.

"Kindly address your rejection to the Charing Cross post office."

The *Life of Francis Thompson* tells the full story of how, when the contents were read, after some delay, efforts were made in vain to trace the author; and as a last resort one of his poems was printed in the magazine – a device that succeeded and immediately brought a letter from the poet. The meeting between my father and the unkempt and diseased vagrant who was eventually found was the beginning of a life-long devotion in my father, making him, who already loved poetry so much, love it still more. The poet was an object for pity, but I doubt if my father could ever pity him. What a transforming thing to him his love of Francis Thompson's poetry has been can be felt only by his family who know how much of the thought and incident of his life have been made of it. Or perhaps it may be guessed by those of his friends who are used to his going to the bookshelves with an open mind to get something to read aloud and who know that his hand falls invariably on a Thompson volume. Francis Thompson's poetry has been more to him than the work of any one poet often is to anybody, so that if one were to imagine the non-existence of that poetry one would have to imagine him a different man.

To my mother the advent of Francis Thompson and his poetry was a less transforming thing. Though she found him a great poet, he did not raise the very status of contemporary poetry, as he did to my father. She withheld no praise from his imagery – "imagery so beautiful as almost to persuade us that imagery is the end and goal of poetry. . . . But Francis Thompson himself," she wrote later, looking back on his poetry, "was soon to learn that these ceremonies of the imagination are chiefly ways of approach, and that there are barer realities beyond, and nearer to the centre of poetry itself." It was when she read certain of the Odes of Coventry Patmore that she considered there was this quality in a living poet, a transcendent simplicity beyond imagery, with imagery's "fervours and splendours put to silence." And when Francis Thompson wrote his third and last book of poems, strongly then under the influence of Patmore and dedicated to him, she thought he took a "yet higher step in his art and thought" through that influence.

At the time when Francis Thompson came the Phillimore Place days were drawing to a close; and it was at my parents' house in Palace Court that he became the utterly dependent friend, – the gentle, late, voluble, flushed, dozing visitor of every day.

The move to the new house was much more of an adventure than the other moves had been. With a part of the little fortune my mother had inherited on the death of her father, a piece of land had been bought in Palace Court, and their idea of a charming house was built for them there, with Leonard Stokes for their architect. At Phillimore Place my mother's busiest writing years had not yet begun; the young family must have taken too much of her. At Palace Court full work and full life awaited her.

VII

THE RHYTHM OF LIFE

THE house in Palace Court was built in a style unusual then. Its red brick, its tall gable, its small-paned windows made a surprising contrast with prevalent greyness and squareness. My father and mother chose the kind of house they liked when they chose their architect. Occasionally there could be seen from the window in after years a party of young men who must have been architectural students standing opposite the house while their lecturer demonstrated to them its points. It was one of the first houses to be built in Palace Court, and was then called Palace Court House; later it became merely No. 47. Here Olivia was born and Francis, the last of the children.

My mother had by this time, in 1889, shown that the masculine art of essay-writing was hers by virtue of her mastery of it. Her imagination had taken essay-shape; her terseness and her pedantry made good essay-manner. In the early part of the year of the move to Palace Court she was writing the essay called "The Rhythm of Life," and following it quickly again and again, as she realised that the power was hers.

The editor to whom these essays were sent as they were written was W. E. Henley. "Henley was the Viking Chief of letters," wrote Francis Thompson of him. " . . . By the intellectual flower of young England, so much of which passed under his personal influence and control, he was worshipped the other side of idolatry." All that an editor needs to be of a masterful, obstinate, opinionated man, Henley was; all the fastidious discrimination that draws from contributors their best, he had. He was ready for the brutalities of editorship, and his approval was the careful genuine approval which is the only kind an editor can afford to bestow. His paper, first called *The Scots Observer*, produced in Edinburgh, became in 1890 *The National Observer*, which was produced in Fleet Street. It must have been agreeable to get from Henley constant appeals for articles. "If you've any more 'Rhythms of Life' I shall be proud indeed to take them on, one of the best things it has so far been my privilege to print." And if this mother of a young family paused: "Are you never going to write for me again?"

But pauses were few. "Mr. Martin tells me," writes Henley, "that he thinks of asking you to write a certain study for a certain portrait in *Literary Opinion*. I have told him in return that I think you would write well about a broomstick." As a mere matter of livelihood suggestions could not be ignored, nor even waited for. "As regards Coquelin et Cie," writes Henley, "one article – on the art, the general quality, of the thing – by all means. But I haven't room for a series, even from you." (A disinclination to appear in *The Yellow Book* must have been an exception to her general readiness, in spite of an inducing note from Henry Harland: "I wish I could persuade you to become a contributor to *The*

Yellow Book. I think I have heard that your feeling for that periodical is not one of unbounded enthusiasm – *raison de plus* why you should lend a hand to the bettering of it. Won't you do us one of your exquisite essays?")

The anxiety and ambition a writer feels about his own work was perhaps especially apparent in Henley, so that when one reads in one of his letters, "I have some verses under weigh which I shall ask you to read with peculiar attention," one smiles to think that there is almost an unconscious threat in such words from that hand. "Your selection" (in a review of his poems by my mother) "has interested me," he writes, "though I don't at all agree with it"; – and to have one of his poems criticised was apt to make him argue that it was undoubtedly his best. He was a man who was able to make the reading of his paper an excitement. "Just think of what was doing then!" wrote Wilfrid Whitten in the *Academy*, when those days were past and he looked back at them. "*The National Observer* may not fill in the memory quite the place that it filled in the eyes of its handful of purchasers; but what a bliss it struck upon the week. We were relatively poor then, my friend and I, and we clubbed our money week after week to buy the paper. How we shouted and wrote each other notes about Mrs. Meynell's 'Rejection' and Mr. Kenneth Grahame's 'Orion' and Kipling's 'Tomlinson,' and the trail of Henley over all."

Essay-writing was surely made the more interesting by that definite figure of an Editor. And it was Henley who gave the first news of a widening public for my mother. "A certain publisher wants, I think, to reprint some of your *National Observer* articles. Shall I encourage him to

74

hope?" And afterwards: "The publisher is Lane. I wrote to him to-day."

The book appeared in 1893 under the name of *The Rhythm of Life*. To examine it apart from all that came after it is to find in it a closeness and economy that would seem more like the final development than the beginning of a style. She did not use too many words on her ideas, she may have used too few. Youth, not age, was crabbed; age unlocked its words a little more liberally. Herself possessing what she found in James Russell Lowell, a "scholarly, linguistic, verbal love of literature, with a studiousness full of heart," she wrote as a specialist who feels so happy a bond with those like-minded who will follow her meaning that she cannot sacrifice one particle of her specialisation. It would have been difficult to convince her that she was often obscure; in suiting herself as she wrote she was suiting those others, those who would follow her exactly as she went, and to whom she must not deny one single subtlety or approval or agreement.

Her subjects were peculiarly her own discoveries. In one essay, that "Domus Angusta " already quoted, she suggests that in your time of emotion, if you have the word to name it with, you sharpen the edge of your feeling in a way unknown to those whose inexpressiveness cannot match it with its word, its description. So that our words, she would make us think, do not merely serve to express our feelings, they enhance them: "We may, indeed, in part know the narrow house by its inarticulateness – not, certainly, its fewness of words, but its inadequacy and imprecision of speech. For, doubtless, right language enlarges the soul as no other power or influence may do.

Who, for instance, but trusts more nobly for knowing the full word of his confidence? Who but loves more penetratingly for possessing the ultimate syllable of his tenderness? . . . And I suppose that even physical pain takes on an edge when it not only enforces a pang but whispers a phrase."

And now, having given this much of importance to the words we speak, she goes still further in another essay to assign to them subtle influence and action. In considering Latin English, as against Teutonic, she finds in such words as "tribulation," "immortality," "multitude" a composure that makes bearable their disquiet: "Without the remoteness of the Latinity the thought would come too close and shake too cruelly." She speaks of Johnson's fear of death, and imagines that his noble English controlled and postponed his terror. But if Latin English will help to put your fears where they are slightly aloof and at peace, that is as far as you want to go, and not as far as some moralists of the eighteenth century whose word of platitude brought not merely peace but indifference. Addison, for instance, she says, "assuredly removed Eternity far from the apprehension of the soul when his Cato hailed the 'pleasing hope,' the 'fond desire.' "

And in the essay on James Russell Lowell, her jealous preoccupation with language is apparent once more when she absolves the writer of too easy or ready-made or exaggerated a use of words. "In his own use, and within his own English, he has the abstinence and the freshness of intention that keep every word new for the day's work. He gave to the language and did not take from it; it gained by him, and lost not. There are writers of English now at work who almost convince us of their greatness until we convict them on that charge: that they have succeeded at an unpardonable cost; they are glorified, but they have beggared the phrases they leave behind them."

With her more easy visual eye alert, she writes of a Suffolk plain with its enormous sky unbroken by scenery, seen as one great construction that confesses the sun as the centre of its design. And the earth, too, is there entirely concerned with the sun; "there are but two views on the plain; for the aspect of the light is the whole land-scape. To look with the sun or against the sun – this is the alternative splendour." A protest is made in another essay against our cheap and slothful use of the flower for all our common ornament, so that a visitor to a furnished farmhouse-room finds everywhere gloomy, interior, un-recognisable posies, – "a dry, woollen, papery, cast-iron garden." The patterned carpet, the table-cover, the wall-paper, the bell-pull, the curtains, the cups, the finials of the sofa and chairs, are all blossoming with the same stale inspiration of the flower. "And what is this bossiness around the grate but some blunt, black-leaded garland?"

In " Decivilized " she complains that the colonist, in danger of mere provincialism, but with his air of the noble savage, when accused of vulgarity is apt to defend him-self against the charge of barbarism; and that when he assures you he does not wear war-paint and feathers it is "difficult to communicate to him that you had suspected him of nothing wilder than a second-hand dress-coat."

But the discovery that must have come from her most vital experience is the rhythm of life itself, the knowledge that, without reference to events, a tide ebbs and flows within our minds, that periodicity rules our lives. Of this rhythm, "distances are not gauged, ellipses not measured, velocities not ascertained, times not known. Nevertheless, the recurrence is sure." She remembers how Juliet will not accept a vow that is spoken in invocation of the inconstant moon, "but Juliet did not live to know that love itself has tidal times." She believes that man does not take count of periodicity. "The individual man either never learns it fully, or learns it late. And he learns it so late, because it is a matter of cumulative experience upon which cumulative evidence is lacking. It is in the afterpart of each life that the law is learnt so definitely as to do away with the hope or fear of continuance. That young sorrow comes so near to despair is a result of this young ignorance. So is the early hope of great achievement. Life seems so long, and its capacity so great, to one who knows nothing of all the intervals it needs must hold – intervals between aspirations, between actions, pauses as inevitable as the pauses of sleep. And life looks impossible to the young unfortunate, unaware of the inevitable and unfailing refreshment." Included in this volume, too, was the essay revealing my mother's unbounded love of Coventry Patmore's Odes.

In making its appearance *The Rhythm of Life* was accompanied by *Poems*, and together the two volumes went out for review. *Poems* was so largely a reprint of the long out-of-print *Preludes* that its publication was a concession on my mother's part – a concession she made easier for herself by expunging what she thought most crude in *Preludes* and by adding a few new poems.

The two books made her famous in the literary world. She was, in fact, pronounced a better prose-writer than poet, and in this decision the reviewers had before them a notable opinion with which to find themselves in agreement. For immediately before the publication of the two books there had appeared in the *Fortnightly Review* an article by Coventry Patmore on her work, denying to her the highest quality in poetry but using about her prose a word which he first defined and endowed with the most magnificent meaning and then bestowed upon her, – the word genius. Thus the critics had to pass under review not only the two books themselves but Patmore's claim for them. Surely rebellion should have resulted – not the less because my mother reciprocated this praise in her own essay on Coventry Patmore.

For thus did these two writers pronounce their utmost of each other. And in the friendship that had now come to them, important in both their lives, nothing could have satisfied them but that their utmost word had been publicly spoken. My mother's article on Coventry Patmore had first appeared in the *National Observer* two years before, when she and my father had a very slight acquaintance with him. By the time his article on her appeared their friendship had assumed its great significance to them.

Because of its influence on her early fame, and because it must surely have been one of the happinesses of her life to receive this testimony from the man whose poetry she adored, the *Fortnightly* article should be quoted here in a few of its salient passages. He speaks of "Renouncement." "This," he says, "like all Mrs. Meynell's verse, is true, beautiful, tender and negatively almost faultless; but it does not attain the classical and only sound standard . . . With extraordinary power of self-judgment she discovered this fact while she was yet a mere girl, and, disdaining to do anything which she could not do, not only well, but best, and notwithstanding the encouragement to persevere in poetry which she received from critics, she gave up the attempt, and has hardly since written a line. But in a very small volume of very short essays, which she has just published, this lady has shown an amount of perceptive reason and ability to discern self-evident things as yet undiscerned, a reticence, fulness, and effectiveness of expression, which place her in the very front rank of living writers in prose. At least half of this little volume is *classical* work, embodying as it does new thought of general and permanent significance in perfect language, and bearing, in every sentence, the hall-mark of genius, namely, the marriage of masculine force of insight with feminine grace and tact of expression. Of the 'sweetness and wit' which are said, by Donne, I think, to be woman's highest attainment, there is in these little essays abundance, but they are only the living drapery of thought which has the virile qualities of simplicity, continuity, and positiveness. The essays of Emerson, of which those of Mrs. Meynell will sometimes remind the reader, are not to be compared with the best of hers in these great merits; moreover the 'transcendentalism' of the American writer afforded a far easier field than that chosen by the English lady. It is very easy to speak splendidly and profusely about things which transcend speech; but to write beautifully, profitably and originally about truths which come home to everybody, and which everybody can test by common sense; to avoid with sedulous reverence the things which are beyond the focus of the human eye, and to direct attention effectively to those which are well within it, though they have hitherto been undiscerned through lack of attention, or the astounding imperfection of common vision for the reality of common things, is a very different attainment. Gaiety of manner with gravity of matter, truth perceived clearly and expressed with ease and joy, constitute the very highest and rarest of prose writing."

Coventry Patmore's estimate was generally accepted by the critics of the two books. Mr. Le Gallienne made the reservation: "She puts too much into a sentence. The words have no room to breathe in"; but to another critic that would only mean that "her sentences need to be read not by the eye only but by the very marrow of the mind." She was accorded a position unique in the literature of the day.

The new fame, the new house, the new children, – this life was full of freshness and the accumulation of things, the heads to count, the pages to sort. The long library table at Palace Court was turned white with papers, the little litter of authorship, the great litter of journalism. Into the book-boxes in the shelves, the papers relating to any event in my mother's literary life found their way eventually, after a few months spent first in the confusion of the table, and perhaps a few years in the indiscriminate depths of the lockers that made the library window-seat. Then the day arrived when my father, always a great keeper and only a fitful putter-away, would find places for all the things he had preserved. My mother on the other hand was an offender in destroying. My father was many years persuading her not to burn the envelopes of important letters – often dated only by their postmarks – even after she had learnt to keep for him the letters themselves. It took him almost as long to learn and believe in her powers of destroying as she his fondness for keeping. Her destruction may have been in part a faintly humorous challenge to the importance of the document. At least, there was something not quite real about her contrition when her sin was brought home to her.

In going through the *Rhythm of Life* papers, which my father has made it so easy to do, among the newspaper-cuttings and letters in strange writings, one comes on a letter in my grandmother's familiar writing – familiar not only in her diaries and letters but in the countless piles she amassed of music of her own composition, for even into her crotchets and quavers she managed to put all the characteristics of her handwriting. This letter strikes a note of family gratification at my mother's success which it is hard to find much trace of elsewhere, for otherwise success seems to have been taken very much for granted:

"My sweetest Alice, – I am sorry to have obliged thee to write. Thou must be heartily weary of holding the pen – but the world is not weary. I copy a passage from a letter just received from Fanny: which ought to gratify thee. 'People are mad about Alice; our chaplain in Genoa, just fresh out, says she is considered the first prose writer of the day, that at Oxford they are fanatical about her. He wished to make my acquaintance simply on the strength of our relationship.' I will not take up any more of thy time. Do go to Dover as soon as possible and oh! do not kill thyself with work! Ever thy loving devoted Mama. A blackbird is warbling divinely amongst the branches of the fruit trees in blossom."

Another letter is from Francis Thompson, in which he says: "Never again meditate the suppression of your gloomy passages – it is a most false epithet for anything you could ever write. . . . How can you call 'gloomy' what so nobly and resignedly faces the terror it evokes?"

And in this year of 1893 my mother was celebrated not only by her own performance but by Francis Thompson's in her honour. His first book of poems was now produced, containing "Love in Dian's Lap," a series of poems inspired by her. Pacing the library floor, or in Kensington Gardens, this volume and *Sister Songs*, published two years later, were composed – "pencilled," says my brother in his biography, "into penny exercise-books. His reiterated 'It's a penny exercise-book' is remembered by every member of the household set to search for the mislaid drafts of 'Love in Dian's Lap' – he himself too dismayed to look."

It is the poetry of remote ennobling love – he disembodied, she almost so. It celebrates her spirit, and his spirit's praise of her – "This soul which on your soul is laid, As maid's breast against breast of maid."

Lady who hold'st on me dominion!
Within your spirit's arms I stay me fast
   Against the fell
Immitigate ravening of the gates of hell;
And claim my right in you; most hardly won,
Of chaste fidelity upon the chaste:
Hold me and hold by me, lest both should fall
(O in high escalade high companion!)
Even in the breach of Heaven's assaulted wall.
Like to a wind-sown sapling grow I from
The clift, sweet, of your skyward-jetting soul, –
Shook by all gusts that sweep it, overcome
By all its clouds incumbent: O be true
To your soul, dearest, as my life to you!
For if that soil grow sterile, then the whole
Of me must shrivel, from the topmost shoot
Of climbing poesy, and my life, killed through,
Dry down and perish to the foodless root.

Sweet Summer! unto you this swallow drew,
By secret instincts inappeasable,
   That did direct him well,
Lured from his gelid North which wrought him wrong,
   Wintered of sunning song; –
By happy instincts inappeasable,
   Ah yes! that led him well,
Lured to the untried regions and the new
   Climes of auspicious you;
To twitter there, and in his singing dwell.
   But ah! if you, my summer, should grow waste,
   With grieving skies o'ercast,
For such migration my poor wing was strong
But once; it has no power to fare again
   Forth o'er the heads of men,
Nor other summers for its sanctuary:
   But from your mind's chilled sky

It needs must drop, and lie with stiffened wings
  Among your soul's forlornest things;
A speck upon your memory, alack!
A dead fly in a dusty window-crack.

The poems are of that kind which in denying any separate
importance to the body manage to give it deathless
beauty:

How praise the woman, who but know the spirit,
How praise the colour of her eyes, uncaught
While they are coloured with her varying thought?
How her mouth's shape, who only use to know
What tender shape her speech will fit it to?
Or her lips' redness, when their joinèd veil
Song's fervid hand has parted till it wore them pale? . . .

How should I gauge what beauty is her dole,
Who cannot see her countenance for her soul,
As birds see not the casement for the sky?
And as 'tis check they prove its presence by,
I know not of her body till I find
My flight debarred the heaven of her mind.

On her resuming the poetry-writing that she had
abandoned, he wrote "To a Poet Breaking Silence":

Too wearily had we and song
Been left to look and left to long,
Yea, song and we to long and look,
Since thine acquainted feet forsook
The mountains where the Muses hymn
For Sinai and the Seraphim.
Now in both the mountains' shine
Dress thy countenance, twice divine!
From Moses and the Muses draw
The Tables of thy double Law!

His rod-born fount and Castaly
Let the one rock bring forth for thee,
Renewing so from either spring
The songs which both thy countries sing:
Or we shall fear lest, heavened thus long,
Thou should'st forget thy native song,
And mar thy mortal melodies
With broken stammer of the skies.

Ah! let the sweet birds of the Lord
With earth's waters make accord;
Teach how the crucifix may be
Carven from the laurel-tree,
Fruit of the Hesperides
Burnish take on Eden-trees,
The Muses' sacred grove be wet
With the red dew of Olivet,
And Sappho lay her burning brows
In white Cecilia's lap of snows!

Thy childhood must have felt the stings
Of too divine o'ershadowings;
Its odorous heart have been a blossom
That in darkness did unbosom,
Those fire-flies of God to invite
Burning spirits, which by night
Bear upon their laden wing
To such hearts impregnating.
For flowers that night-wings fertilise
Mock down the stars' unsteady eyes,
And with a happy, sleepless glance
Gaze the moon out of countenance.
I think thy girlhood's watchers must
Have took thy folded songs on trust,
And felt them, as one feels the stir
Of still lightnings in the hair,

When conscious hush expects the cloud
To speak the golden secret loud
Which tacit air is privy to;
Flasked in the grape the wine they knew,
Ere thy poet-mouth was able
For its first young starry babble.
Keep'st thou not yet that subtle grace?
Yea, in this silent interspace,
God sets His poems in thy face!

The loom which mortal verse affords,
Out of weak and mortal words,
Wovest thou thy singing-weed in,
To a tune of thy far Eden.
Vain are all disguises! Ah,
Heavenly *incognita!*
Thy mien bewrayeth through that wrong
The great Uranian House of Song!
As the vintages of earth
Taste of the sun that riped their birth,
We know what never cadent Sun
Thy lampèd clusters throbbed upon,
What plumèd feet the winepress trod;
Thy wine is flavorous of God.
Whatever singing-robe thou wear
Has the Paradisal air;
And some gold feather it has kept
Shows what Floor it lately swept!

Poems and *Sister Songs* were greeted with strong praise and strong disapproval. If the poet himself was only occasionally attentive to what befell his books, it was my father's constant interest to discover and store every word of approval. There were some rare examples of early, wholehearted, eager discernment to rejoice the household. "My belief is," wrote Arnold Bennett, "that Francis Thompson has a richer natural genius, a finer poetical equipment than any poet save Shakespeare. . . . Well, please yourself what you think. But, in time to come, don't say I didn't tell you." And from Mr. Garvin: "A rarer, more intense, more strictly predestinate genius has never been known to poetry. To many this may well appear the simple delirium of over-emphasis. The writer signs for those others, nowise ashamed, who range after Shakespeare's very sonnets the poetry of a living poet, Francis Thompson."

VIII

"THE PENCILLING MAMMA"

"At her place at the library table," wrote Everard in a few pages of notes he made for the Life of his mother, which he would have written if he had lived, "the pencilling mamma* would sit at her work, the children at scrap-books on the floor or perhaps editing a newspaper under the table. 'My high-water-mark,' Monica might announce after completing a paragraph, a phrase which, having heard it in relation to my mother's writing, we appropriated to our own journalism – though I could never hear it without picturing too literally a Thames jetty with dark water lapping the piles. 'Pot-boiling' was another interesting and suggestive phrase for our adoption. I remember her, at a pause in her writing, running her pencil lightly along the curve of the young eyebrow of the child whose head came hardly higher than her table, and saying 'Feather!' Blandishments we had little of; we were taken to her arms, but briefly; exquisitely fondled, but with economy, as if there were work always to be resumed. We were at once the most befriended of children, yet the most slighted; we fitted into the literary life and business of the household."

Our parents had no immunity from us, for we were not

* This was what she was named in a verse by George Meredith.

nursery children. We had our nurses, generally French; but not beyond the stage of most helpless infancy did we remain the property of the nursery; we sidled into the grown-up surroundings, not because our parents were willing or able to adapt their conditions to us, but because we just managed to be sufficiently adaptable ourselves. We accompanied our father so much on his journeys to newspaper offices that at an almost incredibly early age we were able to perform his errands for him alone.

"On top of the blue horse-bus to Harrow Road," continues Everard, "we went constantly with my father to the Westminster Press, where the *Weekly Register* was printed. We were adepts at waiting in circumstances that provided absolutely no occupation. Then my father would take his half-trotting stages, cutting corners, home from the Press to Palace Court, a child just keeping up a few paces behind. It was a kind of agony and yet one we could never avoid. How we loved to be included in his busy rounds! – facing utter boredom while he dictated letters at Burns and Oates', where he was a literary adviser; or corrected proofs, or wrote extra paragraphs if 'copy' was short in some Fleet Street office; stumbling behind him down creaky wooden stairs in Essex St. – now turned to stone – and half walking, half trotting after his disappearing figure to the *Tablet* office in Wellington Street. Here, too, I have been sometimes with my mother, but she was not an office-woman and would hesitate in such scenes. She was never a Londoner like Lamb; the pavement crowd did not beguile her; she complains that Englishmen do not make good crowds. She was not antagonistic, but she remained more or less unfamiliarised, in a way that she would not have been in an Italian crowd. She never really understood things said to her in Cockney, and it was among family legends that she had said 'I beg your pardon?' apologetically, as if she had missed something of importance, when a bus conductor remarked 'Now we shan't be long.'"

Our parents had a glamour for us that is perhaps lost by parents who occupy themselves more with their children's affairs. They were commonly so absorbed when we were with them that we even temporarily lost our names, and were all called "Child." My father would say "Just post the letters, child!" without looking up to see which of the children stood near him; and the errand would have to be performed in that unidentified manner. I can also vouch for it that when we were out with him my father found that the best way to avoid having to walk more slowly for the sake of a child was to go at the pace of any running game.

Our adoration of our mother was of a particularly persistent kind, for we were not satisfied with being with her most of the day, and managing to be acquainted with all her concerns, but were unable to allow her to forget us even for a few hours. We had a way of circumventing the inevitable partings made by outings and bedtimes; by leaving letters to trap her attention on her dressing-table or on her pillow we managed not entirely to lose her. Another way of detaining her love and interest, even while we slept, was to exact a visit to our bedsides and a sign put to prove to us in the morning that she had really been. "Signs" were a feature of our childhood—a shoe hanging on the wall, a chair turned upside down, a sweet or fruit by our beds.

The book-box called "Infants' Letters" yields some strange contents. Monica, the chief scribe, with an excellent instinct that there is something cloying about mere adoration, and that one must be more amusing than that, adopted a severe tone in those hand-delivered letters that were written nearly every day:

"Dear Mother, – I hope you will in time give up your absurd thoughts about litreture. It makes my mind get quite feverish when I think of the exhaltation your undergoing. I'm getting quite frightened about calling you 'dear Mother' because you will begin to take it quite seriously. Just because Mr. Henley and those sort of unsencere men say you write well simply because they know if they don't flatter they'll never get anything for their paper. Now mother take my advise and don't be quite so estatic, you'll get on just as well in the world and much better because you'll be respected. Now just you see. MONNIE."

It was certainly a good sense of irony that made her turn into dispraise the love and praise that possessed her:

"My dear Mother, – I hope you will never write such a bad article again as you did for the Art Journan the other day, if you do I shall really begin to lose trust in your litreture. You know I love you but it really takes off a little of my liking for you when you write such unconventionan wash as that article if it is worthy of being called an article. From your most indulgent daughter MONICA."

My mother had so slight a degree of physical strength that it is difficult to imagine how the demands made upon it by children and by bread-winning were met. That it was impossible not to feel solicitude as to the effect on her health is shown by many a letter from Coventry Patmore to my father at this time:

"My dear Wilfrid, – I feel alarmed at Alice's liability to take cold. It shows some, I hope temporary, lowering of general vitality. Do not bring her down with you unless every trace of chill shall have vanished, and unless she consents to a good meal of meat and wine just before she starts. I would rather be deprived of the sight of her for a twelvemonth than she should run any risk. If you come, don't let her make its being Friday a reason for not eating meat. There is no such obligation on those who are travelling, even in ordinary weather and in good health.

"If Alice should, at any time, be seriously ill, please telegraph to me asking me to come.

"Yours affectionately, COVENTRY PATMORE.

"She ought not to go to church on Friday morning. Good sense dispenses her from doing so. Piety minus good-sense equals superstition."

He was full of such alarms. "You will not think it intrusive," he wrote to my father, "if I express my hope that you are having the best medical advice for your dear wife. I have seen so much of chest disease. . . . Pray don't let her get up, nor go to the station to meet me on Monday, nor go to her dinner-party on Tuesday. She may *seem* well enough and will want to do both, but don't let her."

In the circumstances of illness Monica's epistolary style is relaxed:

> "My dear Mother, – You know you are very lovely. I now feel so guidy that I can hardly write, but of course I should not grumbel because of course I know you are ill yourself. You know I am very very sorry for you when you are ill. O dear Mother, I love you very much. You know you and father are the two very best people I ever saw in every way in the very whole world. I always remain Yours truly, MONICA MEYNELL."

The praise their mother was receiving from outside also brought the young critics at home more or less into line. The paper edited under the table said: "There are few real writers alive now. Mrs. Meynell is certainly one of these few that are in existance. She has produced two books which the world ought to respect and venerate. They are perfect masterpieces. Her thought is a thought which very few writers got. It is mystical, but excucite. She is a little obscure to readers who are not up in litruture suficciently to understand mystical touches. 'Veni Creator' is a wonderful example of a lady's power. Her works are like her. If you read her work you would tell the sort of woman she was. Hers is a very docile temprement and thoroughly simpithetic. When she is singing a synpethitic song you can tell that she must have some excellent powers in her head."

94

The children, by illness and accident, added brief but
terrible anxieties to these times. Monica, taken by a
friend in great cold to the funeral of Cardinal Manning,
and lingering at a punch-and-judy show on the way home,
became dangerously ill with pneumonia, – the occasion
when Francis Thompson wrote "To Monica thought
dying," for he was making the children, as well as their
mother, the subject of his poems:

  You, O the piteous you!
  Who all the long night through
  Anticipatedly
  Disclose yourself to me
Already in the ways
  Beyond our human comfortable days;
  How can you deem what Death
  Impitiably saith
  To me, who listening wake
  For your poor sake?
  When a grown woman dies,
You know we think unceasingly
What things she said, how sweet, how wise;
And these do make our misery.
  But you were (you to me
The dead anticipatedly!)
You – eleven years, was't not, or so? –
  Were just a child, you know;
  And so you never said
Things sweet immeditatably and wise
To interdict from closure my wet eyes:
  But foolish things, my dead, my dead!
  Little and laughable,
  Your age that fitted well.

And was it such things all unmemorable,
  Was it such things could make
Me sob all night for your implacable sake?

  Yet, as you said to me
In pretty make-believe of revelry,
  So, the night long, said Death
With his magniloquent breath;
  (And that remembered laughter,
Which in our daily uses followed after,
Was all untuned to pity and to awe:)
  'A cup of chocolate,
  One farthing is the rate,
  You drink it through a straw.'

  How could I know, how know
Those laughing words when drenched with sobbing so?
Another voice than yours, than yours, he hath.
  My dear, was't worth his breath,
His mighty utterance? – yet he saith, and saith!
This dreadful Death to his own dreadfulness
  Doth dreadful wrong,
This dreadful childish babble on his tongue!

The next thing to happen was that another child, leaning over the banisters of the wide open staircase on her way down to breakfast, fell thirty feet into the hall below and lay unconscious and unrecognisable, her father bombarding the doctor's house opposite three times in ten minutes while the doctor dressed. A third catastrophe was that Sebastian, the eldest child, who had been sent to school at Ramsgate, developed pneumonia, and his case was pronounced by the doctor there to be hopeless, though my mother, when she reached him, thought that she saw the promise of life and not death in his face. In that anxiety Coventry Patmore wrote:

"My dear Wilfrid, – You and Alice must find it very hard to get on with your next numbers of your two Periodicals. It has struck me that I might help you by sending a little article for the next number of *Merry England* – if it be not too late. Command me also for correcting proofs of *Register*, or anything else I can do for her and you in your trouble. I do hope that she will take care of her dear self. She seems strong, but she may rely too much on her strength which, perhaps, is rather that of spirit than body, and she may break down suddenly and fatally. . . . Give my love to your poor darling. I pray many times a day for her and Bastian.

"Yours affectionately, COVENTRY PATMORE."

Two days later, with an anxiety he could not control, he was writing again:

"My dear Wilfrid, – You will not think it meddling on the part of one who has probably had much more experience than you have had of illness and the very serious effects of long nursing if I venture to caution you against letting Alice watch too long. . . . I have had bitter experience of this in myself and others near to me; and I fancy that Alice requires especial caution, by reason of her splendid spirit, which would keep her up in any trial *while it lasted*. Yours affectionately, COVENTRY PATMORE."

Across this letter, which my father must have sent on to my mother at the school at Ramsgate, she wrote in pencil in returning it to him: "Dearest, I need not say I have not given C. reason to think I was 'nursing' or was tired. It is only the solicitude of one at a distance who does not see the course of things."

The children all made their respective recoveries. But apart from illness, my mother's hard work always remained for an anxious friend to concern himself about and to try to mitigate. Once, on finding a review of his own work in the *Weekly Register*, Coventry Patmore wrote: "I little thought, that day that I sat chafing hour after hour at the claims of the *Register* on Alice's time, that you and she were labouring for me. Kiss her sweet hand for me, and beg my pardon of her." In reply to one of his frequent petitions to be made use of my mother wrote to him:

"My dear Friend, – You must not think of that kindness of coming up to work in my place. I should readily accept it if it were a question of proofs merely. But there are the foreign papers – arriving in a batch – to look through, and an unaccustomed eye would take half a day over the hunt for Catholic news, which my practised glance can do in half an hour. Then, if Wilfrid is hard pressed, there is an article to do in a hurry in the evening. These little things require no talent, but they do require a knowledge of current things, and a perfect familiarity with the habits of the paper. If this were not so it would always be easy to get help. . . . Affectionately yours, ALICE MEYNELL."

It must indeed have been hard for the friend at a distance to know of the stress of work as some of my mother's
letters revealed it to him.

"My dearest Friend . . . I have just despatched
Wilfrid and Monnie to the Isle of Wight, after a very
hard morning's work in making them ready. And now
I am taking Cuckoo [Everard] to call on the Hink-
sons. I think I shall not have a very hard *Register*.
There is a good long law case that makes copy. Father
Cuthbert came this morning but no one had time to
talk to him. You know what it is when I am mending
frocks and everyone is calling me. These are all sweet
duties, but sometimes I am on the verge of crying. Be
sure to let me have the next batch of your proofs.
Always your affectionate ALICE."

78650

But Coventry Patmore had it in his power to give
practical refreshment. My mother's visits to the Lodge at
Lymington were a frequent pleasure. "I hope that you
will be able to come down with your dear Wife," he
wrote to my father, "and stay a night or two, and come
back again to fetch her. Thank you for letting her come.
I can guess how much happiness you give up in giving
up a fortnight of her sweet society by the pleasure which
the prospect of enjoying it gives me." And afterwards he
writes: "I need not tell you and Alice with what gladness
I accept your invitation for the 11th. Since she left us I
have not known what to do with myself for want of her
society; and the prospect of two or three days with her
sooner than I expected is a boon for which I thank you
more than words can say." That my mother's visits to

Lymington could not be pure repose was unavoidable though painful to her host. "Your wife is leaving us this afternoon," he writes, "and I feel that I have been done out of at least half my expected fortnight. Best part of three days' absence in London, and three days more during which she was invisible, except at meals, slaving at pot-boilers! I feel too savage to thank you as I should for the remaining week." From Lymington my mother herself writes home: "Thank you, dearest Love, for your letter. You wrote a very nice one also to Mrs. Patmore. I should much like to know what the *Pall Mall* means to pay me for the weekly articles. I shall not growl at £1 10s.; but £2 would make me very happy. If you suppose I am not thinking of your darlingness at work through the weary day, you are much mistaken. Coventry is so melancholy at my working that I am glad that the Kipling is over, though I enjoyed doing it. We have been for a most exquisite drive, and all the way I thought of my beloved boy sitting beside the fender."

Though our devotion no doubt made our upbringing easy for our parents whose mere displeasure was terrible to us, our misery when we were parted from them must have complicated their lives. Our mother's absences when she went to stay with the Patmores could just be borne, for we were at least at home and with our father; though a letter written on the first night of one of these absences shows that they were not taken too lightly:

"Darling Mother, – I hope you had a nice journey. I woke up about half-past three this morning, and I could not get to sleep again. At last I got out of bed, and went slowly into Dimpling's room, she was asleep, I stayed there a little while, and then went back to my own bed. But soon I got out again and went once more into Dimpling's room; she was still asleep. At last I came out and went slowly downstairs. At last I stopped at Father's door, I waited there till it struck four, and then I knocked gently at the door (no answer). I knocked again, Father came and opened the door, and then I got in his bed and stayed there for the rest of the morning. I hope you found the key of your portmanteau. Send my love to Mr. and Mrs. Patmore. Dear, Sweet, Love, Goodbye. VIOLA."

But there were more cheerful letters to her in her absence:

"My own girl, – I hope you had a nice journey and warm feet and a better head. You're a lovely woman. Tell Mr. Patmore he's a brick for loving you so much, and that I appreciate him awfully. Viola's in perfect spirits now. Miss Swain says I've been an *eccelentissima figlia!* Your girl, MONNIE."

"My own girl, – Thanks so awfully for the lovely letter and rusks. Father's so *awfully* kind. Miss Austen came to lunch on Thursday and told Father all about Mrs. Austen, and so that Father of mine had to do his article at night, and came to bed at one o'clock and actually put a ten-shilling bit into my hand. What do you think of a man like that? I am longing to see your sweet face again. From your own girl, MONNIE."

Our father, too, snatched his rare holidays – such as that of which my mother wrote to Coventry Patmore:

ALICE MEYNELL

"I trust and hope he may find it pleasant. His hostess is
decidedly frivolous. If he can persuade her to read poetry
with him, he will like it; if not, not." To the children such
an absence would be again tolerable, if uneasy:

> "Darlingest of all boys in the world, – I hope you
> had an aggreable journey and a good meal at the end
> of it. You must make up your mind to really enjoy
> yourself. When I saw the lovely sun come out I was
> very glad if it means that you'll have the same. I am
> quite happy, but I miss you awfully. Now and then I
> feel inclined to break down. You've got a darling wife.
> She's full of importance about the *Reggie*.* She's got her
> papers all spread on the table, and no one's to go near
> her; she's a thourough editor. I'll always go to bed at
> nine while you're away darling. I hope you'll be well
> and happy. You're not to work hard. Write and ask
> Father Cuthbert if he'll do a leader and Father Daw-
> son if he'll do a leaderette. MONNIE."

And from my mother to my father:

> "My own Love, – Thank you for your letter, sweet
> and beautiful verses, and flowers. By the same post I
> got a box of roses from Coventry, and I think I am
> the happiest woman in the world. F. T. and I kept
> our noses to the grindstone well yesterday. We sit
> opposite each other in extreme gravity. He is exceed-
> ingly good and offered to play with the children and
> take them out. Never again shall I fear taking the
> *Reggie* for you. But another time I shall ask you not to

* *The Weekly Register.*

102

send copy to the printer but to let me have it; there
has been some duplication already and I expect to
see more in the proofs to-day. I am perfectly capable
of turning out an amusing *Register* with no help except
that of F. T. Your own Johnson."*

And in the meantime the hand-delivered notes from the
children to their mother continued. "Goodnight my own
darling precious. Mind you have a good night (and no
mellolnkily)."

But partings could be more disastrous than that; and
if some of the children were sent away on a visit to the
country, long-planned and hardly-earned by our parents,
they would sometimes almost at once have to be fetched
back again. I can remember what the falling of dusk
means to a child sent away from her parents, when the
horror outside the windows and the horror inside one
meet and unite. We were not readily indulged in our
weakness, or else how could I remember so many of the
cheerful mornings of novelty and the dreadful evenings
that separation meant? Many letters tell their tale of the
nuisance we must have been.

"My dear Mother, – You are so very nice, you
know. I never mean to annoi you, because I love you
so much, you know, or to vex you in any way. I am
sure everyone you meet must think you very nice, and
splendid in all your ways. Mother, I don't want to go
with the others away next summer. I am very sorry I

* This name by which she was often called at home had its origin
in her being regarded as the family's standard dictionary. The
children also had many alternative names: "Dimpling" is Madeline;
"Lobbie," Olivia.

ALICE MEYNELL

weren't nice to Madam, I will be always nice to her
in futcher. Your loving MONNIE."

Francis Thompson all this time, besides Coventry
Patmore, was assisting our parents with the two papers,
though in the case of Francis Thompson the help was not
unassociated with a certain amount of hindrance. His
excellent contributions were not produced to time, and
he increased the inconvenience of his delays by chatting
a great deal about them. He formed part of the pressure
round the library table on those Thursdays when in the
evening I remember the silver soup-tureen perched on
the piled-up papers, brought upstairs because my father
could not stop to go down to dinner. Francis Thompson's
ulster, with its cape, made the outline the child would see
daily who ran to the front-door at a knock, getting down
from the library easily quicker than a maid could get up
from the basement. "He was put to small tasks," says my
brother in his Life, "as much that he might be put out of
train for talk as for the use he was. But no device was
good enough to do that; set him to write and there would
be endless conversation on nibs and paper, of what it
was advisable to write, what to ignore, of his readers'
alleged susceptibilities, and his care for the paper's cir-
culation. In the end, after a hard day, there might, or
might not, be a 'par' to show." Distressingly conscious of
his own shortcomings when he failed, in the way that
people well may be who yet cannot change them, he can
never once have seen in the disappointed editor any sign
of disappointment. "I don't know what I shall do, or
what you shall do," wrote Francis Thompson in one of

many letters of the kind. "I haven't been able to write a line. I am more in a condition to sit down and go into hysterics like a girl than to write anything. I know how vexed and impatient you must feel to hear this from me, when you had expected to have the thing from me this morning. Indeed, I feel that you have already done too much for me; and that it would be better you should have nothing more to do with me. You have already displayed a patience and tenderness with me that my kindred would never have displayed; and it is most unjust that I should any longer be a burden to you. I think I am fit for nothing: certainly not fit to be any longer the object of your too great kindness. Please understand that I am perfectly resigned to the ending of an experiment which even your sweetness would never have burdened yourself with, if you could have foreseen the consequences." In the Life this letter is followed by the comment: "Such fits were treated by my father with a persuasiveness and love that I think no other man could have summoned. In after years Francis wrote letters that seemed to supply no possible opening for the comforter. Read to-day, their desperation offers no outlet but a return to the streets. But no sooner did he come into my father's presence than he was consoled, often without the exchange of a word." To my father, of course, Francis Thompson stood for achievement to such a mighty degree that such failures as made the poet despair did not exist for him.

At Pantasaph, in Wales, where they had sent him for a time to recuperate in the care of the Franciscan friars, and especially that of their great friend Father Anselm, our parents visited him, and he wrote: "The leaves fell from the day indeed when you left." And in a *Pall Mall* article called "At the Monastery Gates," written by my mother after this visit, she could not omit to say: "When the poet comes drifting in from his walks over the tops of the hills, his light Shelley-figure looks as though it were brought home by the sea-wind" – an anonymous allusion to him which she feared, too late, would be taken to refer to the robust figure of Lewis Morris, the resident poet of Wales! But it was not to country hills but London streets that the strange figure of the poet belonged if it belonged any-where, and he rarely left his London quarters, and knocked at hardly a door but Palace Court's. (One of the infrequent visits he paid was a short stay in Whitehall Gardens, whence he wrote to my father: " I have done a perhaps rash thing – promised Doubleday to come to him again when they return after Christmas. I forgot that you cannot be without your dress-clothes continuously!") He occupied a succession of lodgings in the Harrow Road district, where he was near enough to Palace Court to be not more than an hour or so late for every meal he came to. My father's light bantering treat-ment of the despairs that descended on him if on some special occasion he had mistaken the time (evening for morning was a possible mistake with him – Tuesday for Monday), or if there should not be a stamp for his letter, was fairly effective; but Francis Thompson had sensitive griefs that banter could not approach. He said so much about losing a box of matches that it might have been easy sometimes to forget what real wild wounds he took from the passing moments. His devotion to my mother made her in particular a prey to his unhappy imaginings.

His sensitiveness was of the kind that can formulate a suspicion, and gather evidence until not one proof is lacking, of someone's offended bearing to him who is utterly unaware of the meaning words or looks that have been gathered from innocent and unconscious behaviour. Her surprise and her distress must have hurried to his reassurance when he wrote such letters as this, which shall be given with its typical reiterations:

British Museum   *Saturday Evening*

"Dear Mrs. Meynell, – It is a small matter, and hardly, I suppose, worth taking a second thought about in your mind. Yet as I seem to have offended you, and as to offend you is to me the most grievous of things, you must pardon me if to *me* it is a grave matter. I mean the misunderstanding this afternoon.

"I wish then to say that I did nothing except with the design to consult your wishes. When I came in this morning, you told me that I was punctual to my time, but that you must go out; and asked me not to mind. It was clear, therefore, that you remembered our overnight agreement, and that there was no need for me to remind you of it. And it was clear, too, that you understood me to have come early in the morning for the express purpose of keeping my agreement, and there was no need for me to explain my desire that you would go through *A Portrait* with me. Yet you came back from your shopping, and never signified your willingness to go through it; you saw me finish my letter to Madam, and sit down patiently to wait, yet you still made no sign of readiness. Now, delicacy forbade *me* to ask *you;* because it was you who were conferring the favour, not I. Consequently, once I had made sure that you remembered my request, and knew what I had come for, I felt that I could not

delicately, in the absence of any encouragement or signification of willingness from you, press from you a favour
which it seemed probable you had repented. If nothing
had passed between us since I entered the house, of course
it would have been my part to remind you of the overnight agreement. But your own words had forestalled
that; and so it seemed to me that the only thing I could
courteously do was to wait until you signified your readiness to fulfil the agreement which you had already signified your remembrance of. No such signification of
readiness came from you before we went down to lunch:
and, I repeat, I did not like to ask you, lest I should be
pressing on you the fulfilment of a promise which you
had repented. When we went down to lunch without
your having intimated any readiness to commence the
task you had agreed to overnight, I felt convinced that
you shrank from it for some reason – perhaps sheer boredom – and, to say truth, I felt sharply wounded. For if
there is one dread I have perpetually before me, it is to
presume on your good nature and toleration. When I went
upstairs after lunch, my eye fell on the proofs lying in
your place. Then, I thought, I understood the matter. You
were anxious to get your essays revised, in order to send
them to C. P., who had, you told me, telegraphed regarding them. I was very sad that I should unknowingly have
pressed on you my own selfish affair, when, as I now found,
your own work was pressing on your hands, while mine
could wait indefinitely. So I determined that the only
way I could repair the unintentional selfishness I had
been guilty of, was to take my leave of you under some
pretext, and so spare you the task of keeping a promise
wrung from you in the kindness of your heart, but which
interfered with what you desired to be at work on. Great
was my consternation when I did this, and found that you
resented it. I meditated whether I should draw back,
since I had angered you where I meant only to consult

your hidden wishes. But I saw that you were so cold and estranged from me, that the going through the poem would have been a constrained affair, painful for both of us. So I left.

"It seems to me that the more I strive to please you and serve you, and to think always what may be your pleasure, not mine, the more I alienate you from me, so far as a lady so sweet can be alienated from anyone. If you understood one thing, I think, you would have judged me better in the past. It is this. I am unhappy when I am out of your sight; and would pass every hour, if I could, in your exquisite presence, only to feel the effluence of your spirit in contact with mine. But *you*, of course, can have no such feeling in reference to me; and would often gladly be without my presence when my love for you prompts it, and your good nature prompts you patiently to bear it. Now my sense of this inspires me with a continual timidity about inflicting my society on you in any way, unless you in some way signify a desire for it. Hence such misunderstandings as that of to-day.

"Let this be sufficient, and let it not come between us. I know how it must tax you to endure me; for you are a friend, a mother; while I, over and above these, am a lover – spiritual as light, and unearthly as the love of one's angelic dreams, if you will – but yet a lover; and even a seraph enamoured must be a trying guardian-angel to have to do with. Ahi! soavissima Madonna Alice, avete pieta di me! Ever yours, most belovèd lady, FRANCIS THOMPSON.

"P.S. I send you herewith the best I was able to do in the correction of the blank-verse *Orison-Tryst*. But its weaknesses are too inherent to be really removed – they are the texture of it."

On another day he wrote: "I hope you are going to have no headaches, 'wheel' or otherwise, but to be just happy for a while, now the *Register* is done. And that to-morrow, for once in a way, and Saturday, you will do just what you like and take pleasure in doing. . . . And since I think you must have had far too much of my company forced upon you during the last fortnight, if I leave you now as much as may be without me, you must ascribe it solely to my anxiety for anything which might fatigue you; not to neglect, of which I am incapable; or weariness, which no man – I least – could feel in your companionship." But these are among few such perturbed and personal letters to her. Generally his letters were more technical than personal, points of etymology or metre being discussed between them with a special respect for each other's views.

IX

THE FRIEND

Even after my mother had given her immeasurable praise to Coventry Patmore's poetry, the full extent of her feeling remained unexpressed, and in a letter to him she breaks off suddenly to say: "I have never told you what I think of your poetry. It is the greatest thing in the world, the most harrowing and the sweetest. I can hardly realise that he who has written it and who is greater than his words is celestially kind to me and calls me friend."

As far as his teaching, his "gospel," was concerned, she was docile, receptive, impressed. She expounds him intelligently: "That the general purpose of the poems is obscure is inevitable. It has the obscurity of profound clear waters. What the poet chiefly secures to us is the understanding that love and its bonds, its bestowal and reception, do but rehearse the action of the union of God with humanity – that there is no essential man save Christ, and no essential woman except the soul of mankind. When the singer of a Song of Songs seems to borrow the phrase of human love, it is rather that human love had first borrowed the truths of the love of God." But she is bound to tell him at times that this spiritual world of his in all its meaning is a region into which she has not really entered and is "a difficult country."

It is his art of poetry that overwhelms and captures her – "an art so quick and close that it is the voice less of a poet than of the very Muse." That the greatest poetry has a simplicity beyond imagery she had discovered by means of him. "Other simplicities may be achieved by lesser art, but this is transcendent simplicity. There is nothing in the world more costly. It vouches for the beauty which it transcends; it answers for the riches it forbears; it implies the art which it fulfils. All abundance ministers to it, though it is so single." His poetry broke her heart and was the happiness of her life. "I hope you will forgive me for keeping your MSS. a little longer," she writes to him. "They are quite safe, and I cannot tell you what a consolation it is to me to read them as I can get time. But I read them with many tears and my heart is full of sorrow." Again she wrote: "I have read the Odes yet again with a new amazement. And then, after my tears over these, I bought a frock to please you." Again and again she felt that she had not yet spoken all her praise. She writes to him: "On Sunday at Sir Frederick Leighton's we were looking at the pictures, and he told a story of Corinna, the subject of one of them. This, he said, is especially for Mrs. Meynell, for she will like it. Then he said how Corinna had given a lesson to a young poet who had written profusely. The sower, she told him, sowed seed from his hand, and not from his basket. How beautiful it is, and how it makes me feel the human measure and human action of art. And how Greek *you* must be. Sir Frederick said that temperance was Greek, and who has it like you? But I suppose no Greek ever had your passion and power."

But even to Coventry Patmore she was an alert and perhaps troublesome critic of slight defects. Her style in criticism was very frank, at any rate when she praised as well, for blame that is only partial is of course the easiest to pronounce. I can think of many instances of her severe honesty with her friends. To my father, in the early days of knowing him, she wrote: "I am rather tyrannical, am I not? Forgive me for speaking so harshly of things which you admire. I ought not to do so; my conscience always stings me afterwards; and – shall I confess it? – I was afraid the other day that your friendship might not always be proof against all my disagreeableness. – Well, at least you can always trust the sincerity of my praises." Of her friend Aubrey de Vere she wrote: "The gentler things in his work are strong: I imply a certain weakness in the violent things." To Henley (difficult man to find fault with) she wrote: "I think *Piccadilly* is not quite sincere. You have intended it *de parti pris* – very wilfully in fact – and it is out of proportion and exaggerated. And to my mind the slightest touch of exaggeration should be got rid of once and for ever from literature. What a literature there might be without it! The world has never had it yet. Men have never penetrated, or seldom, into a certain secret place quite in the centre of the heart. It is the eye of the whirlwind, where there is a calm set about by tumult. You are in the tumult. . . . After reading your poem I went at once to Coventry Patmore's 'February.' He refuses, against his heart – no, he accepts, against his will (who shall define that lovely postponement?), that which you leap at." On Francis Thompson, too, she used her severity in the midst of her praise.

And so with Coventry Patmore she made her occasional quarrel:

"My dear friend, – You will receive your Volumes which I post to-day. I know you will excuse the boldness with which I have suggested one or two small alterations merely for the sake of beauty. Sometimes the word 'which' occurred perfectly correctly but not prettily several times in one sentence. I have taken it out, substituting 'whereof' or a participle.

"It has been a happiness to read again, through and through, the words of the greatest intellect I have ever known. To me the truth of your teaching is much more than convincing, it is evident instantly; the only effort I have to make is to understand – a most happy effort. But why is it that some passages – a very few and all in the later book – trouble me by getting no interior assent from me at all? . . . I would ask you to reconsider *Distinction*. Believe me, it does such injustice to living writers (so does *William Barnes* indeed) that it is almost a confession that you do not thoroughly know the men you slight. And that is so extremely irritating to people that I am inclined to think it has caused the partial boycotting of your work.

"But worse than this is the quarrel in it with the *Spectator* and the *Guardian*. Your attitude has been always one of singular dignity, and this one incident is not worthy of that dignity. I have always thought so, and I think so more now than ever. Nor does *Distinction* contain anything that does not appear in one form or another elsewhere. . . . A. M."

Her efforts to save him from rash and scornful statements were only partly successful. "Distinction" was
reprinted in the volume in question (*Religio Poetae*,
one of the books of his fine but didactic prose), though
without a passage she particularly objected to. She failed
in another of her persuasions: – the article called "Mrs.
Meynell" was also reprinted here, in which she was called
the only woman of recent times who had achieved distinction of style. My mother sent him *Sonnets from the
Portuguese* and *Wuthering Heights* for a re-reading which
must surely be followed by a recantation. But the
passage which embarrassed her with its untruth was left
unchanged.

But when did a stern and obstinate man ever bring to
a friend so much sweetness as he did? When he praised
her it made my mother feel that all praise was indeed
hers, and she wrote to him: "I ought now once and for
ever to lay aside all vanity and ambition and desire for
recognition – indeed I do." He was a man whom it was
a singular honour to serve. "Don't forget to send me the
books," writes my mother, "so that I may have the
infinite pleasure of being of some little service to you in
giving your work that scrupulous revision to which I have
accustomed myself, and which an author never gives to
his own writings." Though Coventry Patmore's visits to
Palace Court were fairly frequent it was never anything
but a stirring event when he came. He was very much of
a connoisseur, and even ordinary things seemed like
treasure when they passed through his hands. He loved
jewels, but did not know whether a diamond or a haystack was the more attractive form of property. He had

the quality of rarity, in his distinctive appearance and
height, in the importance that was his naturally. On
his visits to town he shared a little in my parents' social
life, even as he liked to share their working life, though
to one so fastidious as he none but the choicest occasions
might be offered. Wilfrid Blunt and the beautiful Lady
Colin Campbell were friends to be made known to him.
"My dearest Friend, will you send me a camellia for
Saturday night, late, for a party at Lady Jeune's?" my
mother would write; and in describing brilliant parties
to him she would try to tempt him to them. The friend
whom Coventry Patmore was of course most bound to
meet was Francis Thompson – when a certain aloofness
on the older poet's part became lost in the peculiar kin-
ship between them. "He bore himself towards me with
a dignity and magnanimity which are not of this age's
stature," wrote Francis Thompson to my mother when
Patmore visited him at his monastery in Wales. "By the
way, he repeated to me two or three short poems addressed to yourself. I hope there may be a series of such
songs. You would then have a triple tiara indeed –
crowned by yourself, by me, and highest crowned by
him." And he wrote again: "It was well understood
between us – by me no less than by him – that it was no
common or conventional friendship he asked of me. Not
therefore has he sought out my Welsh hermitage; and
scalpelled the fibres of me." That it became an uncommon friendship can be seen in glimpses of their correspondence. "Of course, I am quite aware," Thompson
writes to Patmore, "that it is impossible to answer openly
– indeed impossible to ask openly – deeper matters in a

letter. But that is not requisite in my case. It is enough
that my gaze should be set in the necessary direction; the
rest may be safely left to the practised fixity of my looking.
. . . With regard to what you say about the symbolism of
the North, I had substantially discerned it for myself.
Indeed it formed part of a little essay already written.
It will be none the worse for the corroboration of your
remarks; there is always something in your way of stating
even what is already to me a *res visa*, which adds sight to my
seeing."And Patmore writes: "Thank you for your very interesting letter, which shows me how extraordinarily alike
are our methods of and experience in contemplation."

Together my mother and Coventry Patmore some-
times went to Sargent's studio, when the portrait of
Patmore was painted that is now in the National Portrait
Gallery, and my mother was drawn at Patmore's request.

In some light deft verses Patmore celebrated the
incidents of a great friendship:

ALICIA'S SILENCE

A girl, you sang, to listening fame,
   The grace that life might be,
And ceased when you yourself became
   The fulfilled prophecy.
Now all your mild and silent days
   Are each a lyric fact,
Your pretty, kind, quick-hearted ways
   Sweet epigrams in act.
To me you leave the commoner tongue,
   With pride, gaily confessed,
Of being, henceforth, sole theme of song
   To him who sings the best.

O ALICIA SEEKING TO MAKE ME A RADICAL

Dear, either's creed one hope foretells.
　Mine waits; yours, kindlier, hastes—
But what to us are principles
　Who are one in Tory tastes?
Bear in your hat what badge you may,
　The Red Republic's even,
So all your lovely ways obey
　The Monarchy of Heaven.

ALICIA

Ah, sole essential good of earth,
　And sweetest accident of Heaven,
Their best rays, on her lucky birth,
　Beamed from the planets seven.

Her body, too, is so like her—
　Sharp honey assuaged with milk,
Straight as a stalk of lavender,
　Soft as a rope of silk.

It will have been noticed that all the letters that have been quoted are either from my mother to Coventry Patmore (these came back to her after his death) or from Coventry ⊥atmore to my father. The reason for this is that, some years after his death, my mother destroyed nearly all Coventry Patmore's letters to her. What other letters she allowed to survive, therefore, I have thought it permissible to quote from. To my own feelings few things could be more painful than that unhappiness should befall this friendship. That such a shadow came is to be seen in certain phrases in Coventry Patmore's letters to my father. His visits had ceased to be welcome, he thought; and he says: "I have had a very kind note from Mrs.

Meynell complaining of my not having gone to see her since I was in town. She knows that it has been from no lack of a desire to see her." In sending her his love in another letter he hopes that he may not be forgotten in absence – "but this will be too much to hope for, with all her distracting interests." He hears on another occasion that a friend had quoted to my mother some verses from Francis Thompson's poem written to her, "To a Poet Breaking Silence," and that my mother had absently said: "I think I have heard them before; whose are they?" "What fate," says Coventry Patmore, "must my poor verses to her expect if F. T.'s are so soon forgotten!"— and he supposed her indifferent now to praises of which she had so many. My mother having become a friend of George Meredith, Coventry Patmore wrote: "Mr. Pember was here yesterday and spoke of the interest your wife's name is creating in London, especially in connection with her great new friendship. Give her my unalterable love." At a suggestion from my father that he should assist my mother in some undertaking, he writes: "It may seem very absurd to you and herself, but my power of doing anything more in that or any other matter has been paralysed by my finding, from her own words and acts, that my primacy in her friendship has been superseded. I shall be as much pleased as I can be at anything by appearing in her new Anthology, and, as I get no news from her now, I shall be very grateful for anything you can tell me about her." And in the meantime his generous love of her writing, about which at least he could never feel the shadow of a misgiving, was as great as it had ever been. "What Jeffrey said," he wrote to my father, "in the *Edinburgh Review* about Keats's poetry is exactly true of your wife's prose. J. said that K.'s poetry was the test of capacity in the reader for the understanding of what poetry was. It seems to me that the faculty of discerning the merit of prose is almost, if not quite, as rare. Your Wife's prose is the finest that was ever written, and none but kindred genius can see how great it is. I am glad to see that all the few competent judges are gradually coming to confirm all that I have ever said in her praise. If I were you, I should go mad with pride and joy." And in another letter: "I wrote the other day to Father Angelo and said, incidentally, that I considered Mrs. Meynell to have the finest contemplative powers of any woman since Madame de Guyon. You will be pleased with his reply: 'I was much gratified by your reference to Mrs. Meynell. I fully endorse your opinion in regard to her place among contemplatives.' " At the end of 1895 he had written a letter to the *Saturday Review* advocating her appointment as laureate, – the laureateship having been left vacant with the idea that there was no one fitting to succeed to Tennyson. (The thought of their mother as poet-laureate, and the sight of her name on posters in connection with the suggestion, was an excitement for the children. "Francis got five *Pall Mall* posters yesterday," my mother mentions in a letter. "He was much excited, saying, 'We are well off for famousness, Darling.' ") In 1896 Coventry Patmore wrote for the same paper an article on her new essays, *The Colour of Life*, with an avowal of praise – the last limits to which praise can go – such as must have enriched for the moment all the pauses and blanks of his isolation.

In this same year there was published by Heinemann a book of selections made by my mother from his poetry, called *The Poetry of Pathos and Delight*, with an introduction that served to let her give yet another version of her praise. She hoped, by choosing among his less difficult poems, to give to a world that was indifferent or estranged an easy approach to this unknown treasure, —as one might hope for any great good suddenly to befall mankind. Her selection therefore did not consist of "best passages," but of poems concerned with the "human and intelligible" passions of delight and sorrow. "What is here to be communicated is vital and mortal pathos and felicity. Even as far as the reader has capacity to perceive that passion, he is aware that it is greater than his experience, and he confesses that it was uttered out of a greater capacity than his. Compassion with the greater passion is a high and worthy manner of admiration. It may be the 'terror' that Aristotle joined to 'pity.' Compassion in the highest degree is the divinest form of religion. The compassion of the slighter acquaintance with sorrow for the greater, and of the smaller capacity for the vaster, is a remorse of tenderness, lowliness, and respect, the paradox of worship."

"Your dear Wife," wrote Coventry Patmore to my father, " will be pleased to hear that her selections have had a most marked effect on the sale of my poems." But any word that he sends to her now has the sound of coming from a distant unhappy retreat. His health is bad, his heart pronounced dangerous, he writes, adding, "One cannot live long without delight."

It is to be feared that in this friendship, and in others,

my mother did fail to some extent to make her love felt. She was selfless, compassionate, and, one would have said, was made of love, but she could fail to satisfy the friends she loved most, him above any other. And that this particular kind of failure formed a definite feature of her life is clearly recognised in a letter written by her in her latest years. It was written to a nun of extraordinary holiness and intelligence, to whom my mother turned for wisdom and to whom she broke unhappy silences. "All my troubles," she says in this letter, "are little, old, foolish, trivial, as they always were – the troubles of my spiritual life, I mean. But as to sorrow, my failure of love to those that loved me can never be cancelled or undone. So I never fail in a provision of grief for any night of my life."

Probably some explanation is simply that she was so provided with love within her family, so satisfied with her happy occupation of writing, that she did not make those who loved her feel her need of them. There is perhaps always inequality in the love that two people exchange – undiscovered or tolerable inequality. But the inequality where one has need of a beloved friend and the other has not, or, merely, when one has leisure and the other has not, discovers itself and cannot be borne.

And if her love of her parents seemed in her memory to have been insufficient too, and to form part of that failure, this can be accounted for only by the familiar fact that in discovering one's own life and breaking new ground one may seem to some extent to reject what has gone before. Probably few people do not suffer from the same self-reproach. Only thus can these failures be made into something that does not do too much violence to her extraordinarily faithful power of loving where she professed to love.

On November 26th, 1896, death put an end to this friendship that had meant so much. One night when we were all in the library a telegram came to say that he was dead. My mother left us and went into the drawing-room. I can remember having no proper realisation of what had happened, – only horror that my mother should go into a dark room alone and remain there.

X

THE WARES OF AUTOLYCUS, AND MEREDITH

The "Wares of Autolycus" was the heading of a column in the *Pall Mall Gazette*, written each day by a different hand; and my mother's was first the Friday, and later the Wednesday, hand. The articles were unsigned; but anonymity, when it is not mere oblivion, can be something more exciting than a name, and to those who looked particularly for the Friday articles it must have been pleasant also to look for the author of them. George Meredith enquired until he got from the *Pall Mall* editor an answer. Mr. Walkley, too, wrote a letter to "him or her," after an article on Duse had appeared, in which he spoke of the peculiar difficulty of writing about acting: "To find the thing handled at once firmly and delicately is a real delight. Mr. Walkley assumes he is right in attributing some really remarkable papers on Swift's and Steele's womenkind to the same hand." A number of these essays were republished in a volume called *The Colour of Life* in 1896. The *Rhythm of Life* essays had been written at her own prompting, when, with the diffidence of inexperience, only the most important of her ideas received tolerance from her. *The Colour of Life* essays were written in obedience to Friday, and the result is a book to be read with greater ease, with very original and delicate impressions rather than thought-out ideas. In the first book, thinking had gone very far; but the weekly article did not always wait for that, and took whatever the winds and clouds and grass, the eyes of the day might have said to her.

Red, she writes in this new collection, is not the colour of life: "Red is the colour of violence, or of life broken open, edited and published. . . . The true colour of life is the colour of the body, the colour of the covered red the implicit and not explicit colour of the living heart and the pulses." The little figures of boys bathing in the evening in the Serpentine give to Londoners one of their rare glimpses of the colour of life: "The boy sheds his slough of nameless colours – all allied to the hues of dust and soot and fog – and makes, in his hundreds, a bright and delicate flush between the grey-blue water and the grey-blue sky. Clothed now with the sun, he is crowned by-and-by with twelve stars as he goes to bathe, and the reflection of an early moon is under his feet. So little stands between a *gamin* and all the dignities of Nature. They are so quickly restored. There seems to be nothing to do, but only a little thing to undo. . . . All the squalor is gone in a moment, kicked off with the second boot, and the child goes shouting to complete the landscape with the lacking colour of life. You are inclined to wonder that, even undressed, he still shouts with a cockney accent. You half expect pure vowels and elastic syllables from his restoration, his spring, his slenderness, his brightness and his glow. Old ivory and wild rose in the deepening midsummer sun, he gives his colours to the world again. It is easy to replace man, and it will take no great time, where Nature has lapsed, to replace Nature. It is always to do, by the happily easy way of doing nothing. The grass is always ready to grow in the streets. The gasometer even must fall to pieces unless it is renewed; but the grass renews itself. There is nothing so remediable as the work of modern man – 'a thought which is also,' as Mr. Pecksniff said, 'very soothing.' And by remediable I mean, of course, destructible. As the bathing child shuffles off his garments, so the land might always, in reasonable time, shuffle off its yellow brick and purple slate, and all the things that collect about railway stations. A single night almost clears the air of London."

The essay called *Symmetry and Incident* compares Greek symmetrical art with Japan's love of incident, and in an aside concerning the human body she writes: "Exterior human symmetry is surely a curious physiological fact when there is no symmetry interiorly. For the centres of life and movement within the body are placed with Oriental inequality. Man is Greek without and Japanese within."

Too good a schooling in acting in Italy had made her a reluctant play-goer here. In *Donkey Races* she uses her invective against English acting on a point more common then than now – its slowness. The palm for acting was awarded then to the one who lagged and dawdled most through his lines; and, on an occasion when she had heard two actors vie with each other in slowness, she writes: "It was a contest so determined, so unrelaxed, so deadly, so inveterate that you might have slept between its encounters. You did sleep. These men were strong men, and knew what they wanted. It is tremendous to watch the struggle of such resolves. . . . It may be that a determined actor may so compel the other actor, with whom he is in conversation, to get on, as to secure his own final triumph. To be plain, for the sake of those unfamiliar with the sports of the village, the rider in a donkey race may, and does, cudgel the mounts of his rivals." And with her great love of acting sharpening her irony she speaks of an unnamed actress who was said to have come to the front of her profession: "Come to the front, do they say? Surely the front of her profession must have moved in retreat, to gain upon her tardiness."

She notes the townsman's loss in seeing only the top of a cloud, not its base or its altitude or its journey. The shower-cloud "has not come from the clear edge of the plain to the south, and will not shoulder anon the hill to the north. The rain, for this city, hardly comes or goes; it does but begin and stop." Of the Londoner's further misfortune of smoke she wrote elsewhere: "And yet you may, twenty times a day in London, hear the smoke called cloud. Storms are announced as lurking in the heart of the powerless bosom of the smoke, and showers are threatened where there never was anything so fresh as a drop of rain. The puny darkness is supposed capable of lightnings, and out of the grime is expected the thunderbolt. The splendid name of the cloud is given to this poor local vesture of decay."

The praise of her work was such that Mr. Max Beerbohm had to come forward with a good-natured and carefully worded protest. An article appeared in *To-Morrow* in which he deplored that "in a few years Mrs. Meynell will have become a sort of substitute for the

English sabbath." He complained that her style, "quite perfect in its sort," was considered by the critics to be "the one and only way in which fine English could possibly be written. . . . One hears a great deal about her essay 'Rejection' nowadays. I am sure that so sensible a woman as Mrs. Meynell must often smile, when the reviewers treat this, her means, for all the world as though it were an end. She must know that there are they who can do quite as much with their flutes as she with her file." He exaggerates her fame in order to deplore it with the more spirit. "So sacred in the eyes of all London is Mrs. Meynell, that I know this article will be considered nothing less than a brutal and revolting crime." On behalf of other good writers who are not so lucky, he envies her her championship by eminent persons. "Between her and Mr. Coventry Patmore the shuttlecock of praise has flashed incessantly. . . . And now, hark! the infrequent voice of Mr. George Meredith is raised in her honour."

It was in 1896, after a bout of the *Pall Mall* Friday fare, that Clement Shorter called on my mother to tell her that Meredith had few wishes left, and that one of them was to lure her acquaintance. His was the figure that was foremost in literary glamour at that time; our parents, in their love of his prose and poetry, had given their youngest son the names of Francis Meredith. He himself wrote: "I have long been attached to you in spirit, and am indebted past payment." My mother and father made their first day-visit to Box Hill, and from that day for the next few years Meredith was a unique, interesting, even urgent accompaniment to their lives.

"My dear Mrs. Meynell [he wrote], your willingness to come when the auspices are favourable shall water my desert until I see you here. A chance of our meeting is offered for the 6th of May, and I hailed the boredom of a crush to embrace it, with the promise to be in town. If you are at Upper Brook Street that evening, you will perhaps be able to fix your date. At present, I think of you gladly as with your sister, drawing strength from sea-breezes, out of the cage of brick, a visible universe about you, and those winged eyes of yours abroad in it. You write of your not being a talker. I can find the substance I want in your silences, and can converse with them. Your plea in excuse makes me ashamed of my prattle. Let me tell you that my mind is not always with my tongue in the act. I do it for the sake of sociability, and I am well disposed either to listen or to worship the modest lips that have such golden reserves.

"I am ever your true servant, and, the more than any word can stamp it, friend, GEORGE MEREDITH."

And after a stay of hers at Box Hill with some of the children his letter took rhymed form:

"Shall I again have Lilac week?
  The coming days of sequence seven
  I view, and see an aspect bleak
  Beside that flash of quiet heaven
  Your presence gave; till I can think
  An angel in one flitted wink
  Was with me; and because I yearn
  I needs must doubt, almost despair,
  Of such kind season's chance return: –

'Tis but a moment's gasp for air.
A moment more and I behold
Your Lobby in her bonnet white
Among the grasses' blue and gold
So sagely gathering; near in sight
Her tutelary Monica;
And near, their pencilling Mamma: –
The mother with the ready smile,
Who wages warrior fight the while.

A most refreshing note arrives. But the 'three o'clock in the morning' distresses me. Your bequest of the slip of paper and the pencil called out the verses to you, of which there is no end, only breaks and the Post and meals and discretion. Adieu, dear soul, with my love to all whom you hold dear. GEORGE MEREDITH."

Heavy double white violets, unforgettably beautiful, he grew for my mother in a frame, to remind her of Genoa; white strawberries came to us from his garden too. An iris he loved, with pale blue petals and a golden middle, he named *Alicia Coerulea*, and kept her supplied with it. He sent up his gardener with four young poplars for the little patch of back-garden at Palace Court. Having asked to see a photograph of her father, he wrote: "Herewith the photograph is returned, to reach you safely, as I trust. It sent me to read 'A Remembrance' again, and I can conjure up a likeness between the outer and the inner in that devoutly steady tracing by the daughter's hand – which is more than great singing to me. My book of 'The Rhythm' will be flying to-morrow to Henry James, who was here yesterday and earned the gift by his appreciation of the contents. I could not let

him have it until another was on its way to fill the
vacancy. . . . My sweet sister in the Muse shall soar
higher than me without shaming me. My pride will be
to keep the title of brother."

Her greatest concern with any friend was to make
Coventry Patmore's poetry loved as she loved it. "The
worst of it is, he stirs a demon imp in me," Meredith
owned; and her efforts had poor success. "I have read
the Patmore extracts," he wrote. "I think there is nothing
you would like that I should not esteem. As to the 'Angel,'
the beauty must be felt, but I have been impressed in old
days by the Dean, and the measure of the verse, correct
as it is, with the occasional happy jerk, recalls his elastic
portliness, as one of the superior police of the English
middle class, for whom attendant seraphs in a visible
far distance hold the ladder, not undeserved, when a
cheerful digestion shall have ceased." – And so the very
thing happened that she often lamented was likely to
happen to Coventry Patmore's fame; it was injured by
the jog-trot domesticity of much of his verse, – a state of
things for which she had her comment. "It must be
owned," she wrote in an article on Patmore, "that some
of the accessory persons and conditions of the story of
The Angel in the House are unwelcome to poetry as we have
learnt to hold it. But this is an avowal that we are either
content, or very weakly, very ineffectually, ill content, to
live in a social world that we confess to be unworthy of
poetry." Another effort at conversion arose from Meredith's
disparagement of Dickens; and she made one of the
"Autolycus" columns an argument in that interest. "A
good Jack Horner study," he said, meaning that she had

picked out the plums. "Portia as advocate is not to be withstood." In their talk they had for discussion not only the main things of writing but its technique. He wrote from Box Hill: "When you are here, in your own garden again, we will talk upon certain minor points of literary composition, in which I may be useful. By the way, touching the heart – never expect it to be perfectly simple. Not the most educated can be that. And further matter for discourse is there." And another time he wrote: "When you come to me we will have talk of the art and aim of verse, and of Sentiment, and the good thing it is when not pretending to be a kingdom of its own. I shall teach you nothing that can be new to such a mind as yours, but I shall be leaven to your deeper thoughts of Earth and Life." Of a conversation with her he reported in Meredithean style: "We waltzed together on celestial heights!" His examination of her work went minutely into the very recesses of each thought and phrase, and he made a study of her writing in an article called "Mrs. Meynell's Two Books of Essays." "Readers with a turn for literature," he wrote, "have noticed of late a column once weekly in the Autolycus basket of the *Pall Mall Gazette*, considering it princely journalism. . . . The essays have, in these days of the overflow, the merit of saying just enough on the subject, leaving the reader to think. They can be read repeatedly, because they are compact and suggestive, and at the same time run with clearness. The surprise coming on us from their combined grace of manner and sanity of thought is like one's dream of what the recognition of a new truth would be. Conceivably the writer was fastidious to the extreme degree during the term of scholarship, but that is only now shown in a style having 'the walk of the Goddess'; and when she speaks her wise things, it is the voice of one standing outside the curtain of the Oracle, humbly among her hearers." He speaks of the balance to be preserved between the double origins of our tongue, a thing hard to maintain "even when there is no strong predilection for one or the other," and certainly hard to maintain in Johnson, with whom Latin was his "lingual club"; – and in this work that he was examining he traced the love of Latinity. It is interesting that Meredith, whose style is characterised by the studied avoidance of simplicity, specially prized the frugal quality in my mother's writing, "the style correcting wealth and attaining to simplicity by trained art. . . . Her manner," he says, "presents to me the image of one accustomed to walk in holy places and keep the eye of a fresh mind on our tangled world, happier in observing than speaking; careful to speak but briefly to such ear-beaten people, and then only when reflections press. . . . I can fancy Matthew Arnold, lighting on such essays as 'The Point of Honour,' 'A Point in Biography,' 'Symmetry and Incident,' and others that I have named, saying with refreshment, 'She can write!' It does not seem to me too bold to imagine Carlyle listening, without the weariful gesture, to his wife's reading of the same, hearing them to the end, and giving his comment: 'That woman thinks!' A woman who thinks and can write, who does not disdain the school of journalism, and who brings novelty and poetic beauty, the devout but open mind, to her practice of it, bears promise that she will some day rank as one of the great Englishwomen of Letters. . . ." His article appeared in the *National Review*. "It is inadequate – what could be adequate?" he wrote to her. "I have curbed fervency as much as I could." And again: "I failed in doing what I wanted to do, because of aiming with my heart and attempting to make it appear the head; so that neither of them had fair play. Writing as a stranger, I should have done more justice to my design and to you."

But throughout their friendship he had outspoken disapproval for what dissatisfied him. "It is not the soul of her soul," he says to her of something of hers; and again, "this is inartistic on her part." When her "Autolycus" had dealt with some secondary poets: "No more anthologies or minute examination of minor moths!" And when he thought her careless with praise: "I have got through 'Cyrano,' and I marvel at the cleverness of the hand which could hold me all to the end over such a group of 'fantoches.' Near the end I chafed, and read only to have done with a conscience."

He had great eagerness for their meetings.

"Dearest Friend, – Let it be Saturday. A room awaits you at the inn. My cottage offers two for the girls. State the hour of your train. I have the delight of a boy in looking to the week's end with you for the crown of it. Your own, GEORGE MEREDITH."

Sometimes a friend who intensely coveted the boon was taken to be introduced to Meredith; but when it was a question of taking Francis Thompson, so averse from any society but that minimum to which he was accustomed, the favour had to be enforced. Francis Thompson's biographer writes:

"Meredith's invitations he could not permanently resist. At Box Hill he spent a night in June 1896. Meredith had written to A. M.: 'You and the poet will have Heaven's welcome to the elect. But the cottage will be wounded if you desire not to sleep in it after having tried its poor resources. Be kind.' To dine and sleep and wake in that small cottage was to be at very close quarters with nature and a man. With birds at the window, trees bowing and rustling at the back door, and at the front the vivid grass ready for his feet, Francis was thrust into the presence of a showy bit of nature, and was hardly more easy than if he had been thrust at the theatre into a box directly adjoining a crowded stage. He would pull at his necktie, and smooth his coat, and be most warily conscious of the Meredith eye, like a husband's, 'microscopic for defect.' The singing of Meredith's blackbirds would be no less confusing than the stream of Meredith's voice; the nodding flowers and the brisk shadows, the sunshine and the talker, were all too strange to him. For years he had evaded such encounters; here he was forced to be seen and to see in the unclouded atmosphere of this garden on a hill, and during a long drive. To be on tremendously good terms with Nature for her own sake, with talk for its own sake, with French literature, with the Celt, was Meredith's way; Thompson was shy of so much clean-cut ability. Meredith's method was acceptance, whether of birds' song or Burgundy. Thompson's method was of refusal because he knew himself not robust enough to meet the flow of either."

In August 1897 Meredith wrote to my mother:

"My Friend, – Will you listen to me? I have felt very urgently of late that you want rest. I am in my

135

present condition because of working on a starved physical system for years. Now, next Wednesday Riette goes to Overstrand, to prepare her house for husband and children. I go with her, to the Batterseas. Will you not come here as my treasured guest and occupy the cot in perfect repose? – doing only the Autolycus article, if that. Repose will be such good medicine for you, and I think it imperatively needed. Taken in time, you may be spared much wretchedness. I mentioned to Eliza the chance of your coming, and she brightened. Here you are at home, loved, untroubled by worries of the household, in good air, with the garden you like; you could have here, as nowhere else, the absolute rest with just the amount of attention required. Be inspired by me, say you will come on Wednesday or Thursday for a fortnight. Husband and children might visit, but you ought to have the complete change. Perhaps, after two or three days, you would like to have Miss Tobin for companion. The phantom host would bid her warm welcome. I may be back before the end of two weeks. I should like to be with you for a day. I trust to hear on Tuesday afternoon that you will do this really wise thing, under the inducement to make me happy, as it is a sister's duty when her heart's brother presses it. He does. Your devoted, GEORGE MEREDITH."

This plain solicitude brings her back on to the page from which, when his note is only of praise and triumph, so much of her is absent. Meredith gave such a high sound to life; he must always have seemed an exotic friend, far apart from the daily incident and drudgery. He was the reward of writing; probably there was not one of the habitual dropping-in friends at Palace Court who did not better reflect the somewhat hard average of life. Her letters to my father, written during occasional absences in these years, reveal their common cares in writing of necessity, against time, even in illness:

(*1895*)   *Clevedon*

"Dearest Love, – I am just posting my *Album*, and shall jog through my *Tablet* at the same leisurely rate. If I can think of a P.M.G. column I need not hurry about returning, for I am more or less wanted here. The nurse is very good but the two smaller children are wild. Except for the occasional outbreak they are exceedingly happy. It is heavenly weather. If I stay, darling, what would you think of coming down on Friday? It would be purely purely delightful with you. I should like you to see your lovely four on these daisies. I hope my poor little paragraphs will be in time to save you the last few hundred words. Heaven bless my own little Lad! Try not to stoop. If you sit at the low black chair at the table you can't stoop very badly however hard you try. Your JOHNSON."

And during an illness at the same place she wrote: "I feel rather victorious at having finished my Johnson's Dictionary for this week anyway. And an Autoly on Charlotte Brontë – a new view of her style. I have been free from acute pain since the forenoon of to-day. In fact these are the merest retreating growls – so different from the advancing growls."

(*1897*)   *Palace Court*

"Darling . . . This morning I took an omnibus drive through London to the farther end of Clapton, thinking to write about the London Sunday, but there was little to note. There was, however, the dreadful incident of a man's cutting his throat on the pavement in Shoreditch. I took notes of London steeples and I went into a City church. Sweetheart, I am sorry to trouble you with this demand, but I suppose you ought to have it. I wrote a line to the collector to say you were away from home. I would willingly sell my diamond crescent if things are pressing. Your JOHNSON."

She was, incidentally, often landed without money, not really because it did not exist, but because of her general want of anticipation of her own requirements. "Last night," she records to my father in absence, "the messenger lagged so in fetching the 'fiver' that it grew towards the time for my dinner and he was not back. But the cheerful hansom-driver was most willing to come for payment next morning. So I started off. Round a corner he banged into another hansom, both going at a great rate. Our horse could not be stopped and we dragged the other hansom with us. . . . No one was hurt, but we knocked the other cab into splinters. During the whole of the ensuing enquiry I had to sit, thinking of Heinemann's dinner. I could not jump into another hansom, having no money. I was nearly an hour late, but happily Whistler was so too."

"Dear Love, – I am writing in the hope that you are to have a few more days in Rome in Spring. I would work doubly hard in order to enable you to have a rest you need so much – and in those happy circumstances. I follow you on your way all the time. I have left much of my life in the churches near you – S. Andrea delle Fratte, the Gesù e Maria, Santa Maria del Popolo. Oh, see all you can. I am quite proud of the *Register* I posted to you yesterday. The children say I look it. In order to be ready for a tougher tussle next week I am writing my column to-day. Monnie so compelled me to do it that *her* pressure was equal to Monday's. Then I have no Royal Academy this week. The children are most sweet in every way, tender, charming and attentive – Monnie only a little too anxious about me. . . . Now, my own love, farewell. I must turn again to adding up those 1,600 words. Once the *Pall Mall* is off my mind I can face the rest serenely. But before I find a subject for the 'Autolycus' I do feel uneasy. Your faithful JOHNSON."

Periodically she enjoyed visiting her sister at Dover Castle. "Last night," she wrote once after her arrival there, "the hurricane was simply indescribable. At the corner of the drawbridge it was a question whether the horse and carriage would or would not be blown over into the open country. From within the eight-foot walls of this tower the wind sounded like cannon. But of course not a thrill or a tremor in the building. They are all too

ALICE MEYNELL

kind. William came into the room crying 'Well *dear* Alice!' Mimi insisted on moving out of her room for me, because it has its own bathroom where I can have a boiling bath at any hour, and late at night, which makes me sleep." – "When I do not eat a large meal I am followed round the house with beef-tea."

The dropping-in friends at this time at Palace Court included Vernon Blackburn. He was the musical critic of the *Pall Mall Gazette*, one of "Henley's young men," and a most devoted and admiring friend of my mother. He was in his 'thirties, and of a rather unattached habit of life, which allowed him to wander to our house at any time. His chair in the drawing-room was the piano-stool. As he was stout, the agility of his fingers, when his piece required nimble playing, must actually have been a difficult – and to watching children seemed an incredible – thing. His sweet, weak, high voice, too, went oddly with his proportions. There was no question, however, of smiling at him; he was the first himself to find matter for smiling round about him. There can never have been anyone who laughed with more excellent pleasure. His admiration of my mother's writing made his own style as like hers as possible; and on one occasion the proof of a *National Observer* article of hers was sent to him, on internal evidence, for correction. Another friend, who came nearly every evening to Palace Court, and was beloved by the children, was Bernard Whelan ("Brin"). He was an old friend of my father; he was an architect, so dilettante that restoring one church (St. Etheldreda's) and writing one book (*An Architect in Exile*) was about sufficient disturbance of his life's leisure. If my mother had a "school" of imitators, here was the other member. "Brin's article I think the best of his that I have seen," wrote Francis Thompson to my father once. "It is really very good, allowing for the fact that it is essentially imitative writing, and his 'make-up' (to speak Thespianly) must have cost him a world of trouble. . . . Brin, in fact, has made to himself a pair of breeches from Mrs. Meynell's cast-off petticoats. But it is cleverly done, and I did not think Brin had been tailor enough to do it." Brin had a special way of knocking at the front-door, and every child in the house rushed to open it to him. There was a picturesque sprinkling of bearded friars, unobtrusively learned, who helped the editor with contributions to the papers, paid their visits equally to the children and the parents, and brought with them the cheerful humble atmosphere of guests who looked for no particular attention. (There was also an old and invalid priest with a taste for light reading who, according to my father, once wrote to him: "Forsaken by God and forgotten by man, I beg you to send me a copy of *Modern Society*".) A beautiful Californian friend of my mother, Agnes Tobin, began in 1896 to increase the number of our visitors by more than her own presence, our other friends finding themselves unable to forgo the chance of seeing her. The drawing-room at Palace Court was a pleasant room for a gathering; it was beautifully proportioned; it was panelled with old Japanese gold-thread embroideries, and a little collection of Venetian glass was bestowed on an inlaid Spanish table that had belonged to Lord Leighton. I can remember my aunt, Lady Butler, unable to take her eye off one of the storks in the Japanese embroideries once, saying as she looked and worried and pondered: "It is so like someone I know: who can it be, – so like, so like; I can hear his voice," – and her relief and delight when she identified some Colonel of her acquaintance.

My mother had a particularly gracious way of welcoming a guest. It was so inconceivable to her that everything should not be suitable for the entertainment of anyone who came that she offered even very plain hospitality with the slight ceremony that went with the assumption that it was good. This faith had its earlier stage when in her household shopping she assumed the perfect integrity of the tradesman who served her, or of the very hawker at the door. "The advertisements speak well of it," she might in fact have said. Richard Whiteing, whose long friendship dated from these days, in his reminiscences describes the fare at the Sunday evening suppers as being no more plentiful than "just to serve, like the banquets in the Iliad, to put away from you the desire of eating and drinking as a hindrance to the flow of soul." Another writer of reminiscence has related how, after a great deal of talk in the drawing-room, he was invited into the quiet of the library by his host who promised him a treat which his thirst made him interpret in a happy manner. Reaching the library he found his refreshment to consist of having Francis Thompson's early poems read aloud to him. Francis Thompson himself habitually carried up from the table with him a piece of dry bread which he lodged on the library or drawing-room mantelpiece, and which said that his hunger was not appeased. Some other autobiographer has made in-

dulgent comment on Palace Court housekeeping. Had
all such writers been as unanimous on this point in their
books as I am sure they were in their experience, with
what little breach of modesty might quotation have been
made here from their volumes! As it is, these excerpts
must be made even with their approval stressed in the
manner of reminiscences.

In *The Romantic 90's* Mr. Le Gallienne says of my
mother:

"Never surely was a lady who carried her learning
and wore the flower of her gentle humane sanctity
with such quiet grace, with so gentle and understanding a smile. The touch of exquisite asceticism about
her seemed but to accent the sensitive sympathy of
her manner, the manner of one quite humanly and
simply in this world, with all its varied interests, and
yet not of it. There was the charm of a beautiful
abbess about her, with the added *esprit* of intellectual
sophistication. However quietly she sat in her
drawing-room of an evening with her family and
friends about her, her presence radiated a peculiarly
lovely serenity, like a twilight gay with stars. But there
was nothing austere or withdrawn about her. In that
very lively household of young people she was one
with the general fun, which under the direction of
her buoyant genial husband used often to wax fast
and furious and made dinner there a particularly
exhilarating occasion. I give thanks here for the
many joyous hours I have spent at the laughing
board, and I have no other such picture of a full and
harmonious home life to set by its side."

In a book called *More Reminiscences of an Old Bohemian*, by Major Fitzroy Gardner, who must have been one of the casual acquaintances who come and go and bring their generous appreciation with them, he speaks of my mother as "no ordinary highbrow but a very beautiful woman whose presence, as much as her writing, was an inspiration. . . . She had the face of an angel and alas! a far too frail physique. . . . She possessed an instinctively gracious dignity of manner, yet the sense of humour of a frivolous girl. Almost all her guests whom one first met on those delightful occasions one desired to meet again. I remember one Sunday evening, coming out of the house by chance with a woman of the world, more distinguished for her physical charm than for intellect. As we walked towards the Bayswater Road, talking about our hostess as if she had been some minor deity, my companion suddenly remarked, 'I feel somehow as if I must go to church and pray.' "

Sunday afternoon was for callers; Sunday evening was more informal; there was some overlapping from one to the other. Charles Lewis Hind, enthusiastic young editor then, and a friend all the rest of his life, says: "I may say that calling at that house meant arriving at about half-past three, staying till midnight, and meeting in the course of the year most of the literary folk worth knowing." H. W. Nevinson (if all these testimonies are to be taken) records his impression of my mother's courtesy which seemed as if it must be affected and yet "revealed her true nature; and beside her were her sons and daughters displaying a similar grace not only towards herself but, to my astonishment, even towards each other." Aubrey

Beardsley, then a clerk in an insurance office, came with a portfolio of drawings; Lionel Johnson, too pale and delicate even for speech; Oscar Wilde, and Willie Wilde whose wit was found no less than his brother's. William Watson and Stephen Phillips and Herbert Trench were visitors; and W. B. Yeats, whose poetry-writing young friend, Katharine Tynan, was also my parents' much-loved friend. She has made many a note, in the course of a long close friendship, of things concerning my mother: "Even in an intimate friendship she very seldom talked of herself. The same absence of personal detail was notice-able in her letters, beautiful and affectionate letters in the most graceful handwriting, but fuller of the person to whom they were written than herself." She also relates: "Mrs. Meynell was subject to the same headaches as mine. Francis Thompson, who had been a medical student, had a learned name for them – something like hemicranial headaches – because they affected one side of the head and one eye. They were in fact the true *migraine*, beginning with arcs and zigzags flashing before the eye. Francis Thompson, coming out of an abstraction, was very much annoyed by a suggestion which had reached him that anyone but Mrs. Meynell could have hemicranial headaches. When he found that I was the privileged person, he said handsomely: 'Oh, well – per-haps Mrs. Hinkson *may* have them.' "

Her friends never discovered a talker in my mother. Even if they found her at her freest she broke silence less readily than most people. When she spoke at all volubly it was of something she had not just – but had long – thought of; and she made but little use of the spontaneous opportunities arising in conversation. Coventry Patmore, in describing to her a dinner-party of animated talk once, said: "I missed your silence." And Meredith was writing from Box Hill of her short letters: "I am in debate whether I would not barter the noble flourishes in your letter for just one line more." And when William Sharp practised on Meredith his strange and successful deception of taking to Box Hill a woman whom he introduced as Fiona McLeod, the name that was in fact merely his own synonym, Meredith, in describing the visit to my mother, wrote: "She spoke of your beautiful *long* letters. I repressed my start and moderated my stare."

Apart from a natural habit of silence, there was all the enforced silence of work. It was a household in which the intimate visitors sat waiting in the library to see which would arrive first, the time when they had to go or the time when their hosts would be free to talk to them. My mother's rather eccentric needlework was sometimes taken up with the laying-down of her pencil. She sewed always with a double thread, with a determined ideal of strength applied even to flimsy things – a fact which did not prevent the trimming falling off our hats sewn on by her the night before. "It was at once humorous and pathetic," says Katharine Tynan, "to see her mending for the children." Her needle, for putting away, would be re-threaded, with the two ends of thread knotted together, and then it was embedded deep in something, – a danger chained and muzzled, a weapon that was never made familiar by use.

XI

THE CHILDREN

THE children, four girls and three boys, ranging from the beginning to the end of childhood, thronged the house. As one child went out at a door another came in; as one went out of a year another entered it. With all these childhoods about her, my mother found that rare thread of childhood that can be written about. The enchanting children all the world over who have been turned into silliness, boredom and sentimentality in admiring anecdote have something repaid to them when childhood comes under shrewd but exquisite observation.

The children had one nurse, Slark, for a great number of years. She loved the boys devotedly; her attitude to the girls was expressed by an adjective which she always used for them and which contained in its single syllable the discreet abuse of whole sentences. The adjective was "great," and at first hearing it has to be searched for its abuse perhaps; but "you great girls" said in a tone that implied an endearing helplessness in the boys was a sufficient key to her life-long partiality. She intermittently exchanged the rôles of nurse and cook; when French nurses were engaged she went to the kitchen.

My mother kept a watchful eye on the children under a new nurse, in case they should be slapped or frightened.

(This watchful eye had sometimes to be turned to the protection of the nurse.) She was alert to prevent the kind of threat that she yet discovered to have been made to one of the little boys who shouted instead of going to sleep. The man with two heads would visit him. How ineffectual was the love that decreed that children should not be frightened! She tells of her assurances to the child that no two-headed man would come, for no such portent was anywhere on earth. ("There is no such heart-oppressing task as the making of these assurances to a child, for whom who knows what portents are actually in wait!") But in this particular case the child clung to the fear, and would not give up the two-headed monster. "He was earnest in controversy with his mother as to the existence of his man. The man was there, for he had been told so, and he was there to wait for 'naughty boys,' said the child, with cheerful self-condemnation. The little boy's voice was somewhat hushed, because of the four ears of the listener, but it did not falter, except when his mother's arguments against the existence of the man seemed to him cogent and likely to gain the day. Then for the first time the boy was a little downcast, and the light of mystery became dimmer in his face."

A different, not the conventional, unexpectedness of childhood was what her pen constantly found. She felt the touch of a child's cheek in midwinter and she wrote: "The child has something better than warmth in the cold, something more subtly out of place and more delicately contrary; and that is coolness. To be cool in the cold is the sign of a vitality quite exquisitely alien from the common conditions of the world. It is to have a naturally, and not an artificially, different and separate climate. . . . More perfectly than their elders, children enclose the climate of life. And, moreover, with them the climate of life is the climate of the spring of life; the climate of a March that is sure to make a constant progress, and of a human April that never hesitates." And in writing of the winter child she chances on a piece of intangible autobiography, the memory of a glory long ago, of which she knows little more than that it was a glory in winter:

"Another word of the child in January. It is his month for the laying-up of dreams. No one can tell whether it is so with all children, or even with a majority, but with some children of passionate fancy there occurs now and then a children's dance, or a party of any kind, which has a charm and glory mingled with uncertain dreams. Never forgotten, and yet never certainly remembered as a fact of this life, is such an evening. When many and many a later pleasure, about the reality of which there never was any kind of doubt, has been long forgotten, that evening – as to which all is doubt – is impossible to forget. In a few years it has become so remote that the history of Greece derives antiquity from it. In later years it is still doubtful, still a legend.

"The child never asked how much was fact. It was so immeasurably long ago that the sweet party happened – if indeed it happened. It had so long taken its place in that past where lurks all the antiquity of the world. No one would know, no one could tell him,

precisely what occurred. And who can know whether
– if it be indeed a dream – he has dreamt it often, or
has dreamt once that he had dreamt it often? That
dubious night is entangled in repeated visions during
the lonely life a child lives in sleep, it is intricate with
allusions. It becomes the most mysterious and the
least worldly of all memories, a spiritual past."

Of the winter child she says too:

"Now more than ever must the lover beware of
making a comparison between the beauty of the
admired woman and the beauty of a child. He is indeed too wary ever to make it. So is the poet. As
comparisons are necessary to him, he will pay a
frankly impossible homage, and compare a woman's
face to something too fine, to something it never could
emulate. The Elizabethan lyrist is safe among lilies
and cherries, roses, pearls and snow. He undertakes
the beautiful office of flattery, and flatters with courage. There is no hidden reproach in the praise. Pearls
and snow suffer, in a sham fight, a mimic defeat that
does them no harm, and no harm comes to the lady's
beauty from a competition so impossible. But here is
the secret: she is compared with a flower because she
could not endure to be compared with a child. That
would touch her too nearly. There would be the
human texture and the life like hers, but immeasurably
more lovely."

A thing to which she makes constant reference is the
child's sense of time. To children time seems so long that
they and they only have the clue to antiquity!

"When a child begins to know that there is a past, he has a most noble rod to measure by – he has his own ten years. He attributes an overwhelming majesty to all recorded time. He confers distance. He, and he alone, bestows mystery. Remoteness is his. He creates more than mortal centuries. He sends armies fighting into the extremities of the past. He assigns the Parthenon to a hill of ages, and the temples of Upper Egypt to sidereal time. . . . Childhood is itself Antiquity, to every man his only Antiquity. The recollection of Childhood cannot make Abraham old again in the mind of a man of thirty-five; but the beginning of every life is older than Abraham. *There* is the abyss of time. . . . Suppose the man of thirty-five heard, at that present age, for the first time of Romulus. Why, Romulus would be nowhere. But he built his wall, as a matter of fact, when everyone was seven years old. It is by good fortune that 'ancient' history is taught in the only ancient days."

The children were a long time in learning for themselves many things that their mother took for granted that they had been taught. But of silliness they were early made aware, if only by the merest inflection of their mother's manner. Without a word said, the immediate aloofness of her manner was enough to bring a little sense of shame that easily lasts a lifetime; her response simply faded. "Children sometimes attempt to cap something perfectly funny with something so flat that you are obliged to turn the conversation," she has written, – and adds: "Dryden does the same thing, not with jokes, but with his sublimer passages."

But to characteristics other than silliness she had so sensitive a response that the children never knew what it was to have a single susceptibility of theirs offended by her. In an essay called "The Boy" she has the same discernment for a twelve-year old boy of unapproachable pride and reserve as she had in writing of her own father:

"He will not endure (albeit he does not confess so much) to be told to do anything, at least in that citadel of freedom, his home. His elders probably give him as few orders as possible. He will almost ingeniously evade any that are inevitably or thoughtlessly inflicted upon him, but if he does but succeed in only postponing his obedience, he has, visibly, done something for his own relief. It is less convenient that he should hold mere questions, addressed to him in all good faith, as in some sort an attempt upon his liberty. Questions about himself, one might understand to be an outrage. But it is against impersonal and indifferent questions also that the boy sets his face like a rock. He has no ambition to give information on any point. . . . When a younger child tears the boy's scrap-book (which is conjectured, though not known, to be the dearest thing he has) he betrays no emotion; – that was to be expected. But when the stolen pages are rescued and put by for him, he abstains from taking an interest in the retrieval; he will do nothing to restore them. To do so would mar the integrity of his reserve. . . . He is not 'merry.' Merry boys have pretty manners, and this boy would not have you to call his manners pretty. But if not merry, he is happy; there never was a more untroubled soul. If he has an almost grotesque reticence, he has no secrets. . . . His happiness appears through his moody and charming face, his ambition through his dumbness, and the hopes of his future through his ungainly bearing. How does so much heart, so much sweetness, all unexpressed appear? For it is not only those who know him well that know the child's heart; strangers are aware of it. This, which he would not reveal, is the only thing that is quite unmistakable and quite conspicuous. What he thinks that he turns visibly to the world is a sense of humour, with a measure of criticism and indifference. What he thinks the world may divine in him is courage and an intelligence. But carry himself how he will, he is manifestly a tender, gentle, and even spiritual creature. . . ."

But it was wrong just now to say that no susceptibility was ever offended. In the delineation of the reserves of this boy, the very susceptibilities were hurt that were so well understood. In one of his notes Everard remembers "my shame at 'The Boy': stealing the proof and destroying it. I thought it a betrayal – to be made a character in a short essay, when there was the whole of our life together to be considered. It was my revolt against impressionism, selection. To be an article, instead of being a son."

Parental control that had hitherto been so easy – our parents having luckily hit on that economy of discipline in which a word is effective – presented new problems with a younger child, the "child of tumult, whose passions find him without defence," and whose face was "delicate and too often haggard with tears of penitence that Justice herself would be glad to spare him."

"For a wild hour he is the enemy of the laws. If you imprison him, you may hear his resounding voice as he takes a running kick at the door, shouting his justification in unconquerable rage. 'I'm good now' is made emphatic by the blow of his heel upon the panel. But if the moment of forgiveness is deferred, in the hope of a more promising repentance, it is only too likely that he will betake himself to a hostile silence and use all the revenge yet known to his imagination. 'Darling mother, open the door!' cries his touching voice at last; but if the answer should be 'I must leave you for a short time, for punishment,' the storm suddenly thunders again. When things are at this pass there is one way, and only one, to bring the child to an overwhelming change of mind; but it is a way that would be too cruel, used more than twice or thrice in his whole career of tempest and defiance. This is to let him see that his mother is troubled. 'Oh, don't cry! Oh, don't be sad!' he roars, unable still to deal with his own passionate anger, which is still dealing with him. With his kicks of rage he suddenly mingles a dance of apprehension lest his mother should have tears in her eyes. Even while he is still explicitly impenitent and defiant he tries to pull her round to the light that he may see her face."

The child (Francis) grows older and becomes "the child of subsiding tumult":

"The tumults of a little child's passions of anger and grief, growing fewer as he grows older, rather increase than lessen in their painfulness. There is a fuller consciousness of complete capitulation of all the childish powers to the overwhelming compulsion of anger. This is not temptation; the word is too weak for the assault of a child's passion upon his will. That little will is taken captive entirely, and before the child was seven he knew that it was so. Such a consciousness leaves all babyhood behind and condemns the child to suffer. For a certain passage of his life he is neither unconscious of evil, as he was, nor strong enough to resist it, as he will be. The time of the subsiding of the tumult is by no means the least pitiable of the phases of human life. . . . By no effort can his elders altogether succeed in keeping tragedy out of the life that is so unready for it. Against great emotions no one can defend him by any forethought. He is their subject; and to see him thus devoted and thus wrung, thus wrecked by tempests inwardly, so that you feel grief has him actually by the heart, recalls the reluctance – the question – wherewith you perceive the interior grief of poetry or of a devout life. Cannot the Muse, cannot the Saint, you ask, live with something less than this? If this is the truer life, it seems hardly supportable. In like manner it should be possible for a child of seven to come through his childhood with griefs that should not so closely involve him."

The Children, consisting of the earlier of the many essays she wrote on that subject, was published in 1897, and had the same praise as her former books, and the same modest success of sales that dribbled into successive editions.

One of my father's letters to the family about this time gives more idea of parental anxieties than was appropriate to essays. The letter is headed Marine Parade, Brighton:

"Darlings of my heart, – Your letters were all the more a delight to me this morning because I hardly expected them. After I left Palace Court I doubted if you would remember the address. It was like the clever Monnie to go to the right box. I do hope that thou, my sweet wife, art feeling better, and not being fatigued to-day before thy dinner. I hope also that the darling daughter's cough is subsiding. The day here is sunny and cold. I saw Fr. Fawkes this morning for a few minutes. He has a very pleasant room in a very pleasant house – with Hegel's works much to the fore upon his shelves.

"My host and hostess send their love. They are only in lodgings here. The thing that passes for the sea is at their door. But it is not the mighty being: the spirit of the mighty being will not stand a Parade, and the body of the sea without the spirit is a disappointing affair.

"I have read *Ships that Pass in the Night*. It is certainly a book. You must read it. I am pleased to find so much Capucin Christianity in it. Two little passages I have copied you may care to read.

"I envy Everard the Latin lessons with his mother. I should know Latin now indeed if I had had such a dear instructress when I was a boy, tell him. He makes me a little sad when I think of his quite unnecessary crossnesses; but he is so good and true a boy all round that I have no fear but that he will free himself from this defect.

"Expect me to-morrow when you see me. Very probably I shall be home to lunch. I know that my darling Monica will do the prudent thing about going to school with her cough. She knows I could not bear her to be ill and to suffer.

"I love you all so much, my darling wife and children. And even the servants who wait on you have my gratitude. Believe me, with my devotion to all, Your W."

Looking her last, during these years, on the vanishing infancies, my mother found the likeness they suggested. "A poppy bud, packed into tight bundles by so hard and resolute a hand that the petals of the flower never lose the creases, is a type of the child. Nothing but the unfolding, which is as yet in the non-existing future, can explain the manner of the close folding of character. In both flower and child it looks much as though the process had been the reverse of what it was, as though a finished and open thing had been folded up into the bud – so plainly and certainly is the future implied, and the intention of compressing and folding-close made manifest."

XII

PROSE AND POEMS

Tasks multiplied themselves in these busiest of years. One of the chief of these was *The Flower of the Mind* in 1897, an anthology of poems from Chaucer to Wordsworth with an introduction and with notes. The characteristic feature of the anthology was its extolling of the sixteenth and seventeenth centuries, the deposing of the eighteenth. "Her passion for the poetry of conceits" was not approved by critics then. They had a sharper quarrel with her because of her exclusion of Gray's *Elegy*. "My labour," she wrote, "has been to gather nothing that did not overpass a certain boundary-line of genius. Gray's *Elegy*, for instance, would rightly be placed at the head of everything below that mark. It is, in fact, so near to the work of genius as to be most directly, closely and immediately rebuked by genius; it meets genius at close quarters and almost deserves that Shakespeare himself should defeat it." In the storm of dissension that met this opinion she had a rare word of agreement in a letter from Wilfrid Whitten, written about an article of hers on the same point: "I cannot forbear to tell you how much it satisfies me. I think it is the truth. Apart from this the article is so beautifully (and riskily) constructed. You gently lead Gray's genius to the light of

158

Shakespeare's, and we see it pale. It was a beautiful method."

In his notes to an anthology of his own, years afterwards, Walter de la Mare wrote: "Many years ago I had the curious pleasure of reading a little book, and one in small print too (Alice Meynell's lovely *Flower of the Mind*), by glow-worm light. The worm was lifting its green beam in the grasses of a cliff by the sea, and shone the clearer the while because it was during an eclipse of the moon." To the *Flower of the Mind* was due the revival of the anonymous Tom O'Bedlam's song.

Other work done in these years included the translation from French of a book on Lourdes, and from Italian of a book called *The Madonna;* also a collection of essays on London, commissioned by Constable, to accompany photogravures by William Hyde in a book called *London Impressions*.

In the meantime *The Spirit of Place*, a new volume of essays, was published in 1899. More than before, in this book, there seems to be a conscious mastery of happy and successful writing; and more than ever the subjects were suited to an individual fancy. "Have Patience, Little Saint," the name of an essay, is the Portuguese alternative to the silence with which we deny a beggar. There is a brief essay on the never-lapsing perceptiveness of such a mind as Tolstoi's: "there is no relapse, there is no respite but sleep or death. To such a mind every night must come with an overwhelming change, a release too great for gratitude. What a falling to sleep! What a manumission, what an absolution!" She writes of Marceline Valmore, who, like Mme. de Sévigné, loved her child in a way that "effaced for her the boundaries of her personal life. Is not what we call a life – the personal life – a separation from the universal life, a seclusion, a division, a cleft, a wound? For these women such a severance was in part healed, made whole, closed up and cured." (It was Marceline Valmore who wrote to her daughter: "Are you warm? You have so little to wear – are you really warm? Oh, take care of me, my child, cover me well.") Other essays in this collection – "July, Wells, Rain" – show in their beauty that there was a new brilliance in the eye that had looked on these things. *The Horizon* begins: "To mount a hill is to lift with you something lighter and brighter than yourself or than any meaner burden. You lift the world, you raise the horizon; you give a signal for the distance to stand up. It is like the scene in the Vatican when a Cardinal, with his dramatic Italian hands, bids the kneeling groups to arise. He does more than bid them. He lifts them, he gathers them up, far and near, with the upward gesture of both arms; he takes them to their feet. . . ." One of the "Shadows," in the essay of that name, is that which the sick man sees when a bird flies across the blind. "What flash of light could be more bright for him than such a flash of darkness? . . . If he had seen the bird itself he would have seen less – the bird's shadow was a message from the sun." And of high-flying birds on a sea-shore: "Though they have the shadow of the sun under their wings, they have the light of the earth there also." It was George Meredith who had suggested to her an article on shadows, and he wrote: "It is a masterly example of the substance you can put upon a thin suggestion."

The task that stands out for hardness in these years was the writing of a book on Ruskin. It was commissioned

by Blackwood for his *Modern English Writers* series, and it
was a summary of Ruskin's ideas. The children visiting
now their mother's bedside – invading even her last
retreat from them – realised that the books and sheets of
manuscript they saw there represented an unusual strain.
Common as it was for that bedside to be visited by
wandering children and found to be given over to work,
the Ruskin time created for them a new standard in
bedside silence, the spectacle of interminable hour-after-
hour work, a new pitch of headache in their mother.
Requiring the kind of trained thinking along fixed lines
that she never found easy, her wrestle with her greatly-
loved Ruskin left her tired and depleted. Such ambitious
and all-embracing theories as his were hard to simplify;
chaos and contradiction can lie so near the narrow truth,
and must have seemed to be awaiting all words but the
very words he uttered. The book was described as a
handbook to Ruskin; it is mixed exposition and comment. "The warmest praise of the Master is there,"
wrote a reviewer, "and yet courteous alarm-bells are
rung on every page." The analysis she succeeded in
making was something one would have judged outside
her particular powers, so that one almost fails to recognise
her in some of her close grasp of the more political
Ruskin, and especially in her reasoning and her reply. A
very interesting quality of criticism met this book when
it appeared, with well-weighed praise for work of a
standard so good that it could be allowed imperfections.
Of the impression left of her estimate of Ruskin as a
whole, a reviewer wrote finely: "Two words Mrs. Meynell brings into vital relation with Ruskin – Mystery and

Lesson. She shows that, when dealing with the Mystery, Ruskin is great; but 'if ever he has explained in vain, registered an inconsequence, committed himself to failure, it has been in the generous cause of possible rescue – it has been in the Lesson.' The nobility of her exposition of Ruskin dwells centrally in the fact that, while she is sometimes doubtful about the Lesson, or is obliged to show (by its arduous compilation) that it was not too clearly or consistently delivered, or is constrained to deny it as a working precept, she makes us feel how glorious were those dealings with the hidden Mystery which issued in the peccant Teaching." Of this Ruskin book the *Times* at the end of an article containing some excellent cavilling said: "Speaking after reflection, we fancy that few people in England could have written a better book."

But here again there was a quarrel! And the quarrel made with her by nearly every critic was due to a challenging opinion of hers certainly presented in a provocative manner. Here is the provocation. After the quoting of some sentences of Ruskin's there occurred the following passage written in parenthesis: "(Ruskin, at this time and ever after, used 'which' where 'that' would be both more correct and less inelegant. He probably had the habit from him who did more than any other to disorganise the English language – that is, Gibbon.)" And here is the critic's protest:

"Note the intensification of authority by the withholding of Gibbon's name until the air has been darkened with his sin. But is it fair, or quite in the scheme of things, thus to ban Gibbon in a casual

breath; to flout, *en passant*, the reader's probable
cherished opinion of Gibbon as if it were nothing?
We picture Gibbon's own astonishment, when this
judgment is whispered along 'the line of the Elysian
shades.' He may have expected it, may have humbled
himself for its coming; but the manner of its coming
he could not have foreseen. 'In parenthesis!' we hear
him gasp, as he sinks back on his couch of asphodel."

The parenthesis was perhaps due to the fact that she had
already in one of the "Wares of Autolycus" columns gone
more fully into her case against Gibbon; and in her own
mind no doubt she was now merely referring to what she
had already written. But this seemed an astonishing in-
dictment of a great writer. Her complaint against Gibbon, when she had elaborated it, instanced the numerous
faults of style which she considered corrupted the writers
who came after him. "Gibbon's literature was scholarly,
and these errors of his alter little or nothing of the honour
due to his eminent elegance of style. But it was these
laxities that took the public taste mightily, and it was the
'corrupt following' of this apostle that set the fashion of
an animated strut of style. . . . There is surely no author
in the history of our literature who has so imposed a new
manner of writing upon an admiring people. He changed
a hundred years of English prose. The dregs of his style
have encumbered the nation. It is not his fault that
posterity divided this property so lavishly among themselves." The set habit of phrase that was questionable in
him, corrupt in his followers, was certainly to be deplored
by this lover of what was wild in literature; the bad

grammar was bound to be abhorred by the pedant. To a style that might have been treated as the product of its age she gave on the contrary the whole responsibility of all the prim and ready-made phrases that were to come. Even the words hemming in Charlotte Brontë's great style – "reside," "peruse," "communicate instruction," "eligible connection," "small competency," "operating as a barrier" – she called a drift of Gibbon.

After the severe Ruskin task there was a difficult thing to do of another kind. A visit to America in 1901, embarked on with all a traveller's pleasure ("this is part of the romance of my romantic life," she wrote from the ship as she started), was unexpectedly prolonged, by the illness of the friend whose guest she was, to eight months; and the separation from her family for that time will be seen in the letters that follow to have been a hard one.

During this absence in America, *Later Poems* was published. Of the nineteen poems it contained, some had been printed privately in paper covers under the name of *Other Poems* in 1896. Many of these poems had yet another beginning in the *Pall Mall Gazette*, where an "Occasional Verse" was a feature that tempted the poets of the day with its opportunity. That the opportunity it afforded my mother was a wonderfully pleasant one is shown in a letter to her from Harry Cust, the *Pall Mall* editor, in which he says: "I worship your verses, the best of the Occ's, and pray for your nearer friendship."

These poems, accumulated so slowly during a number of years, are to some extent offshoots from the prose that was absorbing her. But in a few of them is a note of new power as a poet, and of that new power these few give a particularly beautiful presentation, before her verse became deliberately less musical in her subsequent poems. In all of them the individuality is striking; there is a rare absence of influences. Some are poems of the contemplative, – but long contemplation, fitted into her poem, is brief even to epigram:

>   Thou art the Way.
>   Hadst Thou been nothing but the goal,
>   I cannot say
>   If Thou hadst ever met my soul.
>
>   I cannot see –
>   I, child of process – if there lies
>   An end for me,
>   Full of repose, full of replies.
>
>   I'll not reproach
>   The way that goes, my feet that stir.
>   Access, approach,
>   Art Thou, time, way, and wayfarer.

"The Shepherdess" is another of the most beautiful of these early though "later" poems, beginning—

>   She walks – the lady of my delight –
>   A shepherdess of sheep.
>   Her flocks are thoughts. She keeps them white;
>   She guards them from the steep.
>   She feeds them on the fragrant height,
>   And folds them in for sleep.

The Boer War was in progress; and her sister's husband, General Butler, had resigned his command of the British troops at the Cape at its outbreak. My mother's last visit to the Butlers before she left for America was at Government House, Devonport, where he was now in command. "Insults reach William by post," she wrote from there; "accusations of accepting bribes from Kruger; and five several copies of *Pick me Up* with a drawing of William being shot by a firing company, their rifles labelled 'contempt,' 'derision,' and so forth." My parents, too, wretched under this cloud of a war they did not believe to be just, were both of that small minority, quickly labelled pro-Boer, who attended meetings of protest against aggression, and to denounce the concentration camps. Boer emissaries who visited England came to Palace Court, and were given individually the justice which no one denied their country at a later date.

When my mother went to America in September, 1901, she could feel that she left her family in favourable circumstances. The children had all put perilous infancy behind them, and could add their own care to their father's for their safety in her absence. Her mother could be left, always composing, always receiving her wonderful gifts of ecstasy from the nature of each day, constantly flitting from some reviled little suburban house to some briefly coveted one, and sending always, at any new doing of her child's, her chorus of interest and praise and tenderness and surprise.

With George Meredith long partings were already made by his ill-health. "I could rejoice to see you, and at the same time hate to be seen," he wrote. His afflictions humiliated him. "I need an arm when I walk, and enliven conversation with the frequent Eh!" "If anything could depress me, my loss of legs would bowl down the mind as well. This war is the cloud on it. My only feeling

for the Boers is that for brave men. Notwithstanding
their intimacy with the Almighty they are hard to deal
with. But it might have been done. Heaven bless you and
all dear to you." And when the news reached him of her
American plan, he wrote:

"My dearest Portia, – What magnanimity in the
husband! And I who am always throwing myself into
other persons' minds and hate to be outdone by them
in this particular, have to confess that it would be
ruefully, grimly, and upon supplication, in sight of a
pained and reproachful countenance, that I, a spout
of doleful forecasts, could be brought to yield the
releasing word. But outside the husband's view, there
is the glorious new for you, a splendid Aurora, a fresh
spring; and though I shall be glad when it is over and
you home again, my sympathy will be running with
you during the course, and for so long as you keep out
of accidents. Otherwise, I shall find a tongue to have
told you so. But no, you will be careful and propitiate
Fortune, who has, in spite of the poet, a divinity for
travellers. Give my love to all at home, and take the
remainder of an inexhaustible heart. GEORGE MERE-
DITH."

The American journey was irresistible with such happy
auspices as were put before her. She was to be the guest
of Miss Agnes Tobin, her Californian friend, in whose
beauty and exquisite and lively mind she delighted; and
there was the prospect of her giving a few lectures, in
order that in her absence she should not abandon her
important rôle of wage-earner.

XIII

IN AMERICA

Sept. 7th, 1901   *U.S.M.S. "St. Paul," Southampton Water*

"Dearest,–We are of course in calm water, but the wind is astonishingly fresh. It always *is*. So I am taking the opportunity while everything is erect and steady. The ship is a hive, but the cells are splendidly solid and large. It would be impossible to imagine anything floating more comfortable. The view of the coast of England is rather pretty. I think I shall be as happy as the day is long, if the sea keeps fairly quiet. The ship looks half a mile long.

" Oh, my own love, it was dear to see you and the children running.

"All the passengers are American. The accent resounds. It is cold, and my coat was wanted at once. Darling, darling, this is part of the romance of my romantic life, isn't it? Keep well. Eat. Have a good night. Love to my most beloved children one and all, YOUR JOHNSON."

September 14   *Murray Hill Hotel, New York*

"My darling, – I did not find myself able to post a letter by the pilot this morning, but I don't suppose any time has been lost. We had a prosperous voyage, and entered New York harbour by sunrise. The news of the poor President's death [McKinley's, by assassination] came on board at about half-past two. I did not turn in, that night, so as to see the dawn and the New Hemisphere together. But I am not a good sailor! That 'St. Paul' is a pitcher and a tosser, and a roller, and, long as she looks, she contrived to do all these in the brief length of my poor bunk. It was not tragic, however. Nor will I let it be tragic to think of the solemn ocean – no one can guess how solemn without seeing it – between me and all I love. The sun comes up three hours late from Palace Court to me. I must say it looks upon an anomalous city, with Italian clearness of air, but nothing Italian to shine on, except ragged harness in strings, high collars on the skeleton horses (which indeed remind me sadly of the Italian horses of my youth – they look better now) and a considerable number of young Italian men at work. As for the noise, never have I heard such a rattling racket. The traffic is quite un-regulated and everything dashes, strains and struggles. Oh, it was wonderful to be in a fog over the 'banks' of Captains Courageous. They are under-water banks, and do not show, just a great region of rather 'shoal' water where fish swarms. We nearly ran through a little boat many hundreds of miles from land, in the night. The fishermen will not show their lights till they are in danger, either from recklessness or – what I hope is not the reason – because they spare their oil. The three men we nearly killed were wild with excitement. Soon after, we entered the Gulf Stream on its way to you, and after a touch of Northern cold it was overpoweringly hot. I have stopped to take an excellent lunch, which I much needed, alone in my nice room with its adjacent bath. The kindness and care of Celia and Edward* are beyond description. I think we shall go to Washington for the President's funeral. I can't tell you the love I send to you and all my dear children. Your own JOHNSON."

September 16   *New York*

"My darling, – I am just on the point of taking my first step outside. I have written to Howells and to Collier, but I am told there is little chance of their being in town. It is tropically hot and steaming. Yesterday, Sunday, I lay up, for I could not get the continent of America to stop rocking under me. Even to-day it swings, but I can keep my feet! I am in the lap of luxury, and the town looks bright in the sun. It is not of English ugliness, you understand. There are none of the box houses left to us by the eighteenth century and the corruption of Dutch taste. On the contrary there is a great deal of tra la la, and it is all bad. But they cook! Nothing in Paris is so perfect. Celia has borne the journey well, Edward is a little ailing. At sea he was perfectly well. I shall be quite strong when the impression of the sea leaves me. I have everything to make me so. Darling Wilfrid, you have the children and they have you, but what have I?

"Let my dearest mother have a line from you to say I am flourishing. I cannot write much yet. Tell the beloved children they shall all have letters in time. Your own devoted JOHNSON."

---

* She was travelling with Celia and Edward Tobin, to join their sister Agnes Tobin in California.

Sept. 19   *New York*

"My love, – To my great happiness the whole batch of letters arrived this noon. How infinitely delightful and touching to see these words written by hands so dear. . . .

"The day before yesterday the heat lifted and we drove about, saw the Metropolitan Gallery, lunched with Ethel Barrymore at the Waldorf Astoria and in the evening saw Mr. Drew in *The Second in Command* – oh how dull is third-class drama! Yesterday we lunched at the Waldorf Astoria, in that kaleidoscope of moving and feeding people amid their palms and marble, then went to *Florodora*, invited by Mr. Drew. In the evening we dined at Sherry's with Bobbie Collier, and that was the most delightful dinner we have yet had. He then took us to a kind of theatre music-hall which is the rage here – idiotic, but with perfect dancing, and redeemed by the talent of two comic actors. Then to supper at the Waldorf Astoria. I need not say I don't eat, but only sample, all these meals. To-day we are going out to Mr. Collier's country house. The heat is all gone happily. I have not worn the stocks once as you did not like them. The satin waistcoat is of the greatest use. All my gloves, shoes, veils, ties are nice, which retrieves my somewhat under-dressed appearance. Collier's attentions are most kind. He gives us all his time. Oh my own Love, how much I think of you! Oh my beloved sons and daughters! Your JOHNSON."

Sept. 24th

"My darling Wilfrid, – This will be my last letter from New York. We go on to-morrow, and Agnes will meet us in a few days on this side of the Sierras, with letters from you. It has been very hard to me to be without letters, owing to our lingering here. Celia has been so unselfish and kind in every way that I could not hurry her to leave merely for my letters.

"We have spent two really delightful afternoons on board the 'Erin,' and have been over the 'Shamrock' – a real angel. There is a photograph of Lipton with the splendid Mrs. Dana Gibson on one side of him and me on the other, and Celia standing by. I wish I had a copy for you. Charles Russell has been very kind. He and Lipton are getting quite morbid about the race. They dream of it. . . . Oh, my Willie, what love I send you and my precious ones! Your JOHNSON."

Sept. 28   *Denver, Colorado*

"My darling, – How hard, how hard, it has been to forgo your letters. Agnes will bring them with her to meet us on this side of the second range of mountains. It will indeed be 'like meeting your' husband."

October 1

"My darling Wilfrid, – I dream, in the strange nights of these trains, of meeting you, on the mountains, in the canyons, on the plains, and you are paragraphing there.

"I wish I had some pars. for you, but though I have plenty of *Pall Mall* matter, it does not take the shape of pars. on the actual journey. We shall hear at Great Salt Lake, I hope, about the third yacht race to-day. I took a real fancy to Lipton – he is so good-natured and such a boy. As for the lecture side of this journey I can say nothing as yet. Agnes strongly recommends a Dickens

172

causerie, as well as lecture, at San Francisco, before a woman's club called The Century. I trust her arrangements thoroughly for she knows her way about. Early tomorrow morning she meets us with your letters, as I hope and trust. The country we are now going through is made of mud that dried in the beginning of the world. Your JOHNSON."

Oct. 4th   *Taylor & California Streets, San Francisco*

"My darling, – We left Denver on Monday early and arrived here on Wednesday night, dear Agnes meeting us at Reno on Wednesday morning on the east side of the Sierra Nevada. Oh, Wilfrid, California is the earthly paradise. All the strange whiteness of light of the plains disappears, and you are restored to sweetness, richness and gold of sunshine. The mountains are like the Alps, the valleys are heavy with fruit, little hills rise with cypress and orange-tree dark in the sun. But the absence of the church belfry prevents it from looking Italian, otherwise it would. San Francisco is a great pretentious city, but not a manufacturing pretentious city like the others. I must stop. Your ever JOHNSON."

Oct. 9th   *Yosemite Valley*

"My Darling, – Here we are for a week or a fortnight, Agnes and I, in the most overwhelming scenery. We took train on Monday afternoon and reached the end of railways on Tuesday, after which we drove four in hand in a rough wagon fifty miles one day and twenty the next up these most magnificent mountains, under a more than

173

Italian sun. Such roads, or rather tracks! I am enjoying
it all greatly. And how happy I was to get your beloved
little letter written on Sept. 21 and my darling Viola's.
To-day, however, my joy is much dashed by what Agnes
tells me of her health. I have noticed how weak she is; she
has a constant cough. She has decided to go to England
with me, but she cannot undertake the journey in her
state of weakness and cannot face an English winter. I
see too well that she ought not to go until the Spring. It
is with tears that I think of staying longer away from you.
How can I? Oh, Wilfrid, I feel about the separation all
that you do, with the poignant pain of absence from the
children added. Write and tell me what to do. This will
be a long long post to you from these wilds. Your poor
poor JOHNSON." *

Oct. 14th   *Yosemite Valley*

"My Darling, – Would you were here in this marvellous
place. The blue of the sky is an hourly surprise. As to the
mountains one is so used to them rising gradually that
one cannot gauge their height when they are perpendicu-
lar, as they are here. One is apt to take a forest on a ledge
for a gathering of shrubs.

"Agnes and I went up one of the heights by an Indian

* Miss Tobin wrote: " . . . I was obliged therefore to entreat her
to consider staying out West till Spring, and taking care of me in
Santa Barbara or Florida. She could lecture in New Orleans, or any
warm place, travelling with me. She is simply overpowered by the
mere suggestion – and is sitting in the next room now, not knowing
what or how to write to you. So I thought I would dash off a few
lines to let you share our perplexity. . . . I hear Alice weeping in
the next room – so I will go and make her send her letter just as
it is."

'trail,' which is a track ingeniously traced on ledges and landing places, up from the valley to the summit. We went up on Californian horses which clambered like cats. In some places the trail was a stair cut in the rock or made with stones. The horses did it all with the utmost cleverness. The guide rode first, then I, then Agnes. We were six hours in the saddle. The rest of the time we have driven about the floor of this valley, which is full of meadows and gigantic trees.

"I have sent, so far, to the *Pall Mall*, 'Atlantic skies,' 'A hundred miles an hour,' and 'The plains.' I hope they will have appeared by the time this reaches you. You cannot imagine how glad I should be of an occasional paper. The American papers do not waste much space on European affairs.

"I believe I am to give my 17th Century lecture on the 30th. The Dickens one will follow independently.* Agnes has made up her mind that I shall turn a penny one way or another. Oh my own dear, I want so much to see you. Your JOHNSON."

Oct. 18th   *Wawona, Mariposa Co., California*

"My darling Cuckoo [her son Everard], – Yesterday was a golden day for me. I received a budget of delightful letters, including yours. It is too irritating to think that a month must pass between your writing and the arrival of my reply.

* One lecture was called "The great transition in English poetry: from the 17th to the 18th century." Another was "The Treble Note," a study of Charlotte Brontë, partly reprinted later in *Hearts of Controversy*. A third was "Dickens as a Man of Letters," also partly reprinted in the same volume.

"Yesterday after days of a sky incredibly blue with such nights of stars – I have never really seen stars before, not even in Italy – and a sun that was much more than you could bear without a white umbrella, some splendid clouds came up over the extraordinary precipices, and as the valley is capable of sudden snow, we resolved to say goodbye to the wonderful Yosemite. We drove the twenty odd miles to this place, which is in a divine valley, from which the expedition is made to the Big Trees. All the trees are gigantic in these mountains, but the Big Trees which are vulgarised by that advertisement (after a life of 2,000 years!) are at a little distance from here. We leave for them this morning and I have got up early to have a moment to write to you. It proved to be not snow but thunder, and we *did* have lightning in the night! But the great sun is blazing again to-day.

"The sea voyage was not nearly so bad as you think. I had two good and enjoyable days at the end. My lecture is put off to the 6th of November. Agnes is herself the Impresario. She is too sweet and dear, she is simply devoted. She has hired the hall, got the tickets printed, advertised, .published portraits, got an article into a paper, and raised H—— generally. Nothing could be better. Yet I cannot persuade myself that anyone will go. How I wish I could turn a better honest penny! Would I had put myself into Major Pond's hands!

"I do not give up hope of returning early in December. My dear love to all – beloved Father and all chicks – Your loving Mother, A. M."

Oct. 24th   *San Francisco*

"My Darling Love – . . . Whether I make any success or not of my lecture (the hall is very small, so it cannot hold a big sum) Agnes has done all that mortal could do for me, Celia helping her nobly . . . I cannot describe to you their cheerful labours.

"I went as the guest of the afternoon to the Century Club. What is remarkable is the wish of everybody to exaggerate in one's favour. It is the old lionizing passion still surviving. They *want* to believe you are the most remarkable woman in the world.

"Nothing could be nicer to me than the Stevensons have been. Mrs. Stevenson* is very ill, but she was indeed friendly and welcoming. Mrs. Lloyd Osbourne calls and calls. Father O'Keefe I thoroughly like. I told him at luncheon of your saying that there's many a slip twixt the Cup and the Lipton, and it was appreciated . . . Your loving JOHNSON."

Oct. 30th   *San Francisco*

"My Darling Viola – I am sending you the only notice I have yet seen of my lecture. I am quite grieved that the man says I have a weak voice. I seemed to myself to be roaring at the people. But it is too true that I saw a priest in the distance with his hand up to his ear the whole time! I looked at him reproachfully. . . . Several people who sat at the extreme end of the hall assure me they heard every syllable, so that priest was deafish! . . . I am so

---

* She told my mother that when her *Essays* and her *Poems* reached Samoa, Stevenson kept them under his pillow lest they should be abducted before he had finished with them.

M   177

glad that you make cakes for your beloved father. O my children, pet him and make him happy. Ever, sweet love, Your mother, A. M."

Nov. 13   *San Francisco*

"My own Darling – . . . To stay three months more would be, for me, a sacrifice I need not dwell upon. It would be a sacrifice for you too, my Dearest, and for my Babes. If I must stay it shall not be with an aching heart, and I shall ask you, for love of me, not to let your heart ache. I could not bear that. Let us improve the situation by a little gain, which will lighten your heavy burden a little. I give my Dickens lecture next Monday. I have also an invitation – only for £15 – from New York, as well as the £20 from Chicago. They will all be modest sums, but Agnes thinks I can repeat them indefinitely. . . . At the worst we will not be too sad, – O my dearest, I beg you not to be. The joy of helping your darling darling weekly addition will keep me up, and the joy of choosing little presents for the children. You don't know how far this will go with me as regards splendid spirits, hurrah! Begin to write again if you have stopped. Your letters and my sweet babes' are my delight. Your most loving and devoted wife, JOHNSON."

November 29   *San Francisco*

"My darling Viola – . . . Yesterday was Thanksgiving, and I went to the Convent which the Tobins support, where many hundreds of poor children were entertained. I took one side of a long table, and served the roast turkey and cranberry sauce, squash pie and mince pie and fruit. There were children of all races. It was a beautiful sight. The Sisters had such fine white table linen and flowers for their poor! . . . I don't forget your dear dear face hidden behind the carriage door when I left because you were weeping, my love. Your most devoted mother, A. M."

November 29   *San Francisco*

"My darling, – Yes, it is settled at last that I stay. Agnes is on her bed again now, looking so drooping that I see she ought to change the air of this too sea-surrounded place. It is so damp that chiffon is turned to crêpe, and the stamps in one's purse stick together. One can compel oneself to most things, and once the decision is taken the sacrifice seems easier. I am in correspondence with Pond, and Lane has seen him on my behalf. If he will undertake my tour I shall start with four lectures, The Seventeenth Century, Dickens, The Children, and The Treble Note. In any case we hope to start immediately after Christmas for Monterey, then for Los Angeles, and if Agnes can bear the roughish travelling, for Mexico. After that our course ought to be eastward to New Orleans, then by degrees up to Washington, Philadelphia, Chicago, Boston, and New York. Thence to all that I love.

"I dream of you night by night, wildly, of course; but always of some sudden meeting. Oh my *Love*. I know you will be comforted in thinking that I am never cold. I never have a bottle in bed, never go to the pretty wood fire which is lighted for ornament after dinner. I am very well, only I get no exercise, because no one else takes any.

And really one cannot very well. The hot damp air does take it out of one's muscles. And the streets are so steep that we can only just manage to walk down. Under their surface rattles the perpetual endless steel rope that drags the cars up and down. It never stops, and the car moves by gripping it, and stops by letting it go. The streets – all but the few business streets – are green with thick grass at the side of the rails. I am as happy as I can possibly be without you. It is a luxurious life, which I should not like to live for long. When Agnes thinks the luncheon at home will not be extra nice she takes me to the University Club where she compels me to eat all the luxuries, or to the Palace Hotel, where we always sup after the opera or play. Your devoted and loving JOHNSON."

December 10   *San Francisco*

"My own darling Wilfrid, – This will cross letters from all of you for my distant, husbandless and childless Christmas. I dream perpetually of a sudden meeting. When I go to ten o'clock Mass I think of you just beginning tea in the drawing-room with a fog outside. When I am going to sleep, the post is just about arriving at Palace Court, and you have already a different date from mine.

"To-day we are going into the country across the bay. Of course the last few letters, written under the impression that I was on my way home, go through and through me. May the lectures give an added sanction to what I was morally obliged to do. I have had no such happy moments as those of posting those absurd little sums to you.

Real joy, that. Have a happy Christmas, my Dearest.
Send me a paper now and then. I am in outer darkness.
I kiss you, my own dear love. Your JOHNSON."

Dec. 10   *San Francisco*

"My darling little Francis, – A merry and happy
Christmas! Let me have the great joy of hearing that you
have had a delightful and good holiday. But the goodness
I now take for granted. The stormy days are over, and
my sweet little youngest child is growing in wisdom and
in grace as well as in intelligence and legs. To think that
four of my children will be visibly taller when I see them
again – or five, for Everard has not finished. My longing
to see you is sometimes too keen. Heaven keep us all well
until the happy day of my return. You must come to
London to meet me. Ever, dearest, your loving mother,
A. M."

Dec. 13   *San Francisco*

"Dearest, – I have had a small disappointment in my
third (Brontë) lecture, and though I have made a profit
– a little one – it is too small to send to your week's budget. We had intended to advertise, and then we thought
we would not, and we tried the experiment of an evening
instead of an afternoon lecture, as a man told me that
more men would go. I also lowered my admission. The
consequence was comparative failure – £12, out of which
I have to pay for the hall and the tickets. I shall therefore
save up a little to add to my next cheque which I hope
will be from Los Angeles. The literary women who came

to the other lectures live out of town, and only come in to afternoon things. One must buy one's experience. Everyone prophesies success for a lecture on 'The Children,' and I wait for 'The Unready,' which I trust is on its way. Major Pond says that he always wants six months to make any serious 'bookings.' Shall I come out again in the summer and have a real innings? I dare say he will do something for me even this time, but not quite what I hoped. I had another tremendous cold, and yesterday I did not know whether I could speak. By I know not what force my voice was preserved clear and strong during an hour and a half's lecture, 'The Treble Note,' and as soon as it was over I could not make a sound. It needed courage. My small audience was exceedingly attentive.

"I send you a sonnet by Dr. Taylor, who gave me the 1844 edition of Coventry Patmore's very first poems – a great treasure. He is also a Thompsonian.

"In the letter I have just received from you I read with grief of Viola's illness. You say 'a chill,' but tell me no more. That Phillips should be attending her means a real illness. I shall be very anxious for news. I should have cabled if I had had better luck with my lecture. I should much like to have news of Mama also.

"We had a lovely excursion into the country, to a house embowered in roses at the foot of Mount Tamalpais, a high peak, in these hills. . . . Ever your own JOHNSON."

December 18   *San Francisco*

"My darling, – This is the first half-week that I have received no letter, and yet the last you wrote me gave me news of Viola's illness. It would be so unlike you to leave me in this anxiety by accident that I cannot rest. It is vain to write this now for you to read a fortnight hence. Your last letter was dated eighteen days ago.

"We three went to the Lick Observatory – Agnes, Celia and I, – drove the 28 miles from San José, spent the night with the Campbells and returned next day. It was very beautiful. I am doing a *Pall Mall* article on it. Yesterday I went to a great luncheon given by the Jewish Woman's Club to the other clubs – very brilliant. We are bathed in sunshine. I see both sunrise and sunset from my windows; sunrise over the bay, and sunset over the hills that hide the Pacific.

"This will reach you on New Year's Day, I hope. Oh may it find all well. But for the first time I have a heavy heart. That all the children should miss that mail seems strange. If she had been gravely ill you would surely have told me? You said it was not serious. My heart is there with you. I sometimes think I have attempted too much in staying. To have constant and quite sincere news is simply a matter of life to me. Your most devoted JOHNSON."

December 25   San Francisco

"My darling Wilfrid, – This morning brought me two great batches of delayed letters, to my joy. At last I hear all about my Viola's serious illness, and I fear she suffered much.

"I went out very early to Church. It is full summer weather. To-day we went to a Japanese garden. Mrs. Stevenson has gone to Mexico. The only thing she said about Henley was that he must have been drunk when he wrote the article on Stevenson. She was naturally indignant, – but that article is not the work of a drunken man. She said there was a particularly disagreeable tone in regard to her, but she took that carelessly enough. . . .

"I am sorry you don't like the cover of my poems. I thought it pretty. Lane writes in a most friendly spirit. But he gave me only one copy. A pile has been melting down in the principal book-shop here, and the other shop had sold out. . . .

"Would you could be in this sun, and see these flowers, humming birds and wild canaries. The town, as a town, one cannot care for much. I could send no presents to the dear, dear chicks. Let us hope for better times. Ever, my most dear, your devoted JOHNSON."

January 9th, 1902

"My darling, – We are here at last, due South, and Agnes has her first good change since the Yosemite. I have had to endure the loss of one mail from you, not because of our coming here, but owing to the delay in the snow-bound continent. It is difficult to believe, here in this paradise of sunshine by a summer ocean, that the whole of America on the other side of the Sierra Nevada is one sheet of snow, with the thermometer below zero at Boston and New York.

"Nothing had come from Pond when I left San Francisco, so my heart is rather sore. He had written so eagerly – spontaneously, before my letter to him, so I had a right to hope. If nothing comes of it, how shall I face you, and my own poor exile self?

"If you have *Across the Plains*, read 'The old Pacific

Capital' again. That is where we are, lodged in the huge and magnificent hotel which R. L. S. speaks of at the close. Oh, Wilfrid, to think that the 'word of three letters' in the assassin article of Henley's was 'cad.' That is really worse than anything else.

"What a place this is, what a place! No, nothing in the astonishing Yosemite was so beautiful. Here is something of the past which was not there. For the Ancient Indians who had always lived in that valley and live there still bring nothing of the past to us. Time is change, and the Indians do not change except by coming, as they have done here, under an energetic, benign influence, such as the Jesuits'. We have something of the seventeenth century in the pathetic signs of the despoiled and destroyed Catholic missions here, the only trace of good – not predatory – dealing with the natives. And yet our histories tell of nothing but Spanish 'cruelties.' The Spaniards alone dealt with the Indian for his sake, and not for their own. South California is sprinkled not only with churches but with hospitals and schools, all built for the Indians, and now either destroyed or turned into barracks, hotels and restaurants. The revolutions at the beginning of the nineteenth century – late and last re-verberations of the thunderstorm in France – did all the destroying and secularizing before American acquisition.

"This hotel stands in an enormous kind of sub-tropical garden, tended by the ubiquitous Chinese. It is itself a wonder of luxury. The little town is unchanged since Stevenson's day. I need not say how joyfully I read your *Academy* and *Pall Mall* articles, and *I.L.N.* Your devoted JOHNSON."

ALICE MEYNELL

Jan. 11th   *Monterey*

"My Darling Dimpling [her daughter Madeline], –
This too beautiful place has already done Agnes good,
and she walks. What an ocean, what a coast, what gardens of palms and cypress! A few Spanish houses remain
– thick-walled, deep-tiled, – with pots of flowers, and
narcissus in the wild gardens. Mrs. Myers, widow of
Frederic Myers, is here with her delightful son Leo, and
we are with them every evening. To-day Mrs. Lloyd
Osborne gave us a Mexican luncheon at Simoneau's.
Simoneau is the old man at whose restaurant R. L. S.
used to dine. He is eighty-two. Poor Stevenson had no
money, and would have starved but for Simoneau, and
Stevenson in after years never forgot it. He is a French-
man, married to an Indian. The old boy came out here
when Louis Philip was King of the French. He is quite
literary, and when I mentioned a certain likeness he has
to Victor Hugo, he immediately quoted the parodies of
Victor Hugo's hard and unmusical early versification,
which were current in his day in France. This is the inscription written in the copy of *Jekyll and Hyde* which
Stevenson sent him: 'But the case of Robert Louis
Stevenson and Jules Simoneau, if one could forget the
other, would be stranger still.' Poor old pedlar though
he is, Simoneau has always refused to sell any books or
letters. His old wife, who is but a squaw, calls him Señor
when she speaks to him. She made us a luncheon – nearly
all chilis and red pepper, and *tortillas*, the cakes which the
Spaniards made as we saw the Indians making them in
the Yosemite – grinding the flour on a stone, then patting
the thin flour-and-water cake flat between the hands, and

baking on a stone. They are but flabby. Then there was *Enchilade* meat, followed by *Tamates*, a really dreadful kind of pancake, with chopped onions and garlic and fish inside. Afterwards we went out in a boat. But a boat does not go with *Tamates!* Mrs. Myers is a dear. My fond love to all the family. Your most loving mother, A. M."

February 7th   *Los Angeles*

"My Darling, . . . I am sending you an absurd £15 to help the budget of one week, my dear, dear worker. I have spent £6 on opals. You mention red opals, and they are very pretty, but I rather prefer an opal to have no local colour. I have chosen some small red ones, however. The children must not expect them big, but as to colour I have taken pains.

"I confess I find it a moving experience to be treated as I was this morning after my lecture. I gave the 'Seventeenth Century' in a large hall, to three or four hundred people. What an intelligent audience, and what attention! They came up to the platform, some even weeping. It is not all the excitement of the moment, for I find by chance how much they know of my little work. I have been much entertained. I was so glad of the *Chronicles* with your dear pathetic witty paragraphs. I fear work is very hard. . . . Your JOHNSON."

February 16   *Santa Barbara*

"My Darling, – We had five delightful days with the Whiteheads; I don't know when I have met such golden people. We were driven many miles along the beautiful valley that opens on the Pacific, to one of the most lovely country houses I have ever seen. It is built, thick and white, in an ancient Spanish manner that is better than Italian, if anything, with a colonnade and a loggia. As I walked into the plain dining room, full of the light of a half-excluded sun, with whitewashed walls and matting, the thought of Castagnolo (the old home of Mrs. Ross) came into my mind, and I was silently thinking of her when Mr. Whitehead said to me 'Will you have some Californian wine, or this red Tuscan wine which I have just received from Mrs. Ross?' I know the children don't think much of my coincidences, but I would just ask them (even Everard) to consider the distance – ten thousand miles or so – and the circumstances all round.

"Our next visit was to Dr. and Mrs. Blair Thaw. How strange and beautiful was the experience of meeting them! Intellect and a passion for literature and such conversation as one seldom hears make a wonderful household. Our third visit is as charming as the other two. This dear Rogers family is equally delightful, interesting, and affectionate to me. And their English beamed house (copied from one in Warwickshire and very well done) is surrounded by a lovely garden, and is not far from the Spanish mission church and Franciscan monastery still in use. . . .

"Mrs. Roosevelt has written a charming note, asking if there is a chance of my going to the White House, but I fear I cannot manage Washington. You cannot count the days more eagerly than I. . . . Your own JOHNSON."

February 23   *Santa Barbara*

"My darling Wilfrid, – Little Agnes left early this morning,* very courageously, but feeling deeply anxious about Beatrice. . . . What a strange ending to my visit! You bet I shall take care of myself on my solitary journey.

"I think you would have been pleased with the lecture last Friday. Each time it goes better, and I have now no nervousness. . . .

"I can hardly wait now the time is drawing so near. I think the hardest time is now, in the leisure of this visit, with Agnes gone. Oh, may all prosper in these weeks still to be lived through! May you all be well; may God protect you. May my journey go well!

"This over-sunned country has at last had a splendid rain, and now everything is brilliant again, and tossing its limbs in a strong and soft breeze.

"I wonder whether you will come to Liverpool. If it was not hard for you on account of work, that is what I should like best. Like indeed! It will be too much happiness to see you. My dearest love to all my own children. Your devoted JOHNSON."

March 11   *Los Angeles*

"My darling Viola, – Here I am at the first stage of my journey. I said good-bye this morning to the Pacific, looking heavenly in its pale and lovely blue. If the sky here is much less mysterious than in Europe, the sea is more so. It is never a positive blue, but has wonderful soft colours in regions. Yesterday I gave my Dickens

* Miss Tobin was suddenly summoned to Paris where her sister, Beatrice Raoul-Duval, was ill.

lecture, in a tiny room, well filled, and made £15. 8. 0. It went off very well. People thronged up to me. It is partly their amiability, but partly also a real interest in a fresh lecture on so old a subject. In the evening Mrs. Cameron Rogers gave a farewell dinner party, with an old Spaniard to sing his ancient national songs in the hall while we dined. They made speeches and drank my health and happy journey, and I can never tell you their kindness. What darling people! The dining-room was a picture with its old oak and beautiful soft blue hangings and white walls. The windows are from some windows in a drawing of Rossetti's. Early this morning Mr. Rogers drove down with me to the station and saw me off, and I am alone now for the first time. I am loaded with Italian novels and I shall not be bored. . . . Your devoted mother, A. M."

March 16   *Indianapolis*

"My darling Wilfrid, – My first lecture in the Middle West (that is what we call ourselves) went very well last night. There was a large and attentive audience. The only contretemps was that the much-vaunted American system of checking baggage played me false, and my things were left on the way, so that I had to lecture in my travelling dress (with the grey blouse I got at Ponting's!) to a great gathering of people in evening dress. It was rather painful, but they congratulated me on the fact that my skirt was not really short. That just saved a remnant of dignity. Mrs. Elder in introducing me very cleverly said that though I liked America I had no reason to admire the checking institution. She said everybody would understand it as an explanation of my dress; and in fact a little explanation goes a long way here. The evening was, strange to say, warm, and the room a hot-house, so that for the first time I felt the effort. After the lecture, the Elders gave a splendid supper to which the most literary Indianapolites were invited. It was exceedingly pleasant. The knowledge of literature struck me as ever – the interest in Coventry Patmore, for instance. They know my work by heart.

"Mrs. Elder went to Mass with me this morning. I feel very fairly rested though I did not get to bed till one-thirty, after four nights' travelling. My love to all my darlings. How lonely I am on this hemisphere! Your devoted wife, A. M."

March 21   *Chicago*

"Oh my Wilfrid, the culmination of the journey was surely yesterday when I gave the most acclaimed lecture of all. I left Indianapolis on Tuesday night, did not sleep more than a snatch in the hot car, got to Chicago early in the morning, made a rather complicated change, driving across the city, retrieved my trunk just arrived from the wilds, went to Beloit, had hardly time to dress for a luncheon-party, then took a bath, met all the professors at a dinner-party, and drove off to lecture in the church! My hostess was an angel, as usual. One of the professors actually travelled to Chicago with me, as there was a change of trains and he wished to help me. At Chicago there was Eames MacVeagh with the carriage. I had time only for a snatch of chicken (looking about me at the wonders of this house) while the maid got out my things, and off we drove to the hall where I gave the Brontes, 'The Treble Note.' There is a law that this club does not applaud, but you should have heard them! They clapped until the President asked me to say one of my poems. I upped and said 'The Shepherdess.' They clapped and clapped until the President said it was for something about the children. So I upped again and described what you had told me of the children's Play, and Viola acting me, and Major Pond, and the two reporters, and no audience. It was the greatest success. Don't think it was an egotistic performance, I simply *had* to do it. Mrs. MacVeagh is kindness itself. Your most devoted JOHNSON."

March 28   *Boston*

"My darling Dimpling, – A fortnight from to-day will see me on the ocean. It is too splendid! What delightful letters I have had from you. One of my Viola's was a real book. I think I told my Everard about the Wellesley lecture. The next day I gave two! – one here in the morning and one at a college club in the afternoon. Then I gave one at a college club at Harvard University. Mrs. Fields had a dinner-party to which came Professor Norton, Ruskin's old friend, and Mrs. Gardner who has that almost miraculous Venetian palace. Tell your dearest Father that Mrs. Fields is indeed a rare creature, with some reminiscence of Lady Taylor about her. I have made only £17 this week. Alas, I must spend a lot of my little haul! A happy Easter, my beloved. Your devoted mother, A. M.

"I find my ship is the *Lucania*."

XIV

THE CRITIC

BACK in England, the lecturing experiment was not carried much further. The Brontë lecture was given in Newcastle-on-Tyne soon after her return; and at the Pioneer Club in 1905 "Dickens as a Man of Letters." But the reading aloud of what probably required deliberation to take it in thoroughly did not really open out a new field of work.

Her writing from the earliest days had included art-criticism, her sister's fame having given her the first opening into that department of journalism. Before her visit to America in 1901 she had undertaken to be art critic to the *Pall Mall Gazette* in succession to R. A. M. Stevenson; and the post was kept warm for her in her absence by my father and by Everard, the art-student son. The weekly "Autolycus" was stopped on her return in favour of frequent art notices. Doing the round of the exhibitions was called "trudging" in the family, as being the word that best expressed the somewhat tired determination with which it was carried through. From now until 1905 she was constantly "trudging." An illustrated art-book called *Children of the Old Masters* was also written at this time, and the nineteen-year-old art student again helped by collecting the illustrations.

Journalism was full of enjoyment to her. An essay she wrote called "The Honours of Mortality" congratulated the artist who is willing to put his best talent into daily drawings for illustrated papers which, once they have appeared there, go "into the treasury of things that are honestly and completely ended and done with" – and who lets permanence and Immortality trouble him not at all. In the parallel line of journalism she herself contributed enormously to that respectable daily appearance and disappearance of things that had been made their best for a moment only. The *Daily Chronicle* had two columns every day of short paragraphs on various subjects under the heading of "The Office Window" – a department edited by Clarence Rook. The paragraphs she contributed could certainly have claimed in a special degree the "honours of mortality"; they were written hurriedly to catch the evening messenger, and their timely little demise took place with the next morning's glance at them. My father and mother contributed rival paragraphs – rival in the sense that when the paper was opened in the morning either of them might be found to lead in the number of paragraphs, and might therefore have more to contribute from that source to their somewhat anxious weekly budget. In this particular competition my mother was handicapped. My father's paragraphs were trusted to the extent of being passed on to the printer unread by the editor, while my mother's, in common with other contributors', were judged and perhaps rejected. She also received the common rate of pay while special terms had been offered to him. This disparity must have been one of the reasons for the half-humorous protest that she constantly made – that she was in reality an excellent light journalist, second to none. "Yesterday at Evelyn Sharp's," she wrote to my father once in his absence, "I was sitting by Mrs. Rook when Nevinson said to her that he had a great compliment to convey through her to Rook. Several editors, chatting, had asked each other who was the best light writer living, and they had agreed that it was the man who wrote the 'Office Window.' I wondered whether, if all were known, some of that should not come my way! Nevinson added: 'They all quoted things, and I must say they were good,' and he smiled at the recollection. I longed to ask him to quote, for I know that I have had the only funny things of late in those columns."

The subjects of her paragraphs were as various as may be supposed from the fact that for many years she contributed one or two or three almost daily. My father's number often reached four or five; it would be an exaggeration, therefore, to say that all his paragraphs were about Cardinal Manning. But there were enough to have made him surely ask himself sometimes whether they would stand yet another!

Hundreds of these paragraphs were preserved in the children's scrap-books. To revive them here is to rob them of their honour of being done for the moment only; but just a few may be quoted as having the actual sound of my mother's voice in them, and as reading like scraps of her conversation. The paragraphs are indeed the closest thing there is to a record of her conversation; the daily, hourly incident or reflection, the things that form conversation, formed also them.

The *petits poussins* that come too young to the dinner-table give rise to some remarks on destruction that conclude: "In any case chickens are less nice to eat when they are so small than when they come to a kind of intermediate time of life, and look about the age of Botticelli's angels." Her horror of the smoke of cities wandered in and out of her talk, in and out of her paragraphs. Herself ruined by cold, she yet found that there was an excuse for a sunless summer of unbroken cold wind in a clean sky. "London has now one great sombre summer of natural sky." Little irritations not quite worked off in brief conversation were given another turn in print only a little less brief. The writers who in transcribing the Londoner's cockney speech insist on writing "sez" for "says," "doo" for "do," "enny" for "any" were always irritating. "How do these writers themselves pronounce these words?" Charles Reade had been before her with amused irritation at the medical man's use of "not unaccompanied" and "not un-attended" (he took the trouble coldly to write "accompanied" and "attended" beneath them when he met them). To these she joyfully added her discovery of "not unseldom," and these negatives reminded her of Miss Martineau passing her prim judgment on the morals of a Charlotte Brontë novel: "I did not consider the book a coarse one, though I could not answer for it that there were no traits which, on a leisurely reading, I might not dislike." The paragraphs adds: "Now how many readers will be nimble enough to find out at once that she says, in this dreadful sentence, the contrary of what she thinks she says?" The use of the word "taint" for the mingling of Oriental with European blood she sharply defines as "one of those insults to the use of which we English have so accustomed ourselves as to have lost our sense of their grossness." The "savage journalese" of the reporter is smiled at who says of the street-boy falling through the ice that he got a "good ducking," while the well-fed skater "sustains immersion." Miniature bursts of indignation followed such incidents as "an eminent poet" quoting a line from Keats with praise for its "perfect sympathy for the yearning of the planet." The paragraphist exclaimed: "Orion a planet, and presumably within the solar system! Why, his very dog-star is a St. Bernard in comparison with our terrier sun!" And one of the numerous paragraphs about words says: "The Italian language is rich in diminutives, and many of them imply a little genial contempt; but some of them are tender and delicate, with a delicacy that makes a grave word most touching. A Roman paper publishes the account of the drowning of a fisher-boy, and adds that the *cadaverino* has been recovered – as if he had said the corpselet." The Italian peasantry may indeed be said to have had in these two columns their organ in England! – so narrowly were their interests watched there. The government was execrated which in this united Italy of Garibaldi's had put a tax on salt and had then sent policemen to patrol the sea-shore to prevent the desperately poor from stealing "their own Mediterranean." The taxing of Italy's poor was a thing she could never forget. "Even in Piedmont, where the fertile land, with its many harvests a year – twelve of hay, for example – is in the hands of peasant proprietors, one less good year means privation, and one bad year means absolute want and a search for wild roots for food. And this is owing to the Triple Alliance and the consequent exactions of armaments." Speaking of the industry of the Italian labourer, reluctant to leave his work, she mentions by contrast a certain *prima donna* at the Handel festival at the Crystal Palace. "At the end of the 'Messiah' come those great sentences – solos and a reply in chorus: 'As by man came death,' sings the soprano, and the phrase is finished by many voices, 'So also by man came the resurrection of the dead.' The *prima donna* sang her words and was off before the first notes of the reply were sung."

The French woman's prettily intimate way of giving her left hand when she shakes hands with those she favours is shown to inflict a disadvantage, because it is difficult for a man to meet the action with ease or elegance unless he uses his own left hand, which he never does. But the Italian woman who gives the back of her hand to be kissed allows of gracefulness all round. Another note gives the condition for gracefulness in a curtsy. "The only thing that made the curtsy graceful was that its processes were a profound secret. The woman dipped and collapsed within her hoop and slowly lengthened again, and it was charming. But it is absolutely necessary that the secret should be kept, and the scanty skirt will not keep it."

It occurred to her to wonder whether Anthony Trollope (whom, lacking present-day enthusiasm, she placed with some nicety as an excellent writer for "say, the second week of a convalescence") had ever unobtrusively crossed swords with Charles Reade: "One suspects a certain intention in the following phrases, published within a few months of each other. A heroine of Trollope's objects, as to a novel she is reading, that 'the people are always in their tantrums.' And slap comes the complaint by a heroine of Charles Reade's that the novel she has failed to finish is 'an ignoble thing, all curates and flirtations.' " A curiosity of literary taste is noted in a reference to the *Golden Treasury* – "the book with which many of us began our abridgements of literary study." The curiosity is this: "Tennyson and Palgrave, putting their heads and hearts together, omitted Keats's 'Grecian Urn.' The present writer once took occasion to ask Mr. Palgrave to explain this amazing proscription – was it an oversight? 'No,' said the anthologist, 'we did not think it good enough.' "

Sometimes the paragraphs were in abbreviated dispute with other papers. The *Athenæum's* dramatic critic had been deciding the sex of Ariel. The use of "he" or "him" in the stage directions purported nothing, he said, because in Shakespeare's day Ariel would have to be played by a boy. He fancied a feminine Ariel. The *Daily Chronicle* paragraphs termed him masculine: "Do stage directions for Miranda bear the masculine pronoun because Miranda was played by a boy? We protest against the 'alluring' emphasis of sex, which the critic attributes to the present actress's performance, as neither spiritual nor Shakespearean. And how 'alluring' would the *Athenæum* have had 'her' howls to be? 'She' had already given tongue, under the spell of Sycorax, so as to 'make wolves howl' in concert." "Will not some manager revive for us the 'Beggar's Opera'?" she asks. "Who in all England knows one of the enchanting tunes that set the eighteenth century whistling through more than half its course?"

About the distress of the poets for the cold season that besets the primrose, she says: "Shakespeare alone is quite explicit, Shakespeare alone has the natural fact at heart and identifies natural fact with divine poetry. Spenser's 'untimely tempest' and Milton's 'forsaken' are both false, for tempest is not untimely but timely during the primrose's life; and the primrose is not forsaken any more than a young virgin is forsaken. Shakespeare every time, Shakespeare for ever."

In the meantime her more serious work had taken the direction which in her essay-writing she was largely to follow – that of studies in literary criticism. As soon as she returned from America she got to work on a number of the Introductions to Blackie's selections from the poets. Another little selection made on her own initiative was from the poems of John Bannister Tabb. Later when he died she added a note on his little-known work in which she enumerates some of his fancies: "The darkness of his blindness in age welcomed as the black face of his dear negro nurse in childhood; those heroes, the champion glowworm raising a spear against the night, and the slenderest shade bearing a sword against the noon; and, perhaps most beautiful of all, the fancy of the poem on the Assumption, in which the Holy Virgin is figured as the mother bird that hears the voice of her Fledgeling, for whom her bosom had warmed the nest of old, and who from a loftier tree now calls her home; then the light epigram about the painter, Youth, and the sculptor, Age; all these and some hundreds more are examples of

the poetry that thinks and feels in imagery. 'Hundreds'
is not here a word of hyperbole; Father Tabb has produced some hundreds of poems in a few slender volumes
and every poem harbours – or rather *is* – a separate
thought, and a thought 'accepted of song.' This is fertility
of a most unusual kind; it is not only quality in a little
space, but – more remarkably – quantity in a little space.
It is for abundance that we must praise him – the several,
separate, distinct, discreet abundance of entire brief
lyrics. Would a slower or longer-witted poet have made
of each of these thoughts, these fancies, these images, a
longer poem? I cannot tell, but I think the longer-witted
one would not have had these thoughts. . . . Such is
one, and not the least, assuredly not to be the last, of the
poets of America. That great nation has looked ardently
for her poets. She has found them in places unransacked.
She must have been much amazed to find one of them
here, in the less literary South, in the person of a Catholic
priest, in the seclusion of an ecclesiastical college, and,
finally, in one of the deprived and afflicted of this
troublous life, a man blind for his few last years but
alight within, who has now gone down quietly to an
illustrious grave." In a letter to her, written in 1906 with
half-seeing eyes, he says: "Your letter has filled me with
gratitude to God for giving, along with my art, the appro-
bation of it that I most craved."

Another and not altogether dissimilar poet who had
delighted her was Winifred Lucas whose few small books
had also this "quantity in a little space." "A lyrical
intellect, thinking brief (not small) thoughts," my
mother wrote of her. . . . "She may never become con-

spicuous, and this last seems a strange thing to say of one whom Nature has made so separately."

Long, important studies were made in the following years. Indeed, so large a part did they play in her writing that it is as critic that she has largely to be judged in her prose. Her criticism may be held to be the best thing in that prose. "In all her criticism," said a writer in the *Times*, "whether of life, of art, or of literature, Mrs. Meynell has remained inflexibly faithful to principles which are as clearly and spontaneously the outcome of impulse and imagination as of a steadfast judgment. That is her time's debt to her." Because in other departments of life she upheld this or that controversial opinion, one expects to be able to find in her literary taste some intruding sign of those opinions, and that is what one cannot do – it was outside all other considerations. If ever she had her private embarrassments when great writing conflicted in its implications with her own opinions, even so her appreciation, her gratitude, her adoration were the same. The nearest she could get to defining the poetry she loved best was to say that it had the quality of wildness. Such a condition admits of no other.

For, since it seems necessary to be able to name what we love, thus did "one for whom poetry is veritably the complementary life" have to seek for the word to describe the poetry that is beyond poetry. "Escape," "flight," "remoteness," – these words only took her on the way to that other word. To speak of that uttermost poetry as "wild" so fitted her feeling that she had even to stop and ask herself whether she did not predicate this particular quality of certain passages of poetry in part because the very word "wild" occurred in them:

In such a night
Stood Dido with a willow in her hand
Upon the wild sea-banks, and waved her love
To come again to Carthage.

If one found that this was wild poetry, it was almost disconcerting that the very word should be there, perhaps itself alone giving the impression that one attributed to the whole passage. Possibly no other single word strikes itself so widely as this across the passage that contains it – so that one must scan the phrase again before it is discovered that it contains not only the word but wildness itself. She found, moreover, to enlarge the definition that one seeks in vain to make, that the skies, the sun and moon and stars, haunt that remoter poetry. "Light is the ruling master of wild poetry, as of painting in any of the wild schools."

The easiest criticism is not praise; but this particular critic was able to communicate her enthusiasms in an interesting way; she could make her writing enter very freshly into this or that paradise of a beloved poet. She never made a dull reference to Shakespeare, though Shakespeare haunted her writing and her life. Even into her last years her newest thoughts were about this oldest feeling. "We all know Shakespeare as it were privately," she has written, "and thus words about him touch our autobiography." It has often seemed to me that a history of her feeling for Shakespeare alone, could such a record be made, would leave not a great deal else of importance to say about her, so much was that feeling at the foundation of her existence. In the beginnings of such a record would be her memory of her mother as a beautiful and blooming young woman taking her two small children to Shakespeare's birthplace, and of her seeing her mother in that room burst into tears with the fresh love and fresh grief which she too had for Shakespeare.

In an article called "Superfluous Kings" my mother laments the passing of kings for no other reason than that Shakespeare's use of royalty will mean less than it did. With kings vanished, vanished are his greatest splendour, his greatest compassion and terror and irony.

> "He confronts us with the uttermost of pride of life in the royalty he sings; confronts us – no, rather brings us to our knees before the arrogant splendour he conceives:

> Where souls do couch on flowers, we'll hand in hand,
> And with our sprightly port make the ghosts gaze.

> It is the pride of life and the pride of death. Only hand in hand with a queen does Antony venture on the prophecy of that immortal vanity. If to him are given the most surprising lines in any of the tragedies, it is only as the lover of a queen that he has the right to them. To him is assigned that startling word, the incomparable word of amorous and tender ceremony, 'Egypt'—'I am dying, Egypt, dying.' That territorial name, murmured to his love in the hour of death, and in her arms – I know not in the records of all genius any other such august farewell. Lear's word is outdone here. Lear a king in every inch of his aged body, but Cleopatra a Queen in every league of her ancient

realm. Has not majesty spoken its one unexpected word in the mouth of such a lover?

" 'Superfluous' kings – Shakespeare's irony could find no other adjective so overcharged with insolence as this. Kings must be as great as he conceived them, for that antithesis. 'Superfluous Kings for Messengers.' . . . Literature, then, will lose this glory, and with this glory this humiliation. . . . When kings are in fact superfluous, Shakespeare's great word 'superfluous' will be cancelled out; when kings are no longer flattered, Young's great word 'unflattered' will be a futile word; when there are no full assiduous courts, his 'thin courts' will suggest no spectres."

Another landmark in her Shakespeare history was a poem written in 1916 at the tercentenary of Shakespeare's death, when the realisation that she had witnessed also the tercentenary of his birth brought the idea of her own years of life stretching before and after his:

> Now that my life has shared
> Thy dedicated date, O mortal, twice,
> To what all vain embrace shall be compared
> My lean enclosure of Thy paradise?
>
> To ignorant arms that fold
> A poet to her foolish breast? The Line
> That is not, with the world within its hold?
> So, days with days, my days encompass Thine.

And the final stanza ends:

> O thou city of God,
> My waste lies after thee, and lies before.

She was not only a good critic within the mood and taste of her time; she kept an independent eye upon the centuries, very much untouched by novelty and reaction. It seems strange, now, that praise of the seventeenth-century poets should then have been a thing of originality and independence. Her love of that period of "spirituality" and "light," her little-love of the century that followed, were harped upon in her criticism. "Indeed I am in love with the seventeenth century!" she exclaims, "when I see how purely it could recall the age gone past, and with what majesty it could forebode the age to come." Her enchantment with that time when "English had but to speak in order to say something exquisite" made her writing never more easy than when she was gathering up rich fragments of the seventeenth century, seeing Andrew Marvell, "cherry-cheeked, caught in the tendrils of his vines and melons," or Vaughan's poetry as "this meditation of a soul condemned and banished into life." Of Marvell she writes: "He, as a garden-poet, expected the accustomed Muse to lurk about the fountain-heads, within the caves, and by the walks and statues of the gods, keeping the tryst of the seventeenth-century convention. And yet this poet two or three times met a Muse he had hardly looked for among the trodden paths; a spiritual creature had been waiting behind a laurel or an apple tree. You find him coming away from such a divine ambush a wilder and a simpler man." Of Cowley she says that he wrote the language of love but left it cooler than he found it. "What the conceits of Lovelace and the rest – flagrant, not frigid – did not do was done by Cowley's quenching breath; the language of Love began

to lose by him. But even then who could have foretold
what the loss at a later date would be?"

Of the transition from one century to the other she
says: "English letters did not suspect their own loss. All
seemed gain, all seemed progress." She could not but
allow the sometimes "exceptional inspiration, the noble
tenderness of Pope," nor that "Cowper was not saved
from the passion of grief by measured latinised diction,
and was not rescued from despair by the heroic couplet."
But she stood in comparative darkness, with the ending
of the century, that century which "at midnight could
speak with the sun."

"The eighteenth century, admired for its measure,
moderation, and good sense, should be considered
rather an age of extravagance, because, in it, imagination, which needs no exaggeration, failed. When it
saw no more clouds and stars, it kindled artificial
fires. The extravagance of Crashaw is a far more
lawful thing than the extravagance of Addison, whom
some critics believe to have committed none. Pope,
and poets less great than he, were all for what they
called 'a rage,' – a poetic 'noble rage.' Of sheer ex-
tremes it is not in the seventeenth-century conceits
that we should seek examples, but in this eighteenth-
century rage. The eighteenth century invented the
art of raving. It was resolved to be behind no century
in passion, to show the way, to fire the nations.
Addison taught himself, as his hero taught the battle,
'where to rage.' Dr. Johnson must have created his
phrase, 'the madded land,' in order to prove that he

too, the poet of reason, could lodge the fury in his breast."

If these were matters not agreed upon, there was reason to discuss them. Of criticism that was mere comment ("poor little art of examination and formula!") she considered there was too much; but for controversy there was a good excuse. That best challenge to criticism – to find that prevailing opinions are not one's own – kept her occupied. Dickens, undervalued in regard to "his watchfulness over inanimate things and landscape," and with his humour half forgotten in the remembrance of his sentimentality, was the subject of a study in which the perfect use of quotation made the arguments of a great devotion seem moderate ones. Another study dealt with Tennyson, too much dethroned because he had, besides his great welcome style, his little unwelcome manner:

"He is a subject for our alternatives of feeling as is hardly another poet. He sheds the luminous suns of dreams upon men and women who would do well with footlights; waters their way with rushing streams of Paradise and cataracts from visionary hills; laps them in divine darkness; leads them into those touching landscapes, 'the lovely that are not beloved,' long grey fields, cool sombre summers, and meadows thronged with unnoticeable flowers; speeds his carpet knight – or is that hardly a just name for one whose sword 'smites' so well? – upon a carpet of authentic wild flowers; pushes his rovers, in costume, from off blossoming shores, on the keels of old romance. The style and the manner run side by side. . . . There should be no danger for the more judicious reader lest impatience at the peculiar Tennyson trick should involve the great Tennyson style in a sweep of protest. . . . There is never a passage of manner but a great passage of style rebukes our dislike and recalls our heart."

She spoke with the decision of a specialist, and sometimes gave to details a specialist's rather than a critic's importance. Her manner in these essays combined humility to literature, authority to her reader. If her opinions as a critic, in their turn, came in for severe criticism, she seemed only hardened in those opinions and inclined to flaunt them. She knew a great deal about yielding, but nothing about it in literary matters. An occasion upon which she defied the then general feeling was when she wrote an essay on Swinburne that struck deeper than in the accusation that his words used his meaning, rather than his meaning his words. She found his poetry without an emotion or an intellect of its own:

"I believe that Swinburne's thoughts have their source in those two places – his own vocabulary and the passion of other men. . . . Other men had thoughts, other men had passions; political, sexual, natural, noble, vile, ideal, gross, rebellious, agonising, imperial, republican, cruel, compassionate; and with these he fed his verses. Upon these and their life he sustained, he fattened, he enriched his poetry. Mazzini in Italy, Gautier and Baudelaire in France, Shelley in England, made for him a base of passionate and intellectual supplies. With them he kept the all-necessary line of communication. We cease, as we see

o

ALICE MEYNELL

their active hearts possess his active art, to think a
question as to his sincerity seriously worth asking; what
sincerity he has is so absorbed in the one excited act
of receptivity. That, indeed, he performs with all the
will, all the precipitation, all the rush, all the sur-
render, all the whole-hearted weakness of his sub-
servient and impetuous nature. I have not named the
Greeks, nor the English Bible, nor Milton, as his
inspirers. These he would claim; they are not his. He
received too partial, too fragmentary, too arbitrary
an inheritance of the Greek spirit, too illusory an idea
of Milton, of the English Bible little more than a tone;
this poet of eager, open capacity, this poet who is
little more, intellectually, than a too-ready, too-vacant
capacity, for those three august severities has not room
enough.

". . . Having had recourse to the passion of
stronger minds for his provision of emotions, Swinburne had direct recourse to his own vocabulary as
a kind of 'safe' wherein he stored what he needed for
a song. Claudius stole the precious diadem of the
kingdom from a shelf and put it in his pocket; Swinburne took from the shelf of literature – took, with
what art, what touch, what cunning, what complete
skill! – the treasure of the language, and put it in his
pocket. He is urgent with his booty of words, for he
has no other treasure."

Such criticism, which Swinburne lovers could hardly
forgive, has now lost at least its surprise. (From Edmund
Gosse it brought reproaches when he and my mother

happened to meet, and undid the good opinion of her judgment he had expressed when in sending her his *Coventry Patmore* in 1905, he wrote: "You will be my severest critic: you are almost the only one for whose opinion I shall care a snap.")

With these studies and many Introductions to the poets, and the comments and allusions of all her work, that old ground was covered, so much of which must be common ground with critics, but covered with an interesting and original note. Her actual judgment was not idiosyncratic; her praise or her blame only might be a little more or a little less or a little sooner than others'; but even in agreement she was individual. The outstanding instance in which her opinion was more than slightly at variance with other critics', and permanently so, was her belief in Coventry Patmore's supreme genius. Never was she so detached from her kind as when she separated herself even from those who praised him, from Ruskin, Newman, Carlyle, or from almost any voice that had ever been raised to commend him. Not only derision at his "domesticities," but praise that missed the centre of the mark, made her suffer all her life on his account the pains of injustice that she imagined could hardly reach his own "haughty soul." But though she knew his pride was content with derision, "who shall say," she wrote, "that he did not undergo, from the 'quaint' of Carlyle, and the 'sweet' of Ruskin, and the 'Aeolian harp' of Newman, a harder experience—the experience of active isolation, a kind of sentence of exile, enduring which the poet says, unlike Bolingbroke –

'The sun that warms you here shines not on me.'"

XV

JOURNEYS

To begin to do things with, instead of for, the children, was a change that gave to family life more variety and more movement. The development of the children can be exemplified by their literary labours. While my mother was in America their magazine of that time, which made sarcastic comment on her lectures, had begun to have articles and drawings with a serious, and generally fatal, ambition about them. This magazine derived its name from the remark of an editor-friend of my father's who had himself just started a new paper. Questioned by my father as to his idea in starting it, he had replied that it was a mere whim, but in imitation of his pronunciation the children's magazine was called the *Bere Whib*. As ambition grew, manuscripts were confided by the children to their mother with such inscriptions as: "Mrs. Meynell's daughter takes the great liberty of offering to her the enclosed for inspection. She will be much obliged for a true opinion of it. She must however beg that Mrs. Meynell will not criticise it in public as is her habit." From that it was not a long stage to my mother's being able to write to my father from her sister's house at Devonport: "I gave my Watercolour Exhibition card to Everard, and impressed on him the duty of doing the

Art Notes. If he is diligent in this, as I know he will be, I shall stay a fortnight and finish Emerson, Holmes and Keats." And there was another letter (which gives also her view of Newman): "How well Everard has done everything! I gave him no help, either in 'Et Cetera'* or the *Evening News*. And he has verified all my many queries in your Newman proofs – a work of hours. It is certainly a delightful little book; and I have only a kind of insensibility of my own to blame for my lack of interest in its subject. I do not love the character at all; the 'beautiful' passage about Ambrose St. John is to my mind a curious inversion of parody. It is a solemn parody of the comic pages of 'The Egoist.' And I don't admire the mere literature. I disagree with George Eliot and Coventry Patmore, and you, and everybody. So the deuce is in it."

The usefulness of the children had an opportunity when in 1903 my father was writing a book on Disraeli. Lord Delaware's flat at Bexhill was lent to him when he needed to concentrate entirely on this task, and one or other of his daughters, enjoying experiments with a typewriter, alternated with my mother in keeping him company there. And a letter from my mother at Bexhill written home to one of the children shows the kind of thing for which they could now be depended on:

"My darling, – I am sorry to have had to write only business communications yesterday. All sorts of difficulties came at once – a dreadful internal qualm about the relative dates of Ariosto and Shakespeare (I had made S. quote A. in a proof now on the

* Two columns then written weekly by my father for *The Tablet*.

Atlantic); an urgent request from Blackie for more
Keats; and then your father's Crashaw doubts. Now
dear Dimpling has settled Ariosto comfortably into
the century preceding Shakespeare's, and I am waiting for her to send the Keats. . . . We are very comfortable. It is colder, however, and sunless. I took a
wading walk towards Eastbourne yesterday, sometimes plunging into seaward-ebbing streams, sometimes taking the long jump. . . . Your loving
mother, A. M."

And in a note from Palace Court to an absent child
about the failure of a surprise, she says: "I did a poem
this morning what *was* a poem, and I called Viola up to
my door, and gave her directions about typewriting it in
secret, and sending it to the *Monthly Review* and watching
for the proof to come; but your father, whom I believed
to be out, was in his dressing-room and heard everything." And as regards a different kind of usefulness an
evening is remembered by a visitor when my mother
suddenly noticed that some family darning was being
done by one of the girls, and for the first time a question
presented itself to her which made her ask in dismay:
"Who *has* darned your father's socks all these years?"

Change of relationship inside the family was accompanied by change as gradual outside it, for there was
taking place all the time that imperceptible shuffling of
friends that happens all one's life. "I do not see you, but
I look about for your work," wrote Meredith in 1906, "to
see where the mind of Portia is active." And again: "You
are with me daily, at the finish of most of my readings,

when I compare our views." But for some time he had been lamenting on his deafness and the infirmities that made him wish to see her far less than he wished not to be seen. His friendship, as far as the outward signs of meetings and letters went, almost ceased. He wrote in 1909: "Though I see little of my friends, I live with them."

Sargent was an acquaintance of many years' standing, seldom seen, but in fairly frequent communication in notes characterised by his moderate and sincere expression. He liked to make my mother know his appreciation of her writing, as when he wrote in the "Autolycus" days:

> "Dear Mrs. Meynell, – I daresay you get many a note written as this one is on a Wednesday evening to tell you that you have given great pleasure – and I can recall at least one that you did not get because it was not posted, for fear of boring. I shall be reckless to-night and give you thanks for many a delight brought home, or for the slight push that sends a doubtful idol toppling. I don't know which I enjoy most. Yours sincerely, JOHN S. SARGENT."

For a book of reproductions of his pictures suggested by Heinemann (of which Sargent wrote to my father: "I confess that I have done nothing yet about the book except to wonder as to whether it would not be the correct thing for me to die before it is published"), Sargent asked that my mother should write the Introduction. This she did, and the book appeared in 1903. "I have just read your Introductory Note," he wrote to her, "with a feeling of gratitude that dates from the time when

you consented to do it, and that is now doubled, for you
have done it well. I am glad of the slight reserves and
distinctions and oppositions which give to your essay the
character of a Study, in spite of its very high praise, and
am honoured that such praise should come from you –
'Wonderful you,' as Henry James says." What the Introduction most praises is the subtle sense of nationality in
a Sargent portrait. "Mr. Sargent paints an English-
woman with all the accents, all the negatives, all the
slight things that are partly elegant and partly dowdy –
one can hardly tell which of those two – the characteristics that remove her, further than any other woman,
from the peasant and the land, further than an artificial
Parisian. . . . It is perhaps almost necessary to have
been an Anglo-Saxon child living abroad in order to have
the nicest sense of the aspect of an English 'lady.' " She
speaks of the accident of a moment being given a place
in his portraiture, adding: "I rather report another's
murmuring than my own if I aver that he tells us, in a
portrait, now and then, such a fact as that a man has or
has not slept well." My mother's and Sargent's mutual
interest somehow did not make easy meetings. "Mrs.
Hunter telephoned," my mother wrote on one occasion,
"to ask me to motor out to her in her motor with Sargent. But I am still headachy. I am sorry, but I and
Sargent would be quite shy. We always are." When he
was making studies for his decoration for the Boston Free
Library, he asked her aid for religious phrases and quo-
tations. "Come to the Studio, and see what I am doing,
and collaborate."

The greatest friend of my father's was Wilfrid Blunt,

poet and traveller, who loved different race characteristics too well to be able to bear the absorption of one
nation by another. This friendship which lasted altogether
for forty years brought many riches with it as time went
by, even to the young family, who found him a pioneer
in the kind of living they admired. He and his wife, Lady
Anne Blunt, a grand-daughter of Byron, and like her
husband an adventurous traveller, had a yearly party at
Crabbet Park, in Sussex, when there was a sale of Arab
horses, and to these wonderful parties the children were
edged in by their father. For two summers, in 1904 and
1905, Wilfrid Blunt lent my parents, for the young ones'
benefit, a one-storey wooden house in the New Forest – a
sleeping-place of his in the wilds, built by his own excellent
design in a mere clearing in the forest. He himself came
driving his fine Arab horses and pitched his tent in the
wood. To what extent the children's interests were here
made uppermost is shown by allusions in my mother's
letters: "I cannot tell you how dear and lovely the girls
are. Viola and Olivia work hard at their 'quotation'
book. Dimpling cooks and markets and mends, but they
all find time to walk a great deal, and they are sweet and
gay."

There were constant visits to Wilfrid Blunt's beautiful
Jacobean house near Southwater. "A glorious day
here," my father reports, "and very pleasant talk with
A. E. Housman and our host and Desmond McCarthy
who is writing a play with Belloc. I was made to read
Modern Love aloud last night – rather an ordeal before
strangers who could have done it so much better and who
knew it in and out." And from Olivia another time: "We

are very happy. Father has talked and read continuously and enjoyed it – to Wilfrid Blunt, Lady Margaret Sackville, and Miss Carleton. Last night we all wore beautiful Arab dresses. I made a remark about Post Impressionists at dinner which Wilfrid Blunt actually thought worth disagreeing with – so I have been quite a success!"

On another occasion, at a cottage at Langport in Somerset, three of the daughters followed their independent pursuits, and one, studying drawing, wrote to her mother: "It is a very perfect life, to live in the country and cook and sew and do everything that you want for yourself. It would be nice not to be following a very shadowy talent, and to give myself up to those things, I think, but I suppose I must sacrifice a few years to seeing whether it can be made any solider."

Our independence received at first a few rare checks from our mother. "I hear," she wrote to my father, "of Olivia's staying alone! in lodgings! with a strange girl! I am indeed glad you are now to be with her. I hope there is no such bachelor-girl project for her. Dimpling and Viola love to alarm me." Opposition was strong, too, to an art-student style of dress which was then inseparable from some of the daughters' happiness. My mother even boasted in a *Daily Chronicle* paragraph of having surreptitiously destroyed a reactionary majenta-coloured flower from her daughter's hat. And another time she wrote to a daughter: "I shall disagree, I know, about the hat not being nice, but it will disappear, and I shall see you in something singularly disadvantageous in its place."

The seats at the Sunday supper-table were now filled with the young. Augustus John and Orpen and Stabb and Wellington, fellow-students and friends of Everard's at the Slade, came to his home. A somewhat later letter of my mother's shows her dealing with our friends in a domestic crisis:

My darling Viola, – Last night we had quite the roughest dinner it has been my once-unforeseen and unexpected lot to give. Everard and Grazia, Miss Radford, her brother (whom I did not recognise and asked him to 'sit next to Miss Radford,' almost introducing them), Chilton, Storer, Murray, Brin, and an Italian whom Carmela sent us – a nice man; – these, with the family, made a full table. Bastian and Lobbie waited, except when Woodnut lurched in, in working clothes, and upset knives and forks with a horrible clash. The food was quite good – a great sirloin, a huge dish of plain potatoes and another vegetable. Happily it was quite eatable of its barbarous kind. A good dessert had been laid in by Lobbie, but was not produced, so we ended on a large savage pudding. The cooklet is *impossible*. Her cooking made your father unwell; – I thought it *negatively* abominable only.

"I have all but settled on a housemaid. She seems nice, but will talk your poor little unlucky head off, or Lobbie's, or both.

"The dancers all went off after dinner, and the rest stayed, and Chilton played me some divine Bach. How you will love it! Lobbie liked her dance, but not ecstatically. How glad I am you are happy, my own love! Your devoted mother, A. M."

In these years there were many journeys for my mother, and in London itself a move took place in 1905. In his capacity as literary adviser to Publishers whose premises were then in Orchard Street and Granville Place, my father had stepped outside his official province in recommending them to turn some disused floors into flats. Having a talent for arranging the redisposition of walls and windows and doorways, he enjoyed watching the growth of two flats, and conceived the idea of making yet another up above for us to occupy ourselves. The Palace Court house would be let; and he would be saved his constant journeys into town. The family viewed at first with derision the confined attics that were proposed for their accommodation; but when a long room had been made for a drawing-room, and extra small rooms snatched from the landings, the flat not only could hold the family, but could show some of the prettiness of the house we were leaving. The gold-thread tapestries were re-hung, the Persian tiles hewn from the old wall and put in the new. From a long passage with round windows like portholes, led the cleverly-schemed rooms, the length and narrowness and whiteness helping the accidental likeness to a ship. My father had so utilised every inch of space, that when, some years later, a lift was added, its only possible landing-place was in the bathroom, and there astonished visitors were delivered if they had shirked the seventy stairs. Never being very fond of conventional apologies, my father boasted to them instead that he possessed the only bathroom fitted with a lift.

Though Francis Thompson remained in his various lodgings in the region of Harrow Road, this move of ours was a move for him too, to the extent that our home was his home. The journey to Granville Place was nothing for his street-haunting habits; his unpunctuality there was no more than the normal. "Francis Thompson has just arrived," wrote my mother from the Flat, "at about eight-thirty, to the seven o'clock dinner, or rather to the one-thirty luncheon, for that was the meal he chose, as he was going to confession to-night. I think it is the same confession that kept him many moons ago." The figure that was in place nowhere was easily shifted. How he struck one observer who knew him through these later years of his London life must be quoted here, as one of the best accounts of him ever written. It is by Wilfrid Whitten, then on the staff of the *Academy:*

"Thompson came frequently to the office to receive books for review, and to bring in his 'copy.' Every visit meant a talk, which was never curtailed by Thompson. This singer, who had soared to themes too dazzling for all but the rarest minds – this poet of the broken wing and the renounced lyre, had not become moody or taciturn. At his best he was a fluent talker, who talked straight from his knowledge and convictions, yet never for victory. He weighed his words, and would not hurt a controversial fly. On great subjects he was slow or silent; on trifles he became grotesquely tedious. This dreamer seemed to be surprised into a kind of exhilaration at finding himself in contact with small realities. And then the fountains of memory would be broken up, or some quaint corner of his *amour propre* would be touched. He would explain nine times what was clear, and talk about snuff or indigestion or the posting of a letter until the room swam around us.

"A stranger figure than Thompson's was not to be seen in London. Gentle in looks, half-wild in externals, his face worn by pain and the fierce reactions of laudanum, his hair and straggling beard neglected, he had yet a distinction and an aloofness of bearing that marked him in the crowd; and when he opened his lips he spoke as a gentleman and a scholar. A cleaner mind, a more naïvely courteous manner, were not to be found. It was impossible and unnecessary to think always of the tragic side of his life. He still had to live and work in his fashion, and his entries and exits became our most cheerful institution. His great brown cape, which he would wear on the hottest days, his disastrous hat, and his dozen neglects and makeshifts were only the insignia of our 'Francis' and of the ripest literary talent on the paper. No money (and in his later years Thompson suffered more from the possession of money than from the lack of it) could keep him in a decent suit of clothes for long. Yet he was never 'seedy.' From a newness too dazzling to last, and seldom achieved at that, he passed at once into a picturesque nondescript garb that was all his own and made him resemble some weird pedlar or packman in an etching by Ostade. This impression of him was helped by the strange object – his fish-basket we called it – which he wore slung round his shoulders by a strap. It had occurred to him that such a basket would be a convenient receptacle for the books which he took away for review, and he added this touch to an outward appearance which already detached him from millions. . . . He had ceased to make demands on life. He earmarked nothing for his own. As a reviewer, enjoying the run of the office, he never pounced on a book; he waited, and he accepted. Interested still in life, he was no longer intrigued by it. He was free from both apathy and desire. Unembittered, he kept his sweetness and sanity, his dewy laughter, and his fluttering gratitude. In such a man outward ruin could never be pitiable or ridiculous, and, indeed, he never bowed his noble head but in adoration. I think the secret of his strength was this: that he had cast up his accounts with God and man, and thereafter stood in the mud of earth with a heart wrapt in such fire as touched Isaiah's lips."

He struck his constant matches through the Shakespeare plays that with friends we read aloud in the evenings. My brother says in his *Life*: "His interruption during a reading of 'Othello' is never to be forgotten. Desdemona was dying when an emphatic voice proclaimed: 'Here's a go, Mrs. Meynell; I have lost my *Athenæum* cheque.' But he found it in another pocket." Though the Flat had these characteristic associations with him, yet intercourse with him was becoming more overshadowed; and memories of him there are slight not only because the Flat knew him for no more than two years, but also because he was more listless in coming, more absent when he came, more sunk in ill-health. When signs were bad he was taken to the country.

The growing-up of the children, the simplification of flat-life after a rather big house, and easier circumstances generally, allowed for my mother more of the journeys to Italy that were too much part of her history to be made much of in the sense of travel, or to be made little of in the sense of the happiness they gave her. "Is it not stupid to leave what one loves?" she wrote once after setting out, but no more than once. And generally part of what she loved was with her.

In 1905 there was a visit with friends to Munich to hear opera, and a little article written then describes also a Passion Play. In it she has been speaking of the crucifixes in scanty fields and on Bavarian hill-tops, but after seeing the living images of the play she writes: "Images that are not living seem made in vain; and no more need be painted or graven, since the German villager held his breath for a while, or took it stealthily, in order to look like a painting of Christ. There is no other image so well worth having. There is nothing in any of the schools that so 'enthralls,' to use Wagner's word. The image at Oberammergau is a person of noble aspect. The hamlet has dedicated its most perfect man to the Passion Play; and he, with the utmost simplicity, keeps his brown locks of the length chosen by the painters, and so goes about his daily work, closer to God than is the altar crucifix, and made by German nature and Italian art in the image of Christ. Not only in the symmetry of the Crucifixion, but in the accidents of every day, shouldering a burden, footing a rough journey in these hard hills, turning his lathe, or gathering a child upon one arm, he carries this perpetual likeness, and turns towards the world this aspect unaltered, until his years shall pass those of the Saviour, when another will take his place. The beating heart, the tide of blood move to the divine purpose, so that the image veiled or scattered among the crowd, distributed, broken, shattered, or grown dull, is gathered up in him, in order and continual consciousness. He lives down the image made by Rembrandt for Emmaus, and that made by Tintoretto for Calvary. The art is theirs, the more than actual beauty, and genius speaks in them. But 'Ah,' the pilgrim remembers, 'there was a wild breeze in the mountains, and I saw the hair of Christ lifted, and His cincture fluttered. I saw His tired breast rise upon a breath.' "

From Munich, she went on alone to Italy, where my father had managed to conduct nearly the whole of the young family to meet her at Verona. That journey from Munich to Verona was made the subject of her poem, "The Watershed."

> Black mountains pricked with pointed pine
>   A melancholy sky.
> Out-distanced was the German vine,
>   The sterile fields lay high.
> From swarthy Alps I travelled forth
> Aloft; it was the north, the north;
>   Bound for the Noon was I.
>
> I seemed to breast the streams that day;
>   I met, opposed, withstood
> The northward rivers on their way,
>   My heart against the flood –
> My heart that pressed to rise and reach
> And felt the love of altering speech,
>   Of frontiers, in its blood.

ALICE MEYNELL

But oh, the unfolding South! the burst
  Of summer! Oh to see
Of all the southward brooks the first!
  The travelling heart went free
With endless streams; that strife was stopped;
And down a thousand vales I dropped,
  I flowed to Italy.

Some of the letters written during various absences
from home in these early years of the new century make
a record of her movements:

July, 1906   *Portelet, Jersey*

"Darling Wilfrid, – We are basking in the sun above a
bay of almost Mediterranean blue, resting after a night
of adventure. Soon after leaving Weymouth the fog began
to drift round us, and late in the afternoon the boat came
to anchor in mid sea, hooting and ringing a bell constantly. In the course of the night the fog lifted and we
made Guernsey, and had to wait there for the tide. At
one time my sweet Viola rather lost courage, though she
kept up a perfectly cheerful manner with two tears on
her cheeks. At 3.30 in the morning we got off at last and
reached Jersey at 5.30, very cold. We drove to this
beautiful place, and we have had another drive this
morning with Mr. Weld. The air is perfect and the sea
heavenly. The scenery is tiny and rather prosaic. Here
and there a hill cultivated in steps charms the eye, and
there are freshets of poplars, but the wonderful sea suggests the mountains of Italy—and this is quite another
thing!

"The little house where I spent a year when I was ten
stands where it did. Not a stone is changed. As yet I have

not found my little old peppermint shop. I am longing for news of you. Your JOHNSON."

Augusi, 1906   *Loch Ailort, N.B.*

"My darling Viola, – We were to have gone over the sea to Skye to-day, but you will be surprised to hear that it has settled down to a good day's rain! It *did* lift for an hour or two yesterday, and Mrs. Cameron Head and I, in the launch, were quite dry! The islands – the Hebrides – looked very wonderful in the blue distances, a great many distances, for there are precipitous islands far and near. I love calm water, so that I always enjoy the Loch, which is really an arm of the sea extending for several miles, winding, inland. This house is at the head. A tumultuous river, which has come through about a thousand glens, all alike, between jumbled mountains, all alike, tumbles into the Loch close by. Two great waterfalls thunder down the steep forest at the back of the house. Sea birds are everywhere, and great seals come quite far up the Loch. It is of course an uncultivated country. In the small space of flat near, a few miserable fields never get dry. . . . Your ever loving mother, A. M."

April, 1906   *Genoa*

"Dearest, – We have had a most prosperous journey and have enjoyed it despite lack of sleep in a crowded train. Italy is under two feet of snow from the Alps to the Ligurian mountains, which happily have kept it away from Genoa. I have never seen so strange a sight in Italy – blinding white, etched all over with the sticks of the vineyards. Nino dined with us, and we went up to his house for the rest of the evening. Oh old, old, wonderful Genoa! Your JOHNSON."

April, 1906   *Rome (at a Flat lent by Mrs. Swynnerton)*

"My darling Wilfrid, – The thought that you may really come is too happy. I don't think I could bear to forgo it now I have had the hope. There is nothing fatiguing in the journey if you sleep (as I think you should) in Paris. I bear travelling all night sitting up, and not sleeping one single half-hour, but you would not. The Modern Hotel at Genoa is in a hideous new street, but very pleasant and comfortable – the journey thence to Rome just not too long. And all the time you are coming to divine things – this sky, this light, this indescribable beauty of climate now we have a real Spring at last. Much is spoilt and vulgarised in Rome, but so much is left! Mimi and I, who feel exactly alike, refuse to see certain things, and keep our eyes for seeing a hundredfold the loveliness that remains. We *do* see. And so does Everard, though he sometimes stops himself from giving in to us. Sometimes, however, he cannot. He is off this morning with damsels to the crypt of St. Peter's, the Tomb of the Apostles. Lanciani thinks the dust of St. Peter and St. Paul was scattered in one of the Dark Ages sieges; but here they lay, and at San Pietro in Montorio was St. Peter crucified. You may stand on the stones where he stood who saw the Crucifixion and spoke with Christ. Constantine built a chapel to mark the place, and there is no reason to doubt it. On your advice, we intend to dine here in the Flat, but coming home to luncheon, such long distances, would be hardly practicable. We begin the dining to-morrow, with

Mimi and Eileen as guests. I hope you got my two articles. If you have not the proofs before you leave, please ask the girlies to read them carefully. Your JOHNSON."

April, 1906   *Rome*

"My darling Wilfrid, – You say nothing in your last letter about coming. This must not be. *Do* come. The sun is streaming over shining Rome. I wonder whether Garvin would endure four articles. I should like to send one entirely on the Vatican Gardens.

"Thank my Viola for her most delightful April fool letter. Everard had not the heart to make me an April fool so far from home.

"We lunched yesterday with **Mrs.** Hunter to meet Mancini, to whom Everard has taken a great fancy. He is very simple. In the evening Mimi, Eileen, and Rhodes dined with us. Maggie, the eccentric, made us a very nice dinner, though a tardy. Your JOHNSON."

April, 1906   *Rome*

"Darling Wilfrid, – What a heavenly day we have had! There was not precisely sun, but a lovely light and it is much warmer. At 10.30 we started in Mrs. Hunter's motor, St. Clair Baddeley being of the party. We sped across the Campagna to Hadrian's Villa, and I thought of you in that incomparable beauty. The hills were the blue of lapis lazuli, but softer, and when we came near we found the lower cultivated parts all misted with almond blossom. Cyclamen and violets were everywhere. St. Clair Baddeley gave us a splendid lesson on Hadrian and his times and his works. Here is Roman history for Everard.

We went over all the stupendous remains of that city –
for a city it was and not a villa – and we pushed through
the olive orchards to places whence you see a visionary
view of Rome and the three ranges of mountains. We
lunched under a giant pine, and at leisure we prepared
for the homeward journey, putting off the Villa d'Este
for another time. So many impressions of vast distance,
exquisite colour, and mysterious form were not to be
disturbed. Cypress, pine, olive, almond, vine – how
lovely are the indigenous things! All the new boulevards
are planted with pale plane and palm, but it is the darkness of the cypress and pine that gives such fine accents to
this pallid scenery, and sends the distances such leagues
away. Delightful letters! Thanks to all the dear children.
Your JOHNSON."

April, 1906   *Rome*

"Darling Wilfrid, – You understand that my object in
the articles I send is to report on the stage of progress, not
to describe Rome. Therefore they sound very grumbling.
That cannot be helped. All I say is true. And I merely
allude to the loveliness that is left. It would be absurd to
begin to make set descriptions of Rome, nor was that
my aim.

"Everard and I spent this afternoon at St. Paul's-
without-the-Walls. After a visit to the magnificent
church, with its jewelled cloisters, we strolled into the
vineyard of a country tavern and had coffee, looking at
the silver country and blue hills.

"I have had a letter from my mother, and she seems
fairly well, which is a relief.

"It is a great disappointment that you are not coming. We propose to go to Mrs. Granet for a couple of days, then home. Or perhaps to stop a day or two at Pisa, which Everard much desires. It has been somewhat more summer-like to-day, but never warm enough for the yellow dress. I never seem to have a moment to tell you how happy we are. We are out all day. We leave after coffee and come in to dine and go to bed, staggering with fatigue. To-morrow we lunch with Mrs. Parrish. Everard seems very happy.

"Dearest Love, when I think that it is with labour and headaches that you have gained us this too, too lovely holiday! Your JOHNSON."

1906   *Rome*

"My dearest Wilfrid, – Please send me any news of San Francisco. I have nothing but the scrap of an Italian paper, and I am very anxious and distressed. Who knows how long it will be before I can hear anything about persons in this wholesale destruction – if indeed it is so bad. One account says that ten houses fell, and another that hardly a house is standing.

"We were all day yesterday – the Butlers, Miss Clemson, and Charles Lewis Hind – at Frascati and Albano in a tremendous duststorm. It all looked wonderfully beautiful in the dreary light – hills, plain and sea blown over by rain and sand. We greatly enjoyed it. Just at the time we were very merrily lunching at the village of Albano, this dreadful thing was happening in San Francisco, in their early morning. If I could only know whether that familiar house is standing!

"When we returned in the early evening we found Alfred d'Andrade. We all went to see the great actor Novelli in Shylock. A splendid performance. But it was rather a long day. There was a great storm and we could not sleep. To-day has been celestial. . . . We lunched with Henniker Heaton and an admirable Sir Joseph Ward.

"The San Francisco earthquake was yesterday, and the news is in to-day's paper. How can I get any account! It seems too dreadful to wait indefinitely. Your JOHNSON."

April 1906   *Rome*

"My darling Wilfrid, – It was splendid to get the telegram when I came in yesterday. I had still enough anxiety left to make the relief very great. I had done little but study maps and plans of San Francisco. I think the papers have frightfully exaggerated the loss of life. Their accounts are altogether sensational. So Hilaire Belloc thinks, who knows the place well. But even so it is a tremendous disaster. Mrs. R. L. Stevenson, by the way, lives well out of the way, I think, of earthquake or fire.

"Hilaire Belloc came to tea on Sunday. He is quite brilliant. My love to all darlings. Your JOHNSON."

TO HER MOTHER

April 1906   *Sori*

"My dearest little Mama, – We have had a splendid time in Rome and here we are close to Villa de'Franchi on the most beautiful coast in the whole world, and in such a spring! We have just been to Mass at Recco. On our journey here from Rome the beauty kept increasing, through the Campagna, Tuscany and Liguria, and it culminates in this magnificence of cypress, pine, olive and sea, with a world of flowers.

"Dear Mrs. Granet is kindness itself. Her villa is not many yards from the dear old villa, and all is unchanged. All my life I have dreamt at intervals of this coast with factories, and there is not one. It is all lovelier than imagination can picture or memory recall.

"Everard is the only one with me. He has immensely enjoyed it, and even after all my prosing about Porto Fino and Villa de'Franchi (all through his life), I don't think he expected anything so wonderful. Ever your most loving ALICE."

September 1906   *Shirley Hall, Langton, Kent*

"Dearest, – I am so very sorry to have missed yesterday's post. I went for a long walk with Anne Douglas Sedgwick, and we altogether forgot the time, and even came back late for dinner. How much I should have liked to do the Johnson column! I fear you are dreadfully overworked, with that and the Acton review added to everything. Miss Sedgwick is perfectly charming and simple, and an excellent talker in a very quiet way. She is very good-looking – a Romney.

"The children may be interested in a game introduced by Miss Dunham. Each player silently chooses a person – famous, whether dead or alive – and describes him by the symbol of a place, a flower, a food, a smell, a sound, an animal and a stone, and the others guess who it is. I will give you one of mine, because Miss Dunham guessed it instantly, even before I had finished:

Place,   close to Italian soil.
Animal,   antelope.
Flower,   Malmaison carnation.
Sound,   a sigh.
Smell,   that of the richer wild flowers.
Stone,   brown diamond.
Food,   country wine in a bottle stopped with a
          vine leaf.

"She cried Duse without a moment's pause. Mrs. Thaw gave excellent ones for d'Annunzio and Hardy, both of which I guessed instantly. My love to all the Dears, Your JOHNSON."

July 1907   *Bansha, Tipperary*

"My dearest Bastian, – I am sorry to hear that it rains so with you. We have had one brief shower. The showers in this heavenly country wing their way from the distant sea and are gone again. What a lovely country! It is very like England inevitably, because the trees – that make so large a part of the landscape – are the same, elm, lime, ash, beech and the rare pine; but it is *more* country. The quality that makes country different from town or suburb is more intense.

"About my telegram, it is surely rather characteristic that the guard of the train at the harbour edited it. I may have my faults, as Viola says, but I don't send 'kindest love' to my family. The guard insisted on writing my message down for me. And he wrote down exactly what I told him: 'Very good passage Love.' It does amuse me that he not only interpolated 'kindest' but changed 'very good' to 'splendid.'

"Thank your father for the *Chronicles*. It is excellent to be able to book my pars, and to spot his. It is delightful here. Would one of you were with me. Your devoted mother, A. M."

February 1908   *Villa Aurora, Rome*

"My dearest little Mama, – I have now been here nearly a week, having spent a week in Paris to help Everard in his researches for his Life of Corot. We went out to Ville d'Avray; Corot's lake was frozen hard and his country looking dismal. We hunted up his little-known frescoes in several churches. Paris was either wrapped in fog or whipped by a bitter wind.

"As to this place, I could never have imagined it – a palace preserved by great masters, on a hill enclosed by a wall that is itself gloriously beautiful, with great trees standing by my window. My room would contain the whole of my flat at home – in layers. It is frescoed with portraits of Popes.

"The Thaws know a great many Noble Guards, Papal Chamberlains and other kinds of princes, but that is easily borne; and indeed, I enjoy the dinner-parties in these halls. I love walking the streets of this beloved city, and as it is I see it generally in flashes from the motor. The weather is celestial. Your most loving ALICE."

February 1908   *Villa Aurora, Rome*

"My darling Wilfrid, – This afternoon there was a musical party at Sgambati's. To think that I knew him tall and young and well set up. I find him fat and shortened down – another man, but still playing beautifully. He pretended to remember my mother's playing. Carolus Duran was there; and Björnson with a most naturally swelled head, the hugest head I have ever seen, and great Scandinavian exaggeration altogether; and a daughter married to a son of Ibsen. Some Finlandish songs she sang were most peculiar and beautiful. . . . Three nice Americans were here at a luncheon-party. One had lately heard Kipling reading my poems aloud. He said they 'rent his heart in two.' At another party was W. D. Howells, very friendly to me.

"The Thaws are everything that is most kind. Rome is too beautiful. It is almost a relief to look at the gasworks and the palms, when one almost aches with love of the pines and belfries. Is it really true that *The Nun** is in a fourth edition, as an advertisement announces? I wonder what the reviews were like. Did they find that dreadfully weak place in the story? But I hope they were touched by the most harrowing book that I have ever read. . . . Would you send a *Nun* to Miss Clemson? Tear out the frontispiece. Would not Eveleigh Nash oblige me by leaving it out from any future edition? Your JOHNSON."

March 1908   *Villa Aurora, Rome*

"My darling Wilfrid, – My ticket is found. The advertisement duly drew the picker-up. I am so glad. There was a heavy reward fixed by law, but that cannot be helped. I should not wonder to hear that a high official jogged my elbow and a member of the Legislature picked up the ticket and passed it to a Senator.

* *The Nun* was her translation of René Bazin's *L'Isolée.*

"How dear are your letters! Ah, could you but join one lunch, one dinner here! Everything is just at the summit of perfection, and nothing exaggerated.

"I am just home from Keats's house, where I stood in the tiny scene of his suffering. He prayed, says Severn, at the last.

"The Elgars took me to their Flat, and Sir Edward played to me all the things he has composed in Rome this time, glorious music. Your JOHNSON."

March, 1908   *Villa Aurora*

"My darling Wilfrid, – On Thursday we got up early and motored a hundred miles, beyond the Sabine mountains, or rather within their depths and over their heights (close to snow) to Subiaco, the place where monasticism began in the West, for there is the Sanctuary of St. Benedict and the retreat of St. Scholastica – monasteries on the high hill-side with a gorge beneath. There Nero built a pleasure house, and there Alexander VI spent his summers. And there the angel St. Benedict prepared himself, in the ruins of their palaces, in absolute solitude, for his great career. His little cave and the surrounding chapels are all painted over with 13th-century frescoes, so that modern art also began there. The great monastery, on a mountain ledge, has a lovely cloister. So has the lower monastery, on another ledge, but still high above the ravine and the torrent. All the oldest parts Gothic, you must understand, of the most exquisite kind. Half the hill-tops have strange little dark cities and villages sitting on them. To one of these we went on our way home. When they have spoilt and vulgarised Rome, it will take them some centuries to spoil and vulgarise these. Will you believe that in these almost inaccessible places they have renamed the climbing streets – Garibaldi, Cavour, Mazzini, and the rest of it! All my love. Your JOHNSON."

May 1909   *Capello Nero, Venice**

"My darling Child, – Lobbie and I agree that you are the most charming of letter-writers. You have it from your father, only he does not give himself such a good chance, for he writes one word in a line, and if it is a long word I have known him write it in two.

"The first words that Chilton said when he looked in this morning, were: 'Now the real meaning of life is' – and Lobbie and I had to laugh, he has said them so often before. We like our hostelry. It is rough but clean.

"Ask your father whether there is any hope of Will Meredith's giving me – if he finds them – the sonnets written to me by dear Meredith. He used to keep them

---

* This one of the journeys, in 1909, was made with a daughter who had written from Mrs. Janet Ross's house at Settignano: "The wild garden, going all down hill from the house, is made partly of sloping fields of olives with purple artichokes growing underneath them, and partly of vines with bright green wheat beneath, and paths and masses of roses. Up near the house are azaleas and lemons and roses of all kinds, in quantities I have never imagined. And flying all about them, large green beetles and white butterflies, and on the ground lizards! We have exquisite weather. Last night from the garden we had a wonderful sight – fireflies amongst the artichokes, the lights of Florence and fireworks three miles away, and stars above. Nightingales are singing all the time. Mrs. Ross is wonderful. She is dressed all in white. She can call like the nightingales, so that they answer her. She exterminated a nest of very large ants this morning with her fingers! Enormous flies, too, in the same way!"

in his revolving desk. They were written in pencil. Your devoted mother, A. M."

May 1909   *Capello Nero, Venice*

"My darling Wilfrid, – All goes well with us. Olivia is the sweetest companion, always considerate, and complaining of nothing. How wise is she who chooses not only her husband but her children's father, and thus has such daughters and sons as ours.

"The weather is so perfect that we expect nothing else. We have strolled through the morning. What enchantment is a stroll in Venice, what dim rosy corners in a sparkle of water-light, what little bridges somewhat too small for the people, as in the back places of a stage, and yet in such a reality of sun!

"We are very quiet in our little rooms, and sleep well. They are only 3 lire each a night, and we live very frugally. It is too hot for real dinners or lunches.

"The *Morning Post* on dear Meredith is good. I skipped the literary estimate, however. I think no one living knows him as I did. Nor can he have loved many as he loved me.

Your JOHNSON."

To her mother, too, she wrote some little time after George Meredith's death, which took place in May, 1909: "I feel the loss of George Meredith is a very great one. . . . No one knew him as I did. He told me that I could have made him what he should have been, and what he could not be without me. He calculated whether there had been a time when he was a widower and I unmarried when we might have met. A retrospective offer!"

Much written to, when she was away, she received this kind of tidings from the young family: "It is after dinner, and Father has been giving us some mental arithmetic – do you remember the kind? ten and twelve and twenty-two and eight and thirteen, etc., very quickly. We jumped about the room and threw up our arms, and then when he stopped we yelled our answers. I think Francis was the shining light among us, though I must not omit to say that on two occasions my answer came ringing out before the others, and correctly. Once, Dimpling, in a frenzy, put her hand on Father's mouth, thus compelling him to pause while she caught up. It was the only thing to do. We all helped her." "You are to stay as long as ever you feel inclined. Of course the day of your home-coming is a thing towards which one's thoughts cannot help wandering. Bill Stabb has already made his early-morning Covent Garden plans. He is going to try and get the Italian roses and flowers you will have been seeing, so on the evening you come back you will have home *and* Italy. And then I have settled your first dinner, which I may as well say at once will be quite English. You will have nothing more nor less than a saddle of mutton, with new potatoes and peas. But perhaps I had better not have said any-thing – I am so afraid you will come home sooner on purpose for it!" "We had a happy Christmas, my dearest, but how I missed you! Oh my darling mother, you are so much to me!" Games loomed large in the young one's letters. "To-day we were to have had a great hockey tournament at our ground at Walham Green, but all the morning was spent in clearing away the snow, which was great fun, and in the afternoon we had one good game. We lit a fire in a bucket and boiled the snow and made bovril for our lunch; it was delicious." The playing spirit took various forms in the large family and was not confined to the young ones. In the middle of a serious letter, written from home to one of the children, my mother reports: "I am glad to say that a plot to make a teazle crawl in Brin's* bed last night came to nothing. It was to be moved by a string that passed under the door. Your father and Everard devoted much time to the preparation, but it did not work." Another time she writes to my father: "Did Viola send you the *Church Quarterly*, and did you send a line to Albert about his F. T. article in it? It is an excellent article, and we all forgot about it, and the *Church Quarterly* was being used to lengthen the ping-pong net."

A crossing-sweeper in Manchester Square my mother kept informed of her absences, writing to him on one occasion: "I shall not be passing your corner for some few more Sundays, and I don't like to think you will forget me, nor do I like you to think I have forgotten you." At the death of this crossing-sweeper she wrote a poem in his memory:

The paralytic man has dropped in death
  The crossing-sweeper's brush to which he clung,
One-handed, twisted, dwarfed, scanted of breath,
  Although his hair was young.

* Bernard Whelan, an elderly friend of the family.

I saw this year the winter vines of France,
    Dwarfed, twisted, goblins in the frosty drouth –
Gnarled, crippled, blackened little stems askance
    On long hills to the south.

Great green and golden hands of leaves ere long
    Shall proffer clusters in that vineyard wide.
And O his might, his sweet, his wine, his song,
    His stature, since he died!

That her charity was subject to rare fits of discrimination is suggested by a phrase in a letter of hers when she was forwarding to my father the request of a constant asker: "I am exceedingly sorry to worry you with appeals," she wrote to my father, "but as I am only too much inclined to let this ass look after himself, it would be too bad not to allow him the chance of your greater kindness."

Up till 1910 she could still find her mother on her return from her journeys, and still receive such welcoming letters from her as this: "My sweet beloved, what a dear and most interesting letter. . . . Oh my wonderful child, how surprising to think of thy being called upon to speak on such an occasion and before such truly great ones. Will the event be reported in the *Catholic Times?* I am so rejoiced to hear that Everard is going to be married to his dear inamorata. I shall hear details when I behold thy lovely face. Good-bye my sweet, my eyes have become so feeble, as is indeed the rest of me, that I can hardly write. It is now hot as the height of summer. I have a sweet garden at the back with a splendid show of flowers of all colours and fragrant with mignonette. Good-bye, my beauty, my wonderful child. Ever thy loving and devoted Mama."

Apart from travel, recreation was not, for my mother, too easily come by. She was not a great reader of new novels; the book by her bed was more often a biography. And in her novel-reading the implied convictions of the author on the conduct of life mattering to her so much, too often dissatisfied her for her pleasure. But she was always ready for her humorous writer; O. Henry she read, and read again as soon as he was forgotten, which was fortunately soon. Her rare visits to the theatre provided few exceptions to the long tale of disappointment. "Percy will have told you that he lured me to the 'Midsummer Night's Dream,' and that I used strong language about the wretched women-players, common little school-girls aping the queen of Shakespeare's fairy land, and the lovely, modest, enamoured girls of his drama. On Wednesday I am to see Nijinski, and that I know will be a pleasure." The opening words of another account surprise one only for a moment. "I am glad on the whole to have seen Julius Cæsar; – it will cure me of wanting to see Shakespeare again. Cæsar was more like an elderly spinster than anything else. The others 'tore' (in the words of poor Shakespeare's own complaint) not only 'passion to tatters,' but mere conversation – as when the conspirators pass the time by a little discussion as to where exactly the sun will rise at that time of year. They yelled it. The two women were quite decent, but the only acting worthy of the name was by the Brutus." But there had been performances that greatly pleased her when Julia Marlowe played Shakespeare here.

The more or less casual entertainment of guests, of which a great deal occurred, was pleasant to her, and often it did little more than add, to the family evening, the incident of chess or a "pencil game." Many formal arranged occasions would have been difficult in a household more adapted to its casual and constant visitors. But this lack of the management of guests often caused an incongruity among them that must have made dull the occasion for many a one. My mother and father had a sympathy and welcome which prevented any system of discrimination ever being set up. My mother was naturally a good deal sought; few people could have more divergent admiration than she. She drew expressions of fondness even from those to whom they did not come easily – such as one that chances to be preserved in a letter from her brother-in-law, Samuel Tuke Meynell: "Farewell, dear sister. If there were in the world a sweeter or a gentler name it should be yours."

The only part that effort might play in her welcome to any guest was in the concealment of tiredness – and that effort as time went on was often necessary, even when the caller was not so late as one of whom she wrote: "At about eleven last night arrived Rosso, the sculptor. I was the only one to talk Italian to him. I think and hope he did not see my deep fatigue." The presence of the casual visitor was often a reason for the reading aloud of poetry. Francis Thompson being duly sampled, my father liked using any opportunity to make known some talent that he found too little known. William Andrew Mackenzie's *Rowton House Rhymes*, and the early poems of Anna Bunston and of Helen Parry Eden, made staple

family reading-aloud. Music, too, was often a feature of
the stray-visitor evenings – if the visitor provided it.
Music, fortunately, was very available, in friends, for my
mother's need and love of it. Especially when Carmela
and Grazia Carbone, two singers, came to London, she
could have her feast, especially of the work of sixteenth
and seventeenth-century Italian composers, exquisitely
sung; and when Everard married Grazia Carbone the
singing was captured into the family.

But sometimes, from very early days, there were
arranged parties on a very ambitious scale, when the
young family earned the excitement of the great occasion
by their very extensive labours beforehand – labours
which, however, surely cannot have produced entertainment of a quite conventional kind! At Palace Court there
were afternoon parties, perhaps one in a year, with music
– "full of ornamental and interesting people," wrote my
mother of one, "(with a lot of diamonds in spite of the
daylight) – As soon as the last At-Homers went away,"
she adds, "we had to dress to go to Ethel Smyth's very
successful opera. Then we had supper at Mrs. Hunter's,
a brilliant scene." At the Flat the parties were lunch
parties, generally planned to introduce some literary
friend to other friends. Of a typical one of these parties
the little cards which my mother wrote for the places at
the table serve as a reminder now, when the presence of
William Andrew Mackenzie was the occasion for the
lunch, and the other guests were Sir Ian and Lady
Hamilton, Mr. Edward Marsh, Mrs. Hart-Davis, Sir
Charles Fitzpatrick, the Duchess of Sutherland, Lady
Lytton and Mr. Snead-Cox. The most exciting parties

she went to in these years were at Stafford House. "On Friday we went to the Duchess of Sutherland's little party," she reports to one of the children. "She is giving 'intellectual' Friday evenings. The Duke of Argyll (who has literary ambitions) was there, the Duchess of Rutland, Winston Churchill, Lord Ribblesdale, Mrs. Hunter, Andrew Lang, Herbert Trench, the Beerbohm Trees, Laurence Binyon, Oliver Lodge, who said he has read all I have written, Mr. Birrell – I cannot remember any more; the gathering was small. Percy Grainger played." And another time: "The Stafford House party last night was very good. Your father came on with Wilfrid Blunt from dinner, and with Lord Osborne Beauclerc. There were a good many people we know, and in any case Violet Meeking stuck to me all the evening, so I was not lonely. Your father and Wilfrid Blunt enjoyed themselves 'listening to each other,' as Violet well said."

She was a diffident hostess. "To-day," she reports, "I am giving a tea at the Writers' Club – your father calls it beforehand 'disastrous,' but I think I shall be able to persuade him to come. Mrs. Meeking will be there to give me the support of her presence and her dress." Neither did my mother often achieve as a guest the enjoyment that self-confidence can bring. She had enough shyness and diffidence to make her feel the need of something familiar beside her, and her whole view of any visit changed according to whether or not she was to be accompanied by my father.

XVI

CERES' RUNAWAY

In 1907 my father took Francis Thompson to a cottage of Wilfrid Blunt's in Sussex. If any circumstances could have improved his condition, these probably would have done so, but he was beyond help. "He returned," says my brother in his biography, "weaker than he went."

"In his extremity of feebleness any hurt seemed grievous to him. Upon an umbrella falling against him in the railway carriage, he turned to me with a trembling: 'I am the target of all disasters!' And when a busybody of a fellow-passenger asked him, on account of his notable thinness: 'Do you suffer with your chest, sir?' Thompson, who had but one lung, and that diseased, answered sharply, 'No!' Even then he did not know the extent of his trouble. In error he attributed all his ills to one cause. My father, seeing him on his return, said to him, 'Francis, you are ill.' 'Yes, Wilfrid,' he answered, 'I am more ill than you think'; and then spoke a word from which both had refrained for years, 'I am dying from laudanum poisoning.'

"My father asked him if he were willing to go to the Hospital of Saint John and Saint Elizabeth. The fact that my sister – the 'Sylvia' of *Sister Songs* – chanced at that moment to be lying ill there, led him to consider the institution without hostility, and the next day he went unreluctant to his death-bed. Consumption was the mortal disease."

In ten days he died, on November 13th, 1907.

An even more personal loss befell my mother in 1910, when her mother died. She attended her through the nights of distress and days of cheerfulness of her last illness. "It wrings my heart to think of that little house where my beloved Mother underwent so much," she wrote to my father after her mother's death. "I never wished her to live when I saw how grave her illness was. It seemed too dreadful that all would have to be gone through again so soon. But no one knows what those nights were – or rather seemed, for they were not as terrible as they seemed, I firmly believe. It would have broken my heart if she, so affectionate in health, had responded to any signs of my love then, but she never did. We ought all to be prepared for a curious change of character in those last days."

Of this and of the few other deaths that affected her closely she barely spoke – especially not of the actual dying. She had a singular reluctance to relate or to hear of the physical circumstances of last illness and death. Great reserve in all the physical things of life culminated in that greatest delicacy of all. The helpless display of death, the exposure of pain and expression and uncontrol, were dreadful to her if they were things to be recorded and remembered. This was a prepossession that made her

248

find in biographies "the disproportionate illness, the death out of all scale." In each silence of hers about dying it was impossible not to feel that she was as it were establishing a precedent according to which she might trust to have silence in her turn. But she could ignore none of the pains of loss. To her family her griefs were the most incurable and inaccessible in the world; they knew that she hid intolerable regrets from them.

The children had begun to leave their parents. The eldest daughter, Monica, was married in 1903, the second, Madeline, in 1907, and Everard in 1910. But these were only half separations. "I have never known anything, and never can know anything, like your kindness to me," Madeline wrote from her honeymoon. "My life has been perfectly happy until now, and now the only unhappiness is leaving you both. If I had known how hard it would be I don't think I could have undertaken to do it. I thank you with all my heart for all your wonderful goodness to me. And I thank God for having given me such parents and such a husband." The children's home ties were too strong ever to be broken, and when they married they remained in almost daily touch with their parents.

The growing-up of the children had brought them something new from their mother. Her tenderness and solicitude towards them had always been the things on earth they could most count on; but, as with years their cares and joys and opinions grew in importance, they had changing and exquisite signs of their growth of importance in her eyes. It was, of course, not merely that she shelved her authority, and that into her manner there came the vigilance and courtesy that people use towards greatly honoured friends, and even a formality of attentiveness to those who had left home, in case mere tenderness should not take enough pains. For, beyond anything that was conscious and designed, the humility of her passion for them made her prize their grown-up love as if it were more than she could expect. She was punctilious to observe all occasions, knowing that mere taken-for-granted tenderness varies so little from indifference. "My darling Dimpling, – Welcome home. I long with longing to see you and the babes again. To-morrow to lunch. I have two angel servants, who will take an interest in the happy banquet. Your devoted MOTHER." From those of the children whose tastes were specially literary ones, she waited for praise or blame of her writing; she said of a daughter's opinion: "Your praise is worth all the rest of the world's to me," and it was true. In the success of those who did any writing on their own account as time went on, she was even more interested than they themselves could be. From her son Everard, for instance, whose powers as they developed in future years she admired, and to whose reserve she accommodated herself, she seemed to ask no more than to lean upon his mind. "Let nothing come between you and me, for the love of you and trust in you are my life," she wrote to one child when she might have written a reproach.

In the early years of the century the long family was still in process of growing up. My mother, with her strong literary ambitions only partly fulfilled, had reached a pause. She had passed the time when her days were crowded with her work. Though her middle-age showed little outward sign (her hair remained black all her life, as her mother's wonderful hair had remained during hers), yet the energies of earlier years had begun to relax. The battle against headaches was more constant; her eyes were allowed to close in her fragile face while she waited for the headache to pass; there were stretches of time when her life was empty of writing. That emptiness was not rest; it brought distress and agitation. "I don't think I shall be quite well so long as my poor literary career is so at a standstill," she wrote in 1908 to my father. "It makes me unhappy." It was six years since *Later Poems* was published, nine years since her last book of essays.

The happiness of accomplishing a good piece of writing – that feeling which she called unmistakable – only she could give herself; but my father could give her every other kind of encouragement. "I am much happier after getting your letter," she wrote after such encouragement. She was read widely and continuously; within the limits made by the nature of her writing she had that kind of fame which sends from far and near its almost daily signs and surprises.

The firm of Constable had published the last volume of Francis Thompson's poems; and it was with them that now in 1909 *Ceres' Runaway* appeared. Some of these essays are made of the mere delight of natural observation; they read as easily as seeing. Others are not easy first thoughts. Of her work Mr. Garvin once wrote: "Each verse or essay contains part of the essence distilled from a deliberate and vigilant life; you cannot apprehend a year of hers by a moment of your own." Neither does the familiarity of a mind with its own idea always allow for that unfamiliarity which makes the most willing reader lag a little behind the writer unless he is carefully given the same advantage. But in this volume may be felt how the powers of its writer's mind were still growing.

Ceres' Runaway is the sprinkling of green that crops up in forbidden places in towns: "One can hardly be dull possessing the pleasant imaginary picture of a Municipality hot in chase of a wild crop – at least while the charming quarry escapes, as it does in Rome. . . . The wild summer growth of Rome has a prevailing success and victory. It breaks all bounds, flies to the summits, lodges in the sun, swings in the wind, takes wing to find the remotest ledges, and blooms aloft. It makes light of the sixteenth century, of the seventeenth, and of the eighteenth. As the historic ages grow cold it banters them alike. The flagrant flourishing statue, the haughty façade, the broken pediment are the opportunities of this vagrant garden in the air. One certain Church, that is full of attitude, can hardly be aware that a crimson snapdragon of great stature and many stalks and blossoms is standing on its furthest summit tiptoe against its sky. The cornice of another Church in the fair middle of Rome lifts out of the shadows of the street a row of accidental marigolds. . . . The municipal authorities, hot-foot, cannot catch it. And, worse than all, if they pause, dismayed, to mark the flight of the agile fugitive safe on the arc of a flying buttress, or taking the place of the fallen mosaics and coloured tiles of a twelfth-century tower, and in any case inaccessible, the grass grows under their discomfited feet."

Another such essay is "The Tow Path": "An unharnessed walk must begin to seem to you a sorry incident of insignificant liberty. It is easier than towing. So is the drawing of water in a sieve easier to the arms than drawing in a bucket, but not to the heart. . . . No dead weight follows you as you tow. The burden is willing; it depends upon you gaily, as a friend may do without making any depressing show of helplessness; neither, on the other hand, is it apt to set you at naught or charge you with a make-believe. It accompanies, it almost anticipates." And of the "bounding and rebounding burden you carry (but it nearly seems to carry you, so fine is the mutual goodwill)" she says: "There never was any kinder incentive of companionship. It is the bright Thames walking softly in your blood, or you that are flowing by so many curves of low shore on the level of the world."

There was a spot on the Thames at Pangbourne where she grew familiar with river-water. "Tethered Constellations" are the stars reflected in "a darker and more vacant field than that of the real skies," in the pool, the river, the flood. When the constellations flash in the restless water "you imagine that some unexampled gale might make them seem to shine with such a movement in the veritable sky. . . . At moments some rhythmic flux of the water seems about to leave the darkly set, widely spaced Bear absolutely at large, to dismiss the great stars, to refuse to imitate the skies, and all the water is obscure; then one broken star returns, then fragments of another, and a third and a fourth flit back to their noble places. . . . The dimmer constellations of the soft night are reserved by the skies. Hardly is a secondary star seen by the large and vague eyes of the stream."

An article called "The Little Language" draws attention to the "inability" of dialect. Goldoni and Gallina, she says, "laid none but light loads upon it. . . . Their work leaves it what it was – the talk of a people talking much about few things," the currency of those who lack literature but do not lack silence. "It may even well be that to die in dialect is easier than to die in the eloquence of Manfred."

"Tithonus" is an essay which scolds the ingenuity spent in making building as permanent as possible, and condemns discoveries to withstand Time, "refusing his pardon, his absolutions, his cancelling indulgences." The essay was written when, for the stencilling of the new decorations in St. Paul's, a method was discovered which was imperishable. "Posterity is baffled." The resolute tyranny of one age in thus coercing future ages, this victory over our sons' sons, is pronounced to be one of the strongest of human desires. "Obviously, to build at all is to impose something upon an age that may be more than willing to build for itself. The day may soon come when no man will do even so much without some impulse of apology."

"The Audience," by an inversion of parts, treats a theatre audience as performers themselves by virtue of their turn of laughter and applause. "The audience are the players. Their audience on the stage are bound to watch them, to understand them, to anticipate them, and to divine them." The audience's too-easy laughter brands them as bad players; the players' too-willing pandering to that laughter makes them a bad audience. "The time may come when a national school of dramatic audience shall not accept artifices that could not convince the fool amongst them; when one brilliant moment of simplicity on the one side of the footlights shall meet a brilliant simplicity on the other. Which troupe, which side, to begin?"

One of the most excellent of her subjects is the mad maid of the poets, the maid who is crazed for love. "I have not met elsewhere than in England," she says, "this solitary and detached poetry of the treble note astray. At least, it is principally a northern fancy. . . . It is as a wanderer that the crazed creature visits the fancy of English poets with such a wild recurrence. . . . Trouble did not 'try' the Elizabethan wild one, it undid her. She had no child, or if there had ever been a child of hers, she had long forgotten how it died. She hailed the wayfarer, who was more weary than she, with a song; she haunted the cheerful dawn; her 'good-morrow' rings from Herrick's poem, fresh as cock-crow. She knows that her love is dead, and her perplexity has regard rather to the many kinds of flowers than to the old story of his death; they distract her in the splendid meadows. All the tragic world paused to hear that lightest of songs, as the tragedy of *Hamlet* pauses for the fitful voice of Ophelia." Out of literature she passed with the passing of the Elizabethans. "Crabbe, writing of village sorrows, thought himself bound to recur to the legend of the mad maid, but his 'crazed maiden' is sane enough, sorrowful but dull, and sings of her own 'burning brow,' as Herrick's wild one never sang; nor is there any smile in her story, though she talks of flowers, or, rather, 'the herbs I loved to rear,' and perhaps she is the surest of all signs that the strange inspirations of the past centuries was lost, vanished like Tom-a-Bedlam himself. It had been wholly English, whereas the English eighteenth century was not wholly English."

Ceres' Runaway met with great praise. Though an author may surprise with each new book he produces, he cannot at any rate recreate the first surprise of all, which is as it were the surprise of his very existence; but, apart from that, no volume of my mother's was more appreciated than this.

It was seldom that she did not have on hand a number of the minor tasks incidental to authorship. The manuscripts and books sent by their writers for an opinion were never neglected. My father tried to save her from the burden of a heavy correspondence by writing letters on her behalf; and in later years, when he tried to save her everything, even a daughter had to write to her: "Some day when you have time, and Father isn't looking, will you do me the great favour of writing out your 'Intimations of Mortality,' as I haven't a copy and often want to remember it exactly." When she feared he might consider that a letter required no reply, she was likely, hastily, to answer it herself. "Please don't say that it need not be answered, merely because it is sent to other people as well," she begs him in forwarding a printed letter; and when later my father would allow her to write none of these official letters she watched their prospects anxiously and counted the hours of postponement after a certain time, dreading discourtesy. She had herself an occasional grumble. "It is a good thing to be nice to the poor dear

Miss B——'s of this world, but the result is that they bring you their poems to read on the spot, in front of them."

In 1910 the death of Sir William Butler left her sister bereaved. "I have never truly realised what widowhood means," my mother wrote, watching her sister's collapsed health and collapsed happiness. A few months after his death a long visit to Bansha Castle, in Tipperary, her sister's home, had a special object. Sir William Butler had written his autobiography, and my mother's literary eye was to scan the soldierly proofs:

Nov. 1910   *Bansha*

My darling Lobbie, – Yesterday we lunched with Canon Ryan, a very delightful ecclesiastic, the most interesting and amusing of Tipperary neighbours. The kind of priestly hospitality was very characteristic; and, being a fine musician, he played old Irish music beautifully, smoking all the while, and wearing most majestic red-bordered garments. He is a great reader.

"I am delighted with the Francis Thompson poem in the *Athenæum*, in fair type this time. And I think your father's Note most felicitous and charming.

"The last batch of proofs arrived this morning. So we shall shortly be turning our way homeward. The proofs are real hard work. No one could have quite taken my place at them, so I am pleased with this serviceable visit, but very anxious about your aunt.

"You don't say what you were going 'as' to the Wells's dance. I shall be rather indignant with my Viola if she threw over her other engagement. There are some little sacrifices (not worthy the name) we have to make for friends. Your devoted mother, A. M."

Will Meredith, George Meredith's son, asked her to prepare his father's poems for the Memorial Edition he was publishing – an exacting task in regard to which he wrote, when she had finished: "I have the satisfaction of knowing that these poems have now been corrected and put in final form by the one person most competent to deal with them."

For the 1911 edition of the *Encyclopædia Britannica* she wrote the account of Mrs. Browning. Many a one of the incidental literary occupations brought the pleasure of discovery and praise. "I am now writing to Fred Page an opinion of his Patmore paper," she says in a letter to my father. "I should like some things altered, and he is only too ready. But as I could not have written so fine an essay, I hesitate." Another paper on Patmore which drew her warmest approval was by John Freeman, and the fact that he could speak of Patmore as "the poet I chiefly love," was enough alone to constitute a friendship between them. Her admiration of Walter de la Mare made him write to her: "I never expected your encouragement because I valued it so highly." And of Lascelles Abercrombie she had to decide that he was a major poet though one capable of "reaching a breaking-point that power should never know." Charles Williams, whom also she considered a true poet, she read with the attention not only of a reader but of an adviser. "Poetry is a region of the mind, and the author of the *Silver Stair* lives there," she wrote in reviewing his book.

In 1913 she was writing to my father: "We are struggling over the collocation of parts of Everard's *Life of
Francis Thompson*. We have worked closely at it to-day,
and, I think, with good effect. I am sure you would be
very much impressed by his digest of F. T.'s philosophy
and theology. It is excellent. He and I together have
pruned the rather strange phrases that sounded too much
searched for, and were often difficult for the reader to
grasp." And again: "You will think Everard's last two
chapters most beautiful – just right in sincere feeling
without too much of the illness which, as you know, I
think ought not to be for the public. It is indeed beautiful
writing, of which anyone might be proud, but with no
display of authorship."

One of the literary tasks at about this time was the
making of a selection from Dr. Johnson for Herbert and
Daniel's "Regent Library" – a task upon which she could
spend a little of the love of a lifetime for "one of the
noblest of all English hearts." The pleasure of this work
was increased by the fact that she was to some extent a
collaborator with Mr. Chesterton, for he provided the
preface for the book. "I hope I shall see the reviews of
Johnson," she wrote when it appeared. "There is nothing
to say of my part of the work, except the inevitable complaint of omissions, which no doubt I too should make in
reviewing. I hope the papers are nice to my Chesterton.
He is mine much more, really, than Belloc's."

The chief enthusiasm in the contemporary reading of
all her later years was this for Chesterton. She found him
to be at once the wittiest and the most serious of living
writers. The habit he was charged with of turning things

upside down was to her mind the setting-right of things that had been standing on their heads. Exhilarating blows and buffets she felt to strike her from his pages. Her enjoyment passed beyond a reader's detached approval:– "If I had been a man, and large, I should have been Chesterton," she asserted with a smile, really feeling that there was something more than mere agreement between his mind and hers. It perhaps takes this announcement of hers to suggest any likeness between them; but, once suggested, it becomes real. Instances of such a likeness were provided in this year of 1912. Readers of both authors might hesitate which name to put to Chesterton's preface to the Johnson volume if it lay unsigned before them – indeed, they have so hesitated, characteristic though it is. And my mother's work, produced this year, a book called *Mary, the Mother of Jesus,* written for the Medici Society, has its occasional likeness to Chesterton, and yet seems only the more truly her own for that. Their characteristic in common was a standard so constant and so pervading that by it they adjusted freshly things long established.

From the last years of Palace Court for the rest of her life she had a slight personal acquaintanceship with Mr. and Mrs. Chesterton – an acquaintanceship that concealed, rather than expressed, her admiration. She was able also to know his critical approval of her own work only by references to it in his essays. She was about as pleased with a mention from him as if it was the first time she had seen her name in print. In 1912 the Ladies' Pioneer Club gave a dinner at which, Mr. Chesterton and my mother both being guests, he paid a great tribute to her in his speech. Across the letter of invitation to this dinner, she wrote, afterwards: "One of the happiest evenings of my life followed, for Chesterton spoke of me."

Mary, the Mother of Jesus, is so good a piece of sustained writing that it seems a misfortune that other long studies were not put in her way. This, more than her Ruskin study, has the effect of thronging one's mind with whole fields of work which should have been hers. She often lamented in these years the absence of regular work, having no obligation to produce an essay week by week, and in retrospect that lament increases. Mere chance commissions (needed in her case to replace male enterprise) could have drawn from her a far greater variety of work; her happiness would have been better served by more of the opportunities of a Chesterton.

In the Scriptures, in tradition, in poetry and art, in influence, Mary is traced in this book, and to give an idea of its manner some of the phrases on tradition shall be quoted – the "tradition at work where the Scriptures are silent":

> "A sense of art mixes with our modern piety. We are apt to admire the evangelical reticence for its dignity, as we admire, in this passage, what Dante does not tell, and in that, the sudden detail that carves his narrative like a blade. Such details are these: – the interruption that weeping imposes on Francesca, and the poet's swoon, when the whole business and pageant of Hell are suspended . . . or the centaur's putting aside of his beard so that he may call audibly in the infernal gale. In like manner

we are apt to respect the Scripture narratives with their few intense details, their close events and their great omissions alike, for their simplicity, and – it is to be feared that our literature leads us so far – for their 'effect.' "

But in the great Dark Ages and the great Middle Ages, "within the monastery and in the little town were childish minds such as will not be satisfied with a story divided by pauses," and those pauses were filled with a search that became an exploration and at last a ransacking, for that which had "all the immediate vivacity of good news, history conveyed by vital voice to vital voice . . . history full of pulses that were full of life, history that had never lapsed, and had never held its tongue in a book":

"Soon upon authoritative Tradition followed eager fancy, urgent conjecture. Nothing was to be suffered to escape. Scrutiny came home with triumphs, such as: Well, and who do you think it was who was married when the wine ran short? Who but Saint John, the beloved Disciple. And who was she? Why, Mary, the sister of Lazarus – no other! The popular passion for identification, for lessening the numbers of the actors in any history, for heaping upon one figure that which befell many, for concentrating, for knotting together, for centralising – a popular passion that may be noted whenever a hero is hero enough to the people to become the subject of their own song and their own story – this passion was delighted by all the later legends, gathered into the enclosure of the Scriptures. The great power of imagination and the little power of ingenuity alike found matter there; and we cannot wonder that the officious power of invention also went to work."

And of Mary:

"Before the pens of the four greatest writers in the world had been set to their task, the New Testament lurked in one woman's memory and in her watchfulness. It was her work to choose and to reject what should be said. Tradition may have preserved something credible: we are free to think so or not; but for what the Scriptures tell we have her word who was for a time herself the New Testament and the Church."

Her work on this book must have had its interlacing in her mind with the general reconsideration of what dignities were due to woman – at this very time a matter of general attention. On this question of where woman should stand she had written:

"No more instructive historic contrast could be set before us than a comparison of the Gospel according to Saint Luke, and Genesis according to Milton. In the great epic of the English language woman appears so entirely in direct relation to man that she is expressly debarred from a relation with God. This birthright of all the children of men, which the savage in his place and manner possesses, and the criminal in his, and the idiot in his, the Eve of Milton was denied."

The now absorbing question of political rights brought this question freshly before many people. But she who had written in her teens, "O my dream, my dream! When will you be realised to gladden my soul, to redeem my trampled and polluted sex? O my Shelley, if you were alive you would help me to fulfil my golden dreams!" had also in her early essays shown how readily her thoughts sharpened to this subject: "In France, in the time of the revolution, the rights of women were officially recognised in no grudging measure, for no one denied her a public appearance on the tumbril. Although she was forbidden political life, that seems a trifle when you consider how liberally she was allowed political death. Olympe de Gouges claimed, on behalf of her sex, 'a right to concur in the choice of representatives for the forma-tion of the laws.' Olympe de Gouges was guillotined. Robespierre thus made her public and complete amends."

Such opinions were of course bound to be joined to the movement for women's suffrage, and to express them-selves by the machinery of that movement. As president and vice-president of suffrage societies, as a writer for the suffrage papers, and a marcher in the processions, she contributed to the work of the devoted women she ad-mired, such as Mrs. Despard and Miss Abadam. From the militant suffragists she held aloof on the whole. At any rate some of her divided family were more successful in keeping her averse from militancy than others of them in making her approve it. "Everard champions the women all through; Francis will join riots in protest if the leaders get bad sentences," reports a daughter. "These lovely days have been perfect for paper-selling. I hope you will not object, when you hear about it." "I am so glad," wrote Everard to his mother, "that you have not hardened your heart against the window-smashers – although they have made a mistake. I have never before found myself so drawn to the cause, as now in its weakness and desperation. . . . Did you see me in the *Daily News*? – a somewhat foolish appearance, but during the dearth of words on the women's behalf, one is glad to say anything." Some criticism of hers of militancy brought from her friend, Evelyn Sharp, a stern and well-argued letter, ending: "Forgive my writing at this length, but as you seemed to think that I might agree with your criticism, I felt I had to make it clear that I do not." Laurence Housman, to whom she had written to invite him to accompany her to the house of a friend, replied uncompromisingly: "Very many thanks, but I find it quite impossible, with suffrage work added to my usual tasks, to add to my social pleasures. Will you convey my regrets to Mrs. Meeking, and tell her that if she will give a drawing-room meeting for the suffrage (either militant or constitutional section) I will come like a bird." My mother lacked only such absorption. "The meeting was magnificent," she writes, after an evening at the Albert Hall. "I have never seen anything like it; but the papers say little or nothing. Zangwill was full of fun – 'I will not say hammer away, I will not say spare no pains!' I don't think he excuses the smashing, however. But what a shameful letter is Sir A. Wright's in the *Times*!" To this letter on the subject of "Medical Women,"* she replied in *The Times*:

* Part of Sir Almroth Wright's argument may be gathered from the reply – the latter part of which refers to his opinion that "the mind of woman is always threatened with danger from the reverberations of her physiological emergencies." He said also: "When man is

ALICE MEYNELL

"Sir Almroth Wright avers that modesty is injured by consultation of a man doctor and a woman doctor. But what of the colloquy of a man doctor with a nurse? It is the nurse who has the most intimate and the most painful knowledge of her male patient's diseases, and must discuss them with the male physician. And what of the woman patient who is, or was until this more recent time, obliged to give every privacy of her nature into the medical hands of a man? It is her modesty that has brought the woman doctor into office; but that is a modesty which Sir Almroth Wright ignores. The different modesty assigned to the woman doctor who is to be condemned and to the nurse who is to be used, must be explained by difference of social caste. Fastidiousness as to the modesty of a lady is not respect for purity, but respect for caste.

"As to Sir Almroth's estimate of the normal insanity of women, it is surely the disproportionate estimate of one who has to deal with the abnormal. Sick women gather – out of the innumerable multitude who are not sick – in the consulting room. But we had hitherto believed that the physician had eyes and judgment for the outer world.

"It is a fact of human life that 'sex' troubles man at least as much as it troubles woman, but it does not disfranchise man. The foolish habit of our speech almost confines the word to womanhood. But George

a witness of the tendency of woman to morally warp when nervously ill, and of the terrible physical havoc which the pangs of a disappointed love may work, he is appalled."

266

Meredith was delighted when a woman who was his friend interrupted a remark about 'the sex' by the question 'Which?' "

To the correspondent of a weekly paper who quoted Scripture against the vote, she responded: "Your correspondent is right – St. Paul says that he does not suffer a woman to teach. Then out with the impious governess, Sunday-school teacher, schoolmistress – away with the nun from her class! St. Paul also says that he does not suffer a woman to usurp authority over a man. Then out of the calendar with the very good queens; and the Pope no doubt will send no more Golden Roses to the fairly good among them. No woman shall give orders to her gardener, or dismiss a footman, or direct her chauffeur, or summon a taxi-cab driver. What a havoc!"

The processions had incidental smiles, and incidental fatigue.

Granville Place

"My darling Dimpling, – I wish you could have seen the procession. I think it must be called a great success. Lobbie and I went to the Embankment and took our places with Evelyn Sharp, May Sinclair, and the author of *Diana of Dobson's* around the 'Scrivener's' banner. It was a great big banner that acted like a sail in the high wind, and what Evelyn and Diana of Dobson's went through in carrying it is beyond description. The band of our 'block' was just in front of it, and the man with the drum was frequently bonneted by the sudden collapse of the banner over his head. The crowd laughed. In fact it had three jokes – poor little Evelyn's sufferings; the name Scriveners, which it changed to Scavengers; and the presence of Careless [our dog]. For I have to confess that Careless, much excited by the band at such close quarters, insisted on joining. Your father had him in the crowd in Trafalgar Square, but when he saw us he came in, and was a great nuisance. The crowd called 'Come out, Ginger!' to him. Humanitarian women near us made a terrible fuss about his fatigue and fright, so we were delighted when we saw that your father had cut us off again in Piccadilly and persuaded him to fall out.

"The crowd was enormous. It reached the whole way of the march, and was generally quiet. We who marched lost the show, of course. I wish I could have seen the graduates and doctors in their robes, and all the other interesting incidents. I had a ticket for the Albert Hall. It was a wonderful gathering, but it was a cruel thing that many owners of boxes and stalls refused to let them, so that there were great gaps in the audience, while hundreds and hundreds of women were unable to get in.

"I was so tired at night that I could not write. Yesterday I was again tired to excess. I have the Women Writers' dinner to-night. Your most loving mother, A. M."

For two or three years, until 1914, the enthusiasm, agitations, embarrassments and despairs of that movement were ours, if not the actual sacrifices.

Family journalism in these years was at a tremendous

pitch of activity; for, as my father's habit was to refuse
nothing that came along, an almost incredible variety of
tasks had collected about him, in succession to his
finished editorships. Art Notes and book-reviewing were
normal and expected; the strangest pages that were produced in this unlikely factory were social and personal
pages – well-paid contributions to the weekly *Sketch*,
with headings such as "Small Talk" and "Crowns,
Coronets and Courtiers." Useful commissions like these
my father undertook and started with a swing, and then
would foist his son Everard upon slightly doubting
editors as one able to supply these pages as well as, or
better than, himself. Everard, a collector of rare books,
an expert on the inside and outside of his copies of Donne
and any seventeenth-century poets, but with his arduous
way to make in the world, could in fact transform himself
with equal skill into a "society" chronicler. (Occasionally the suitable subjects were lacking. "Thanks for your
pars.," he wrote once to my father, "but you had no
sooner left than Goddard wrote to say that he thought
there had been enough of Rome in the Socials. G. was
quite nice: 'good as they are,' he said, 'perhaps there has
been enough.' ") In all the anonymity of journalism,
there could not be a much more surprising identity concealed; he was a bearded bookseller by now, for he had
opened a shop for the sale of rare books and prints and
manuscripts, but he was also "Marigold" of the *Sketch*.
As his days were spent at his Serendipity Shop or in sale
rooms, his writing was done at night; and, though he no
longer lived there, it was done at his parents' Flat. His
father's help was constantly needed in the desperation of

lateness and insufficient subjects, and every page before going to the printer was read by his mother for errors. Even when it became a little less of a struggle, and he was more independent of help, he still came often to his parents' Flat to write – as if their mere ink was a brand that suited him.

In the meantime there had arisen amongst us, by 1911, the anticipation of having some country dwelling of our own. My father was urgently looking forward to giving this extra pleasure to his young family who, on walking tours, were now becoming familiar chiefly with Sussex, and lodging in its inns. Our acquaintance with anything but town-life still being new, this idea of my father's seemed not an ordinary development in our lives but a great adventure.

For many months a search was made – the sense of adventure rather reduced by each trip of inspection to the house agents' plots and villas and estates. In our inexperience it was often difficult to name one single flaw in a place that yet threw us into the deepest dejection. In fact it was not until we saw what my father actually bought that we knew what we had been looking for.

The second daughter, Madeline ("Dimpling"), had married Percy Lucas, the younger brother of E. V. Lucas, and he had a cottage at Thakeham, near Storrington, in Sussex – the Storrington where, many years before, Francis Thompson had stayed and written. Through Percy Lucas my father heard of the forthcoming sale of some land three miles from Storrington, under the South Downs. There was just time for him to make one hurried visit to it before the auction sale took place in London.

XVII

GREATHAM

"I FEEL I shall love the place if only you love it too,"
wrote my father. "I do love the Property," replied my
mother. "If I complain of anything it is of isolation and
inhumanity. But the very look of our homestead does
away with much of that." She loved tilled fields better
than any other form of landscape; and at Greatham the
tracts of bracken, the common-land, and water-meadows
flooded in winter, prevented our landscape from being
purely agricultural. But no sooner had she discovered
pasture and tillage on our very border than the objection
vanished.

The eighty acres, as they came to be known, gave
garden, orchard, field and wood, besides what was
common-land and marsh. A small seventeenth-century
farm-house and an old cottage were at opposite ends of
the land. Of this piece of country Hilaire Belloc wrote in
The Four Men: "At this place the flat water-meadows, the
same that are flooded and turned to a lake in mid-winter,
stretch out to a sort of scene or stage, whereupon can be
planted the grandeur of the Downs. . . . This is the
foreground of the gap of Arundel, a district of the Downs
so made that when one sees it one knows at once that
here is a jewel for which the whole county of Sussex

was made, and the ornament worthy of so rare a setting."

Wilfrid Blunt, driving four-in-hand over from his own wild, oak-overgrown piece of Sussex that he loved, set the seal of his all-knowing approval so strongly that through his eyes our treasure grew. Visiting Wilfrid Blunt at Newbuildings, my father wrote to my mother: "We are just back from a visit to the Property. W. B. thinks the place perfect, and that we must have used some magic to get it at the price or indeed to get it at all. I took further observations and the more I see the Property the more I like it." But while Wilfrid Blunt's approving glance would rest most on the bracken and heath and owl-haunted fir trees, my mother's would sweep the great corn-field which from our lane rose gently to the horizon, with a group of giant elms where the sun sets. (Even in gardens she preferred use to ornament, so that she could write from a friend's house: "There are several beautiful gardens, bowling alleys and lawns and woods. But I like the kitchen-gardens much the best!")

The little house had been used as two cottages. Re-united they still were not big enough. The fact that there was a good deal to do, even building, added to the pleasure of possession. Thenceforth the family was divided between London and Greatham. My father's idea was to give to each of his daughters a small separate cottage, as well as to enlarge his own house. When his youngest son, Francis, meeting Lutyens, described Greatham's needs, it was exciting to hear that Lutyens had rapidly sketched something on the back of an envelope. But part of what was originally planned, including a chapel, was postponed on account of expense, and soon my mother was writing: "I am sending you Lady Baker's terra-cotta prospectus, now that I fear the Lutyens idea is failing." In the end, Courtney Crickmer designed the addition to the house, and Basil Procter the cottages. My father's talent was earliest at work in the matter of changes, and in the winter, before anything was ready for my mother, he was there, with Eric Gill for Greatham's first visitor, in the cold bare rooms that were still strange, with snow lying outside, and wood burning in the great open chimneys.

If, during the progress, my mother was in town, she sent urgent advice or congratulation: "Forgive my telegram. I am more than ever anxious that the colony's water should be directly heaven's. I am uneasy about the danger of well-holes in that garden or near it; and, besides, there are all the metallic or mineral things that are in all well-water. I have just heard of a rain-tank, like Bastian's, that is always full, summer as well as winter, and always pure. I know I prose, but it is with good reason." "I am so glad to hear there are cowslips as well as everything else that is adorable in our Sussex." Or from Greatham to my father in London: "Your Greatham is looking heavenly. May it be all a joy to you, my own dearest."

She had always been more mindful of harvests than most town-dwellers; an extreme consciousness of the world's needs had often made tidings of crops be received at the high London Flat above the traffic as if fields of grain and hungry people were all the world outside. Now in the country, with the thrashing-machine humming across the road, and the hay-carts rolling about the fields, and the farmer to be pressed for news, she kept an eye on this miniature version of the world's supplies.

With the constant separations, inter-family corre-spondence increased. "I hope to be strong and well and do some work now. I feel very young," wrote my mother after an unwellness. A slightly disorganised state of things, domestically, which marked the beginnings of country life was not particularly conducive to work. Part of the family would disappear to Greatham, perhaps with the cook, or some other essential aid. "In regard to the Henry question," wrote my mother, "I suppose we must make up our minds to the necessity of enough servants to keep town and colony going. The girls think that Henry could be transferable between the Flat and the Colony, and Margaret also. I have no dislike to this picnic kind of life, but it is almost impossible for guests. I have just washed the whole of my room – good exercise but not literary." On another domestic point my father replies to her from Greatham: "The only thing that it occurs to me to report is Olivia's opinion that posterity, reading your touching appeal to me to pay the laundryman, will say I have no heart and no purse."

The great number of books that had been holed-and-cornered in the Flat had good shelf-room in the new library at Greatham. Books and papers became better sorted – though searches for lost letters and manuscripts and books were still, as always, a feature of family life. "I should say I left it," my father would write, of some paper he required, "on the window-sill nearest the library door, but I might have taken it up to the table by my bed or have restored it to its place in the lowest shelf in the F. T. compartment" – explicit enough places, if only it were in any of them.

A letter written by my mother to Greatham, in March 1912, gives an account of London doings:

Granville Place

"My darling Wilfrid, – We are very glad to have Bastian here for a little town life. On Saturday we all seem to have had some dissipation – even I, for Thorplet took Viola and me to hear Mrs. Besant who weekly fills the Queen's Hall. She is simply a good Mediocrity. Her moral teaching is excellent and might be that of a good governess giving her class a lesson on the gospel of the day. But she talks as though she were making a new revelation, and refers all this wisdom to someone she calls the Master whom she interviews in her astral body. The combination of familiar teachings and mystical hints is the only surprising thing, and it sounds silly. Some thousands must have been hanging on her words. She speaks well but without distinction. In this respect she is just another disappointment, for I had heard for years of her great power.

"Carroll lunched with us, and Dimpling's babies were very charming. No one called except a poor dear woman whose husband recites Ruskin, struggling to bring himself into notice by this 'great gift'! Storer came in the evening. He is getting tired of 'mockery,' to which he had given himself lately, he owns. His poetry society or club had had an evening party at which an awful Countess had smashed some of the furniture and thrown things at the heads of the guests and made Storer pay for her taxis. This made him tired of irony and the light touch!

"Did I tell you that Albert sent me his essay on me and my work? I have very nicely asked him if he will omit the personal description and tone down the ecstasies. Your JOHNSON."

Another note concerns an absentee black cat and a newcomer black cat – possibly, but not certainly, the same animal. "A beautiful pussy – Black Jackman? – has just come to stay. Isn't it rather sad that we shall never know whether he is B. J. or not? Complete blackness gives so few indications. As to character, he answers well enough, being perhaps a trifle less affectionate than Black Jackman, but still affectionate. He is smelling everything, but whether for novelty or old acquaintance I can't tell."

Under the growing roof-space at Greatham, not only the sons and daughters but their infants collected, either as residents or as visitors. The roadless cottage that lay across the field and through the pine-wood was occupied by Madeline and Percy Lucas and their children, when a few new rooms were added to its old beamed ones, and when Percy Lucas, with his country knowledge and outdoor industry, had put the mark of his labour upon it. Two other cottages were put up, and a third was made under the old roof and within the old walls and wood of the cattle-shed.

In the winter of 1912-13 my mother left both her

English homes to visit Rome once more, her last visit, and the last time that she set foot in Italy.

January, 1913   *Rom*

"My dearest Bastian, – You, who have seen the Oriental sun, can hardly perhaps imagine the joy I take in the mere Italian – the reflected light from one side of the street to the other, the darkness of the cypress and the ilex in the sun. I could not rest for the beauty of it yesterday, and I wandered everywhere, except to St. Peter's, which is for to-day. This is my *sixth* visit to Rome, yet it is always a surprise.

"The temple to the divine Victor Emmanuel, as I call this really idolatrous monument, is even worse, now it is finished, than I expected. It is beautiful in itself, but it is out of all proportion, and from the top of the Capitoline Hill it crushes the whole of Rome as though you took the town in your hand and crumpled it up. It is dead-white too, and Rome is old living yellow and brown. They call this violated city the 'third Rome' – characteristically ignoring the Middle Ages, but it is the fourth. Ancient Rome was destroyed by fire and sword, Medieval Rome by the pick-axe, Renaissance Rome – the most flagrant and triumphant of all – is being superseded by the jerry-builders. . . . Your loving mother, A.M."

Her sister was with her in Rome: "She is so profoundly sad, underneath all her pleasure in this place. We are now in the dear old narrow street where we were as girls with our parents. Our rooms get the sun, and your aunt has a nice terrace with aloes in pots, the charm of which you perhaps do not understand. We are within a walk of St. Peter's and the hill that commands Rome. (But everything is really within a walk in this little city.)" My mother had many friends: "People are really too nice; they keep one from the real Rome." And Rome was apt to be too rich. "There is a kind of excess in the luxury of society here – the canopies of flowers, the regiments of tall servants, the gold and silver plate – which I don't and never shall really enjoy in such a world of want. But the 'palace chambers far apart' are glorious and majestic indeed. I shall never really care for a room with a low ceiling again – except Monica's and Dimpling's and the Flat's!"

January 1913   *Rome*

"My darling Wilfrid, – The luncheon at Mrs. Mulhall's yesterday was grand – scene, food, appointments little less than magnificent. I sat between Abbot Gasquet, whom I tried to amuse, and Sir Alfred Molony who is a humorous man and amused me much, when he was not talking about his ('practically') one meal a day. I find a lot of people keep this rule 'practically,' which by the comedy of language means that they don't keep it, – 'a hegg here and a hegg there,' as the cook in *Punch* said of a Highchurch fasting family. Bishop Hedley has almost given up talking, and is a difficult guest. He sat by Mimi – took her in, as Sir Alfred took me; for here we are taken in to luncheon and even taken out again, along corridors. Our hotel is not bad, or will not be when I have got a good room on Mimi's terrace. The atmosphere is good. The smart hotels (except the dear Beau Site) have those infernal round doors that keep out the air. If Dante had known of them he would have made them the gates over which the famous inscription was placed. . . . Your ever JOHNSON."

Among the tea-parties was one at the Excelsior: "Casting my eye over that scene of vanity, it lighted on Hall Caine, who looked pleased to be spotted. Talk rather lively but gossipy – nullities, separations, the Rodd's fancy-dress ball, which is the topic. The sky, the evening star, the wonderful, wonderful evening sufficiently rebuke an Excelsior tea."

March, 1913   *Rome*

"My darling Wilfrid, – . . . Presents for the darling families will have to be Genoese sweets merely. Smart things here are inordinately dear, old things are probably fakes; and though the opals and amethysts at the rag-fair are beautiful and cheap, the setting is such an undertaking.

"We had a great day at Ostia yesterday, the Parrishes taking us in their delightful motor. Ostia, where St. Monica had her last colloquy with St. Augustine, and where she died, is now a great uncovered city with its league-long streets towards Rome laid bare, and some fine statues discovered now and then. On the way we were held up in a village to give help to a boy who had run a knife into his side. Without the loss of a moment, the grandmother, the father, and the mother who carried the child, climbed in, and we turned back towards Rome, and gave the little family to the care of the still smoother train on its way to the hospital. These people took the service and the little money I gave for the child in absolute silence and as a matter of course. Emotional people as they are, they were quiet under their great anxiety. They never looked at us or spoke to us. When we returned to the village a kind of head man made us a brief speech of thanks, beautifully and with real dignity. Everyone we met on the road no doubt thought we had run over the boy. He was conscious but dreadfully pale, and had no expression of pain. His mother's chief care was to keep the air from his face, poor child. . . . All my love. Your JOHNSON."

Her scruples gave her not much peace when she was spending money on herself. "I don't want to stay here inordinately long," she wrote, "spending such oceans of money." "Oh what it is to be rent in two! Mimi is so urgent, and friends entreat me not to go back to the fogs and cold. What shall I do? Will you make up my mind for me? I want to go home, yet I love Rome. Telegraph 'come' or 'stay,' and I shall with joy do either. Literally with equal joy." She had been unwell before leaving England: "I have loved Rome much. I thank you for the joy of it, which perhaps you can hardly understand. Nothing but Italy could have drawn me away from all I love – not any number of aches. But really that arthritis is wonderfully quiet now. I must be looking better since a man – English – told me my portrait ought to be painted and 'sent to the Academy'! The last compliment (out of my own family) of my life!" "When I read of your sixteen degrees of frost I know that I have saved the benefit of my visit by staying. Nietzsche would thoroughly approve of me." "Ah what dear friends I leave in Rome! How generously loving to me!"

In Genoa, on the return journey, she renewed, as she always did, the cherished ties with her Italian people, her Italian half-sister, and all the beloved place. "The sea lying absolutely still and silent, as though it were a little lake and did not clasp African shores and Cretan and Greek – a tender white-blue seen through pine and cypress – made me think yesterday as I travelled along the coast that there is no beauty in Rome or anywhere equal to this beauty. It was a cloudless day and hot. This morning is dull and dark, so I seem to be doomed not to see my Genoa looking bright."

Just after her return to England a spirited controversy took place on the laureateship, the last poet-laureate's appointment having left many people in doubt as to whether the office should be continued. Some of the papers printed eminent people's opinions as to who, if anyone, should follow; and there was much unexpected, and even popular, opinion in favour of my mother's appointment. Sir W. Robertson Nicoll wrote in the *Observer* plebiscite: "Would continue the Laureateship and appoint Mrs. Meynell"; adding in the *British Weekly*: "I will not go so far as Mr. Garvin and say that Mrs. Meynell is the greatest of living poets, but I will say that she ranks with the very best, and I believe there will be no disposition to dispute her claim." The appointment of this "lady laureate" was advocated, too, by James Douglas; and in the *Pall Mall*; and someone writing in the *Daily Mail* said that to ignore her would be "to hand the laurel wreath half way up the ladder." A plebiscite in *T. P.'s Weekly* favoured her next to Kipling – with Masefield, Hardy, Robert Bridges, Yeats and the rest in the rear! A letter to her from a daughter announced the fact: "I congratulate you on *T. P.'s Weekly*. You beat everyone by an enormous number – except Kipling. I had asked two people to vote for you – just so that you should not be entirely out of it! But I needn't have troubled."

In this year, 1913, appeared a volume of her Collected Poems, in which the two former volumes were reprinted, and a number of new poems added. Before she started for Italy the arrangement of the book was being discussed, when my mother's comparative dislike of her early poems made her wish that they should be placed at the end of the book, instead of in correct chronology, for there is a note from her to my father across the outside of which she wrote: "Quick, before I lose courage!" and in which she says: "I have just received your letter about the poems. Yes, place them as you like them best. I cannot say I like that order but I can sincerely say that I trust your judgment. Or perhaps, even more truly, that making you unhappy about the book is intolerable to me. Oh, let the word *Early* be conspicuous!" Some of the volumes followed one order, some the other; and from Italy she wrote: "So some of my volumes have the cart before the horse and others the spirited, thoroughbred horse before the rather conventional old cart. Think of that now!"

She was always convinced of her duty to obey, and she could only cling to literary disagreements when they did

not involve some practical issue. In mere argument she
held her own vigorously. The young family would hear
at intervals Tennyson's greatness disputed, sometimes in
the early morning, called from one room to the other, my
mother's defence of him very spirited and unyielding
because no action hung on it. A later instance of her life-
long sense of the duty of obedience (not perhaps that of
any wife to any husband, but herself to her husband) is
described in a letter to one of the children: "Here is a
little bit of news which involved the giving up of my own
wish. A committee, formed of the Laureate and Gosse and
other poets, intend to present to Hardy a book containing
poems of living poets in their own handwriting. I, being
asked to contribute, thought I never would agree to join
such a self-advertising and intrusive assault upon Hardy.
I had written a courteous refusal. And lo! your father
quashed the answer, not yet posted, and now I am to say
Yes. I should have thought it a moral impossibility."

The *Collected Poems*, like the *Collected Essays* that appeared in the following year, achieved that concentration
of her work that carried it further than before; and in
that form it has its permanent demand. "The *Times'* was
a notice, wasn't it?" she wrote – "I think I have never
had anything so good, so interested. Three cheers. I
wonder who wrote it."

Among the new poems, "The Rainy Summer" alone
is simply descriptive:

> There's much afoot in heaven and earth this year;
>   The winds hunt up the sun, hunt up the moon,
> Trouble the dubious dawn, hasten the drear
>   Height of a threatening noon.

No breath of boughs, no breath of leaves, of fronds
    May linger or grow warm; the trees are loud;
The forest, rooted, tosses in his bonds,
    And strains against the cloud.

No scents may pause within the garden-fold;
    The rifled flowers are cold as ocean shells;
Bees, humming in the storm, carry their cold
    Wild honey to cold cells.

Others are poems of imagination and of religion, such as
"The Unknown God":

One of the crowd went up,
And knelt before the Paten and the Cup,
Received the Lord, returned in peace, and prayed
Close to my side; then in my heart I said:

"O Christ, in this man's life –
This stranger who is Thine – in all his strife,
All his felicity, his good and ill,
In the assaulted stronghold of his will,

"I do confess Thee here,
Alive within this life; I know Thee near
Within this lonely conscience, closed away
Within this brother's solitary day.

"Christ in this unknown heart,
His intellect unknown, – this love, this art,
This battle and this peace, this destiny
That I shall never know, look upon me!

"Christ in his numbered breath,
Christ in his beating heart and in his death,
Christ in his mystery! From that secret place
And from that separate dwelling, give me grace."

And "Christ in the Universe":

With this ambiguous earth
His dealings have been told us, these abide:
The signal to a maid, the human birth,
The lesson, and the young Man crucified.

But not a star of all
The innumerable host of stars has heard
How He administered this terrestrial ball.
Our race have kept their Lord's entrusted Word.

Of His earth-visiting feet
None knows the secret, cherished, perilous,
The terrible, shamefast, frightened, whispered, sweet,
Heart-shattering secret of His way with us.

No planet knows that this
Our wayside planet, carrying land and wave,
Love and life multiplied, and pain and bliss,
Bears, as chief treasure, one forsaken grave.

Nor in our little day,
May His devices with the heavens be guessed,
His pilgrimage to thread the Milky Way
Or His bestowals there be manifest.

But in the eternities,
Doubtless we shall compare together, hear
A million alien Gospels, in what guise
He trod the Pleiades, the Lyre, the Bear.

O be prepared, my soul!
To read the inconceivable, to scan
The million forms of God those stars unroll
When, in our turn, we show to them a Man.

In this same year a little book called *Childhood* was commissioned and appeared. "I am getting on well with my *Childhood* (the cheerful book for Batsford)," she wrote from London to Greatham, "so that the solitude has not been really unwelcome. Solitude *with letters* is in fact useful. In my old 'Autolycuses' are several capital columns on children, written after my book *Children*. I am sure you would agree with me that they could go in bodily or with little recasting? By their aid I have done more than half the booklet." In the newly written part of the little book the children who entered were now sometimes the children's children.

The youngest daughter, Olivia, was married to Murray Sowerby and living at Clifton, and my mother paid frequent visits to them there. She writes: "Hermia was baptized in deep slumber to-day. . . . This place is really magnificently scenic. . . . They make me very happy, and I try to add to Lobbie's beautiful serene happiness." And two years later she writes to Olivia, when she has been consulted about a name: "I so deeply respect a father's choice that I hesitate to tell you with how little favour Judith is received in this Flat. A hard, beheading Old Testament name seems to accord so badly with the sweet and sprightly name of Hermia." – "What about Juliet? Shakespearean, charming, not too far-fetched, yet somewhat fetched, which is well. The great virgin patronesses of Christendom had noble names – Catherine, Agatha, Dorothea. Greek is very nice in names. If I had had yet another son I should have called him Agathon from Plato's *Symposium*." On another occasion she wrote to Everard's wife, when a new child was named Vivian, the name of her own lost infant: "Dearest Grazia, I am very glad that you have given your little son the name of one whom I can hardly think of without tears. He was a most adorable little child, and it is very dear of Everard to have thought of repeating his dear name. Are you calling the boy Vivian Everard? I hope you will continue that beautiful name also."

And at Greatham the Lucases' three children added to her happiness. "The children are *too* lovely together, hiding in the fern." In her absence her letters follow their doings. "Thank Christian for her monosyllables." "So Barbara has cut her lovely little intelligent forehead!" To Sylvia, the eldest little girl, she had written in infancy some verses recalling the poets' sentimental version of a child's early death – how its youth was preserved by its death:

Long life to thee, long virtue, long delight,
    A flowering early and late!
Long beauty, grave to thought and gay to sight,
    A distant date!

Yet as so many poets love to sing
    (When young the child will die),
"No autumn will destroy this lovely spring,"
    So, Sylvia, I –

I'll write thee dapper verse and touching rhyme
    "Our eyes shall not behold – "
The commonplace shall serve for thee this time:
    " Never grow old."

For there's another way to stop the clock
    Within my cherishing heart,
To carry thee unalterable, and lock
    Thy youth apart.

"Thy flower, for me, shall evermore be hid
  In this close bud of thine,
Not, Sylvia, by thy death – O God forbid! –
  Merely by mine."

In 1913 this Sylvia had an accident, cutting her leg with
a knife with such disastrous consequences that even her
life was in danger. For months her desperate illness and
suffering, at the age of five, when she seemed too small to
be so much hurt, and did not even know the words with
which to describe her own distress, were a terrible experience to the family.* My mother's letters often spread
the reports that were so eagerly waited for then. "Yesterday we began to have a little hope that the anti-toxin

---

* A verse written by one of them describes her helplessness.

The Vocabulary.

The child was hurt and lay
Day after day
For doctors to perform their task.
She could not ask
For cause or reason, – she was still too small
To match the agony with words; and all
She cried, lying there damp and flat,
Was, "I don't like your doing that!"

O come away,
It is too horrible to stay!
Come into the next room, and close the door . . .
But now you only listen more,
And still you hear the whispering voice complain,
The sudden scream of terror and pain,
Never less sudden though day by day goes past,
Then her high words at last.
And swift she uses all her art
To speak the protest in her heart
Against this agony that comes and goes, –
Her most violent words she knows,
The pain to fit:
"I don't *like* your doing it!"

treatment, following on the second operation, would succeed. Dimpling was happier yesterday than she has been
since they came; and it is a great thing for her to have
Percy with her. She is heroic beyond description. I believe she had never broken down once. The room is as
full of jokes and of flowers as we can make it. Sylvia is a
shadow of herself." "I was with Sylvia on the roof
yesterday" (of the Hospital of St. John and St. Elizabeth)
" and pleased on the whole with her state though she
looked very ill. For the first time she had needed no
anæsthetic." "A physician (no. 4 round that tiny bed) is to
investigate her heart to-day, for her pulse is very fast."
For years the fate of that leg was inseparable from the
thought of a beloved child; and Sylvia haunts my
mother's letters. To Sylvia herself she writes of "dear
dear priceless lovely Mrs. Badleg," and to her mother:
"My love to the three angels, but a special cherishing
love to my own adored Sylvia."

In April of 1914 my mother wrote from Clifton:

"My darling Wilfrid, – Celia (Clark) writes that I
am to be invited to visit the Panama Exposition next
year – one of four women: Mme. Curie, Mrs. Sidney
Webb and Helen Key being the others. These are the
first names. In case of refusals others would be substituted. Celia is on the Women's Committee and
sends me this preliminary notice. I can't go, can I?
The whole expenses are paid, of course. I have to
answer at once. If I were a little younger, so as to be
more presentable, I should fly. What do you think?
Send me a line by return. Your JOHNSON."

"My darling Viola, – A most happy Easter, sweetest! Happy in every sense, in the interior world and in this lovely exterior world of spring and friends. . . .

"Shall I go to San Francisco? I say Yes and No all day. Murray says 'Yes,' Lobbie says 'No.' I must write to-morrow.

"How are you, my ever precious? This suspension bridge is a bad dream to me. I shall not go near it again. Seen from below! My love to the darling Flat group. Your devoted mother, A. M."

"At least delay to refuse," wrote my father. "But if *I* am converted to your going, how desirable must that going be! It is such a compliment to you, and I am persuaded of its opportuneness. And you look so beautiful!" – "Well, there! I am cabling acceptance to San Francisco," replied my mother, making at last a decision which the War was to render futile. "I am writing to Celia also to say that of course illness (but nothing less) would stop me. You see it is nearly a year off! I shall be a year older!"

In the early part of 1914 the *Collected Essays* appeared, beautifully produced under my father's, and his son Francis's, care, and with a reproduction of Sargent's drawing of the author for frontispiece. "My 'Collected' are out," she wrote to a daughter. "If I could suppress the portrait I should be wholly pleased, for the book is exquisitely produced." My mother had to keep Greatham informed as to reviews. "In case you didn't see the *Times* I enclose it. A very fine article and uncommonly well written." "I much liked the *Westminster* – as intelligently good as anything I have had except Dixon Scott and the

New Statesman." "Alfred Noyes has written to Francis: 'What a marvellous volume – far and away the most significant and beautiful collection of Essays in the English language'!"

June 1914   *Granville Place*

"My darling Wilfrid, – On Friday I fly to you. . . . It is a great relief to find that Elmslie ratifies Trotter's judgment about Sylvia. But he does not think the knee will ever be quite normal. The new splint is being made. Dimpling is heroic. I am very well. Delighted with the look of my book and with the sales. Oh if I can make another nimble ninepence to help with Sylvia! . . .

"What is the news about Chesterton? I can think of nothing better than his reviewing me – except his reception into the Church. I do love him so.

"A lovely, lovely review in the *Liverpool* something – not all praise, but such as an author loves. Viola is ordering some copies and I will send you one to-morrow.

"Margaret [a maid] had a kick from a horse on Saturday – not serious – but her arm is much bruised, and she fainted. Her last thought, under the impression that she was dying, was of you; and she weeps in telling it, saying she is deeply attached to you. So, by the way, is Mrs. Cale Young Rice (of *The Cabbage Patch*) on whom I called. I did three calls without a taxi, and I find the shining streets intoxicating, and love walking in them. Ever my dearest, Your JOHNSON."

ALICE MEYNELL

July 30, 1914   *Granville Place*

"My darling Wilfrid, . . . D. S. MacColl has sent
a messenger to ask whether he may 'run round,' so I
am awaiting him. Everard and Grazia dined last
night, Everard hard at work till midnight. I was able
to do him a couple of feeble art pars. He was forcing
an article on the Austrian Ambassador.

"MacColl has come. All he wanted was my signa-
ture, with Asquith's, Lady Ritchie's, and all Gallery-
Directors', in an address of sympathy with Robbie
Ross. All the papers are alarming us this morning.
Your devoted JOHNSON."

In the *Collected Essays*, a little section called "Women
and Books" gathers together articles which do a kind of
literary and yet feminine justice to some women of the
past. Dr. Johnson's wife, Tetty, especially, is reclaimed
from the ignomiy of Macaulay's and other biographers'
indignation:

"Men who would trust Dr. Johnson with their
orthodoxy, with their vocabulary, and with the most
intimate vanity of their human wishes, refuse, with
every mark of insolence, to trust him in regard to his
wife. On that one point no reverence is paid to him,
no deference, no respect, not so much as the credit
due to our common sanity. . . . Not to any writer
has it yet occurred that if England loves her great
Englishman's memory, she owes not only courtesy,
but gratitude, to the only woman who loved him
while there was yet time. Not a thought of that debt
has stayed the alacrity with which a caricature has

been acclaimed as the only possible portrait of Mrs. Johnson. . . . And English literature has had no better phrase for her than Macaulay's – 'She accepted, with a readiness which did her little honour, the addresses of a suitor who might have been her son. . . .' The meanest man is generally allowed his own counsel as to his own wife; one of the greatest of men has been denied it. 'The lover,' says Macaulay, 'continued to be under the illusions of the wedding day till the lady died.' What is so graciously said is not enough. He was under those 'illusions' until he too died, when he had long passed her latest age, and was therefore able to set right that balance of years which has so much irritated the impertinent. Johnson passed from this life twelve years older than she, and so for twelve years his constant eyes had to turn backwards to dwell upon her. Time gave him a younger wife."

In the case of Prue, Steele's wife, the rescue is from the hands of Thackeray and the banter of the nineteenth century. In the case of Mrs. Dingley it is from the romanticist who will not let her sufficiently share Swift's correspondence and his love with Stella.

Up to the very brink of the War these things had their importance, and then suddenly such literary justice or injustice became indifferent and far away. A declaration of war puts the figures of the past not only into a reasonable oblivion – it gives to their deadness a new alienation, increasing a thousandfold their absence and ignorance.

My mother was at Greatham when war was declared.

"All are well here," she first writes to my father, "and keeping up each other's hearts. It is heavenliest weather. How we hope you will come to-morrow, bringing the last news. But we no longer hope for peace." The harmless scattering of her children became uneasy to her. "I do want to keep together as much as possible, so that I long for the Everards and Francis to be stowed here somehow." "It is very difficult to live through this time in decent calm." "I look forward so to your coming. I bear absences less and less well."

XVIII

THE WAR

Her attitude to the War was that which people expressed by the phrase that it was a war to end war – the attitude which has since seemed so mistaken, and which now may still be right. The belief that a warlike power was to be rebuked and defeated was for her as for others the argument of that time – one might almost say the pleasure of that time, by contrast with the horror which no argument could reach.

She was stricken with an inner suffering about the War compared to which anything that she might express was mere alleviation. If she wrote or spoke of the miseries of the War, these were her easier moments, her moments of distraction. For it became one of the griefs which tormented her privacy, and which were too much for her.

She was filled with a sense of her uselessness in the world, making her especially grateful if anything was done for her, or humiliated if she thought that more was done than she was worth. "My darling darling," she wrote to my father, "ever too kind and ever too good to me and to all, but especially to me." She was very dependent on our affection. "O my Lobbie," she wrote, "what a pleasure it is, even in this unhappy year, to see my beloved children, and to have the assurance of their love – so much more than I have ever deserved." She was sometimes moved to tears merely by her own humility or affection – these things become too poignant to her against the background of the War. These were the years when her fragility was sharpening itself to actual illness, the heart that had to bear the brunt of great distress being a weak and damaged heart.

Fortunately there were great distractions, and the one nearest to the distress itself was the conviction of her country's integrity. "You know," she said, writing to a daughter, "that our *entente* with France (a real alliance, we all see now, kept secret from the nation) has been my horror and my dismay for the years it has lasted. An alliance with so much that I detest against so much that I respect!" But apart from deploring that, she found that "everything adds to the security of our conscience in this war, and defeat itself will not degrade us now." "I hope you all saw the *Times* full report of the Notes between Grey and Berlin. Nothing could be more honourable to us. I do think there is such a thing as distinctively English honour." Moved by any love shown her or service performed for her, she was similarly overcome by the good-will and participation of other countries with hers. To a French soldier, a great reader of English poetry, who wrote to her in the midst of the War to ask for a scrap of her writing, she replied: "I am touched by your request. You are the first French soldier with whom I have exchanged a word in the war. Therefore you must let me tell you that the gratitude I feel to all Frenchmen who are fighting for justice against iniquity is almost too much for my feeble heart." And when America joined the exhausted countries she wrote in a letter to a friend: "As to America, coming out of her prosperity and peace and separation, she has saved us and all the present world. I think it is the greatest deed done by any nation in recorded history."

She took to herself another distraction, that of renewed activity in her lifelong happiness of writing. One of the few poetry-writing periods of her life occurred now – bringing with each poem a sense of achievement that was little short of glorious to her in contrast with unhappiness and failing health. She prized the writing of these latest poems more than the writing of anything before, but that was partly because they carried more than their own merit: they reopened the question for her of living and of accomplishing.

The Shakespeare poem which has been referred to was of this time, and the poem called "A Father of Women"; and these two at least are the very perfection not only of her later kind of poetry but of her whole art. Two other poems were borrowed from her own prose, or rather emerged again from that constant place where some thoughts are the intermittent companions of one's existence. The idea that the very young have experienced as much sense of the length of time as the old recurred now to enable her to feel that the early dead in battle had actually the longest time of life behind them.

> Irrevocable good –
> You dead, and now about, so young, to die, –
> Your childhood was; there Space, there Multitude,
> There dwelt Antiquity.

The other subject that had already figured in her prose

was the fact that the primitive painters looked with the
sun, not towards it, until Tintoretto, chiefly, who put
his figures between himself and the light:

> Master, thy enterprise
> Magnificent, magnanimous, was well done,
> Which seized the head of Art, and turned her eyes –
> The simpleton – and made her front the sun.

Two of the poems have more of Nature in them than this
poetry of intellect and religion was otherwise concerned
with – one written when, at Greatham, she lay and
heard the thrush before the dawn.

> A voice peals in this end of night,
>   A phrase of notes resembling stars,
> Single and spiritual notes of light.
>   What call they at my window-bars?
>   The South, the past, the day to be,
>   An ancient infelicity.

> Darkling, deliberate, what sings
>   This wonderful one, alone, at peace?
> What wilder things than song, what things
>   Sweeter than youth, clearer than Greece,
>   Dearer than Italy, untold
>   Delight, and freshness centuries old?

> And first first-loves, a multitude,
>   The exaltation of their pain;
> Ancestral childhood long renewed;
>   And midnights of invisible rain;
>   And gardens, gardens, night and day,
>   Gardens and childhood all the way.

THE WAR

What Middle-Ages passionate,
  O passionless voice! What distant bells
Lodged in the hills, what palace state
  Illyrian! For it speaks, it tells,
    Without desire, without dismay,
    Some morrow and some yesterday.

All-natural things! But more – Whence came
  This yet remoter mystery?
How do these starry notes proclaim
  A graver still divinity?
    This hope, this sanctity of fear?
    O innocent throat! O human ear!

And the other called "Summer in England, 1914," where
the contrasts of that year are drawn:

. . . Most happy year! And out of town
  The hay was prosperous, and the wheat;
The silken harvest climbed the down;
  Moon after moon was heavenly-sweet
Stroking the bread within the sheaves,
Looking 'twixt apples and their leaves.

And while this rose made round her cup,
  The armies died convulsed. And when
This chaste young silver sun went up
  Softly, a thousand shattered men,
One wet corruption, heaped the plain,
After a league-long throb of pain . . .

Another poem called "In Sleep" gives a fundamental
sense of religion in the episode of a dream:

I dreamt (no "dream" awake – a dream indeed)
A wrathful man was talking in the park:
"Where are the Higher Powers, who know our need
  And leave us in the dark?

299

"There are no Higher Powers; there is no heart
In God, no love" – his oratory here,
Taking the paupers' and the cripples' part
    Was broken by a tear.

And then it seemed that One who did create
Compassion, who alone invented pity,
Walked, as though called, in at that north-east gate,
    Out from the muttering city;

Threaded the little crowd, trod the brown grass,
Bent o'er the speaker close, saw the tear rise,
And saw himself as one looks in a glass,
    In those impassioned eyes.

Ten of these poems were first printed by her son Francis,
who had now started on his career of printing and publishing at his Romney Street Press, in a small quarto
edition limited to fifty copies. These ten poems were
then published, with more added, in 1917, under the
title of *A Father of Women, and other Poems*. "I am naturally
delighted," she wrote, "to see my tiny book getting such
an august reception: I am also surprised."

In 1917, also, appeared *Hearts of Controversy*, a book of
six literary studies, the Dickens and the Swinburne and
the Tennyson among them, reprinted from the periodicals
where they had originally appeared, but newly revised.
"I confess," she wrote to her son Everard, "that I think
a great deal about the prose, hoping rather than
believing that it is good."

Besides the praise given by critics to these two books,
even a world at war was still accumulating its knowledge
and appreciation of her work. The new, discovering

praise given her in her early writing days had become something less vociferous, but it was now praise spread over the general reading world where English was known. In the case of Francis Thompson, it was from the moment he died that his fame had become wide-spread, but already her fame, sometimes companioning his where circumstances linked them, had travelled far.

At the end of 1914 she was elected to the Academic Committee of the Royal Society of Literature, when Sir Henry Newbolt delivered an address to her in which he spoke of her poetry having a "union of wit and religious emotion as rare now as it was characteristic of the seventeenth century in England"; and said of "Renouncement": "I cannot foresee the generation which that poem will not delight." "That Literary Society affair was lovely," she wrote in a letter to Olivia. "I could not have wished for a better welcome than Gilbert Murray's and Newbolt's."

A fitful literary occupation at this time was reviewing for the *Dublin Review*, of which my father became the editor in the absence of his friend Shane Leslie on a mission in America. Another letter from my mother, written from the Flat after an afternoon of visitors, relates the kind of anecdote that she knew a daughter enjoyed: "The drawing-room is in a state of chaos quite indescribable since the *Dublin Review* is edited on the writing-table, on the piano and the chairs and the floor, and in the fender. So I have no ink. All are well here. But it is a dreadful scene of umbrellas. Mrs. Spicer's – a very special one – was taken, perhaps by Euterpe Craies, we thought; and Ida Taylor's by Viola or Dimpling. I went to Euterpe's, and we hunted up all hers, and found one with a name and address engraved on the silver band. Tiny engraving, and we had up the porter and the house-keeper and they could not read it, but at last I managed it, and the name was – Craies! The lack of ink or a corner of a writing-table to use for answering all the letters about the umbrellas is maddening." A little stray reviewing was done elsewhere than in the *Dublin*, such as that of Laurence Binyon's war poems which she considered "noble poetry," reviewed in the *Observer*.

Greatham, during these years of war, provided a love-liness and a distracting traffic of family life that was good for a mind that craved for things that were slight and yet absorbing. Percy Lucas, Madeline's husband, had gone from Rackham into training in the army. "I give him," she wrote to Madeline, "a mother-in-law's blessing from my heart! Some people would think that comic; I pity them." She liked trying to do some of the tasks of those who were absent. "My dearest Mary," she wrote to the eldest grandchild, "Greatham is very eager to see you back, for agriculture is the order of the day. We found chaos. The potato patch was a kind of small forest, in which potato-plants were hardly perceptible. You should see it now – orderly rows of flourishing banked-up potato-plants, promising Irish stew for months, and not a weed to be seen. Viola has been particularly masterly, but I must say I bore my part. I do *eradicate*." She lingered round the bonfire. She enjoyed the weeding in the garden which she did with an amateurishness of attitude beyond that of most amateurs even, but certain to get her root. "The whole company of dandelions is seeding by many thousands," she wrote, "and I give up the fight. I think a whole lawn of them would be the most beautiful thing in the world – but not exactly a lawn."

Such games as she could play were more than a mere relaxation – they were a saving and a mercy to her. "Croquet has set in with great success over at Rackham," she wrote, "barring the slight disadvantage of the lack of a lawn there. But we crawl under the apple trees and Lobbie makes splendid shots." "I am glad you and Father are enjoying croquet," an absent daughter wrote to her. "Do you ever beat Father? What happens? Is it like when you play draughts? Does Father have his shots twice over? Do you play croquet in gloves?" A small alarm about the house occurred when part of it was being whitewashed. The debated point as to whether it should be whitewashed or left red-brick, was decided, by the way, when my mother from a little distance saw John Drinkwater clothed for tennis standing against the house-wall, when his whiteness happened unexpectedly to serve her eye as a test of the effect! The work was done during an absence in town, and just as they were about to return to Greatham my parents realised that they had not told their man not to do the old grey stone front, assuming that he would not – as they now assumed, in their alarm, that he would. On their arrival at Greatham my mother wrote: "The front is untouched. How we craned out of the carriage, telling each other that it would be quite pretty, white. I am thankful to say that kind of resignation is not required of us. Otherwise, whitewashed Greatham looks delightful. There is some obscure memory in my mind of a 'maison blanche' some-

where in childhood abroad that makes me like it so."
Interesting visitors constantly found their way to Greatham. "Wilfrid Blunt has been here to lunch. He brought
the *New Witness*, with G. K. C.'s article on Louvain –
and me!* It is delightful about me, but too wrong-headed
about the Germans. He must have no music in him when
he says they have created nothing – music being the one
creative art, and German music the greatest that is or,
surely, can be." "We had croquet yesterday at Dimpling's, and I fell over a hoop. What is literary renown
compared with this humiliation? Yesterday the Parrishes
came to fetch your father for a delightful drive to Ports-
mouth. He is a consolation to Mr. Parrish, who complains, with a pretty American apology to me and to his
wife, that he has only women to talk to." "Yesterday Dr.
Henry Head and Mrs. Head came to luncheon and we
much enjoyed them. I find in Dr. Head a most admirable
adviser as to questions of science and our faith. No one
has ever been so valuable to me. I like his wife and find
her attractive. Dr. Head and I had our talk apart. He
had been preparing himself for it, remembering something I had said." "Sir John Ellerman and Winifred came
to tea. We talked war finance all the time, my contribution to the conversation being remarkably crude." She
loved blackberrying or the garnering of any little harvest,
delivering her spoils to the pot – admiring immensely
the skill of those who could deal with them there. "Viola
and Eleanor Farjeon are jamming in 'Shed Hall,'" she
wrote to Madeline, "and Grazia jamming at Monica's

---

* "Mrs. Meynell and the Destruction of Louvain," an article on
the indestructibility of ideas, written after reading her Essays.

(Monica's pretty things put away, and the lovely rug rolled
up). Apples and blackberry." Though her own assault
upon the dandelions might be hardly known to the dandelions, and her various harvestings almost invisible, there
was in her eldest grandchild sufficient real agricultural
energy to delight her with its wonderful efficiency. And,
in this war-time, women were working in the fields of a
neighbouring farm. When a little magazine concerned
with land-workers asked her for a contribution to its
pages she therefore had it ready in some verses called
"The Girl on the Land":

> "When have I known a boy
> Kinder than this my daughter, or his kiss
> More filial, or the clasping of his joy
> Closer than this?"
>
> Thus did a mother think;
> And yet her daughter had been long away,
> Estranged, on other business; but the link
> Was fast to-day.
>
> This mother, who was she?
> I know she was the earth, she was the land.
> Her daughter, a gay girl, toiled happily,
> Sheaves in her hand.

The delicacy of her health was becoming more apparent
and more acute. Her nights were short. She had not herself done that which she counselled a daughter to do when
she wrote: "I hope you sleep well, my ever darling. I fear
you have not yet learnt to compel agitating thoughts to
wait till daylight. But go on, and teach yourself." She

was at the mercy of cold weather. "I slowly cool at night under a mountain of blankets and with a hot bottle." In the beginning of 1915 she was writing in answer to questions: "I am going on well. I believe I am as well as I was in the summer, when I remember telling people about my rag-time heart." "I am decidedly mending. But I must mention that for the first time in a lifetime of 'wheels,' I had, the other night, wheels in both eyes at once – a record."

In July of 1916 her son-in-law, Percy Lucas, died of wounds in France. What the nature was of that life that was extinguished is described by Everard, who, though he could never again speak of him, could write this one memorial:

"Ever since I read the War Office telegram I have been trying to reconcile his death with the many signs of life he has left behind here at Greatham, and particularly over at Rackham, at the far end of this property, where his overgrown garden speaks of his past labour there, and waits in vain to be curbed and cropped again by his masterful but gentle hands. Those hands had a way of shepherding his little world of children and flowers into order, rather than forcing it. They were at once tolerant and sure, restrained and industrious; they never shirked a hard job nor made much of one. It is because I loved his hand and because he now and then laid it in affection on my shoulder that I need to write of him – because I loved him very well rather than because I knew him very well. He and I were good friends, pleased to meet, but not sedulous to make occasion. I can, to my regret, count the times when he sought me out; but for my part I cannot count the times when I made some effort to join him, or make sure of him in a family gathering. All we did together was touched with a sense of companionship – to me, pure luxury. . . . He was indifferent; but which of us can recall the ghost of a snub from him? He was exclusive; but which of us ever felt excluded? Of his affairs he said not a word to me. When he became a Catholic he told his Catholic friends no more about it than he would if he had been joining a faith alien to them. He neither sought help nor sought to give it. He held his counsel, but never reserved the smile that was kinder and better than all advice. That he was never, for an instant of time, a bore, was a characteristic of which all who met him must have been aware, for he always told one just a little less than he might have done about the things one wanted to know, and not a word about anything else.

"On rare occasions, such as on the evening before he went to France, he did, very moderately and shyly, but quite certainly, convey to us that nothing marred our relationship, that nothing was on his mind. Even though he did not care to say whether he was glad or sorry to be going, he made sure of putting those he left at their ease. I do not here allude to his care for those for whom he was bound to have a care, but to us of the second line. I know now how thorough were his arrangements for those other more important ones; I know of the letter of good-bye to his wife he left in his brother's hands, to be delivered in case he died; and I saw him classify and pack away the papers – innumerable bundles – connected with his genealogical studies and businesses – before he left Rackham. Those bundles, so practical and yet so unutterably pathetic, are witnesses to his method. Nothing – (and this is the chief thing I have to say) – nothing in his cottage, or elsewhere, carries a hint of reproach to his memory. Everything he leaves is testimony to the man we admire. No evidence of even a minor selfishness, or such small luxury as is possible to a poor man, lingers in those rooms. No derelict hobby, unreasonably indulged, is there to tidy away. He made no preserve for himself that may now be turned over to the children. There is no one niche that may be kept as his memorial. It is all a memorial to the slenderness of his needs. An able cricketer, he left only the apology for a bat in his bag; his tennis racket is made good with grocer's twine; and a brass cigarette box hangs on his wall, but is as empty as it often was when he might have wished it full. Not one bottle is there, though had there been dozens they might all have reasonably ministered to the thirsts that follow driest toil. The style of the man, rather than a care for clothes, kept him always in good looks – the ideal of an English officer. Sun-faded and rain-stained, his garments took the colour of Horsham stone – the colour of the great slab of it of his own finding which he had hoisted on a chimney high above his roof to keep the rain from beating down on his wood fire – and which now remains as the memorial of the active amateur. When he came to pack his kit, it was noticeable to the on-looker that no feature of it was extravagant. His baggage, spread open on the floor alongside a friend's, looked like a thing of many campaigns, and yet was homely, as if half of it had been gathered from a country dressing-room. In the friend's were all the new toys of warfare – a trench-dagger to be fondled and a certain swagger soldierliness about the leather trappings. But in his were no toys and only the supplies that had been pressed on him, and, for his only book, an odd volume of Borrow he had rescued from a friend's throw-outs.

"Spartan in little things, he would amuse us by snatching embers from the fire to light up with, as if he could not burn himself. I have seen him dig a thorn from the palm of his hand as unconcernedly as if he had been sharpening a pencil; and once, on a walking tour, when he tore his side on barbed wire in a way that would have taken most men to a doctor, he refused so much as sticking-plaster. No risks checked him. He had a way, when tramping across country and coming to an uninviting brook, of throwing his coat over first to make sure of following. I do not know when he made up his mind to enter the army, but I think it was in his mind from the first day of the war. When in those early months he worked double time among his genealogies, dug the upper portion of his garden with more than usual vehemence, rising early and knocking off late, and doing besides all things required of him in the house, I think he was testing the alternative, the home task, to see if it sufficed. He was more than friendly, too, to see if that were enough. But once the test failed him, he decided to enlist. He left us humbly and cheerfully. Having no thought for any of the lesser awkward chances, he refused, at the last moment, to take a reserve of money. That the main ill chance was in his mind and faced with supreme courage, we all knew, even while he bade us good-bye without a flicker of regret save such as was sufficient for the day and a temporary absence.

"Once in France he prayed for the wound that would bring him home to all he loved, but I doubt if he hoped for it. . . . He was on such terms with his men that they had all been shown the photographs he carried of his wife and children, one of which he sent home just before the advance, because he thought it too precious to risk. Having given up all else, he gave up that photograph as well – even that little paper shadow of his world. Heaven knows what the effort of it all cost him; but he died in peace, ministered to by a priest."

In the beginning of 1917 Everard himself went through the disguising process of becoming a soldier when he enlisted in the Artists' Rifles. He closed down his Serendipity Shop in Museum Street, where many a layman in soldier's uniform had liked to handle books again and to penetrate into his rare knowledge. ("Ralph Hodgson was at the Serendipity to-day," he wrote once to my mother, "full of your poems. He puts above everything 'Free Will' and 'To Sleep.' He said that he went

back to his patrol work a happier man for reading them.")
In a letter from town to Madeline in the country my
mother writes: "It is difficult to think of anything except
the war. The news is good but how sad is all good news.
Everard goes into his camp on Friday. He keeps up his
spirits well. At first the cutting-up of all his interests and
occupations which he had worked so long to establish
seemed to overpower him, though he said nothing. He
has had a little show for the family of his own old paintings. *That* would have been a career for him – a really
great one." She had constant anxiety for his health which
was not robust: "I am told that you look well though
thin. I long *deeply* to see you." He wrote of his name being
put down for a machine-gun instructorship. In a letter to
him she says: "I am hanging on to the hope of that appointment. It is never an hour out of my mind." He was made a
gun-instructor and a corporal – an odd soldier, or as
E. V. Lucas said, "perhaps the only corporal in the British
Army who has written a Life of Francis Thompson." He
was moved to Oxford, and she wrote to him: "I am deep
in the Colvin Life of Keats – a longish article for the
Dublin, and so out of practice of work that I find it very
difficult to lay hold. My sole recollections of Oxford are
those of brilliant Commemoration festivities, and of being
taken over colleges and gardens by attentive under-
graduates many and many a year ago."

In January, 1918, she wrote to Olivia: "We are much
excited to hear you are going to move to a house at Flax
Bourton. I dreamt about it last night – idiotically, of
course, but with admiration. Frederic Myers thought
that what was immortal in us and would survive death

was the mind that dreams. If so what silly asses we must look to be!" While the Sowerbys were still at Clifton she went to stay with them there, always loving those surroundings – "all radiant white, and Brabazons, and engravings." There were pleasant drives in the lovely country to inspect the new house at Flax Bourton. "Is the new house very nice?" wrote Everard from Oxford to his mother, "and where is it? I imagine it has style, if not gables; and a good larder which Lobbie will fill with Steinlens and portfolios and discarded Morris dresses; and a wine-cellar for Murray's boots and fishing-rods (so much for the ancient jest, indulged in deference to Viola who originated it); what I really want to know is something about a house where Hermia and Elizabeth will some day entertain their cousins and their cousins' children."

During this visit to Clifton she became suddenly, sharply ill. It was an illness which contained a different presence from anything that had been before; it brought to the two of her family who were with her a revelation of what the fear of loss could be. A child of hers, however grown up, could still depend utterly, for everything in life, upon her life.

Back in town she was chivvied, like the rest of Londoners, by the Zeppelins, from roof to cellar – an experience she rather enjoyed, having for danger a zest that, speaking of it in other connections, she thought must be put down to "something rash in the feminine character." She had enjoyed danger whenever it came her way. Once when Wilfrid Blunt's horses had bolted with her sitting beside him waiting for the crash which eventually came, she summed up her sensations afterwards by saying: "If life contained many such moments it would indeed be a gift beyond price." Certainly she was invigorated, unlike the rest of her family, even in the gloomy cellars to which we retreated. After the bombs had fallen a few streets away, she wrote: "Your father wished me to think the great thuds were guns, but I do know a bomb and I always shall!" "As to that old raid," she wrote in answer to an enquiry from Olivia, "I must confess there is a pleasure I cannot account for. I am glad Viola was at Greatham this time, as she does not enjoy raids as much as I do." From Greatham she wrote to Everard: "Three raids on consecutive nights sent us down here, to avoid cold vigils and short sleeps. It is beautiful here, but cold. Jack Squire and Mrs. Squire have spent the week-end with us."

The war was in the verses she continued to write. A phrase of Richard Hooker's "Lord, I owe Thee a death," prompted the lines:

> Man pays that debt with new munificence,
> Not piecemeal now, not slowly, by the old;
> Not grudgingly, by the effaced thin pence,
> But greatly, and in gold.

And some lines "To Conscripts" gives them their parallel in the "compel them to come in" of St. Luke's gospel:

> You "made a virtue of necessity"
> By divine sanction; you, the loth, the grey,
> The random, gentle, unconvinced; Oh, be
> The crowned! – you may, you may.

You, the compelled, be feasted! You, the caught,
  Be freeman of the gates that word unlocks!
Accept your victory from that unsought,
  That heavenly paradox.

Holiday time at Greatham, when the different families
left their London quarters and their schools, and flocked
there, was cheerful. With their going, there was comparative solitude. "You don't lose very much here," her
mother wrote to Madeline, "though it is very beautiful.
The hurricane never drops, and the brief snatches of sun,
which make the white cottage radiant, come between
lashing and roaring rains." At another time: "Your
father mows, and I even do a little weeding. All the
common on the right (going south) of the road is to-day
in flames in preparation for tillage. I am pleased, as I
have always longed to see England more cultivated. And
I don't like commons. I think it is a reminiscence of my
loathing of Putney and Wimbledon as a small child –
the suburbs after Italy!" A sense of solitude was what she
could bear very little of now; and the cold and damp of
the country would soon send her to the high-and-dry Flat.

It was neither at Greatham nor in London, but in the
train between the two, that the news of the armistice
came to her, conveyed by the wild hooting of the engines.

XIX

LAST POEMS

THE years after the War are full of letters to a family growing more scattered. From my father she was rarely away. Her dependence on him was not on account of his constant service, for she was never very much aware of the difference between comfort and discomfort, and had as few needs as anyone in the world – a characteristic for which Katherine Tynan supplies a beautiful reason when in writing of her she says: "She had grown up in Italy, and like many more for whom the sun has been all-sufficing, she had few yearnings after material comfort, none at all after luxury." But she depended utterly on my father for reassurance and equability and companionship. "My ever darling, keep up your invaluable heart," she wrote to him in family anxiety, pleading for her own strength from him.

She went about very little, but the impression made on those whom she did meet at this time was not an ordinary one. Sylvia Lynd wrote later, when she had been reading her poems after her death: "Reading these poems, the conviction presses in upon me that when I met the faded, remote, slowly-speaking woman, with her sweetness, keenness, and unexpected humour, I met a being whom my sceptical mind must reluctantly name a saint."

Mr. Squire has recorded his impression of her as she was then. "I, one of many who were honoured by her kindness and benefited by her wisdom, shall carry her gracious memory to the grave. There, in her London Flat or in the ample library-room of her country cottage, she would sit in her corner: a woman with unwhitened hair, very upright and calm. She still gave an impression of youth and beauty . . . a saint and a sibyl smoking a cigarette." And John Drinkwater was among those who found her as untouched by age as she would have wished to be: "It was not easy, perhaps, to think of Alice Meynell as a girl or a young woman, but it was impossible to associate her with anything of old age. Witty, generous, of the simplest and most tender humanity, there was also in her some austerity, not of personality, but of spirit, that suggested the women of Greek tragedy. I have never known anyone so ageless. Youth, maturity, and fulness of years were here strangely at one. . . . In her home, humorously intent upon the succession of family cares and gossip, she was yet the seer always. To be with her was to be at ease in the presence of a great lady. Let the talk be of what it might, she was never withdrawn or indifferent; but behind the gayest of her occasions there was a quietness of mood that gave precision and authority to everything she said. Here was a perfect example of the original as distinguished from the eccentric mind. She never startled you, but she never failed to delight your attention."

She was fortunate in her friends, with their seeing eyes.

Her poetry-writing continued, and because there was an element of argument in these poems that she wrote now, argument entered to some extent into the comments made on them, sometimes baffling that exaltation with which they were written. "No one cares for 'Reflexions,'" she said in a letter to a daughter, "though even Francis does care for the 'Rich Man,' which is an ethical study but not a poem at all. It does not matter. If no one ever cares for 'Reflexions,' it is written. And it has succeeded in *singing* the highest thought of intellectual passion and emotion of which I am capable." "I am disappointed that no one here *begins* to understand my *Mercury* poem – the antithesis between the human, local, new, single human poet, and the birds who are *general* all over the world and in all times – I should have thought nothing was plainer or more direct." "If you don't like my new poem I shall be vexed, though it is not so good as 'Shakespeare' (my one, *one* masterpiece)." My father tried to protect her from the disappointment of being ill-understood, but she could not make up her mind to elucidate anything, at least without appeal. "My dearest Everard," she wrote. "Will you do me the kindness to read the enclosed poem, and tell me whether the heading of No. 1 is sufficient (as I think) or whether the heading of No. 2 is necessary to explain the sense (as your father thinks)? I want your good and impartial opinion. It seems to me that I have given the sense, even with redundancy, in every stanza, and that the thing becomes a vain repetition with the No. 2 heading. If you get all the meaning, which is plain though rather fantastic, from No. 1, I have won; if not, your father has won. Your devoted Mother." Everard replied: "Dearest Mother, I mastered the most beautiful poem without the help of the second version. The process of mastering poems often takes me a couple of days, but this time I did it between the courses of my supper, so I suppose you win. The second title makes the position more directly intelligible, but may be open to the charge of flattening the point somewhat. But if Father really thinks it needs the explanatory heading, it probably does from some points of view. So I don't really know who wins, except that as you scored in writing the poem, it's his turn now. Your devoted Everard."

The gift of a car from Celia Tobin, who was now Mrs. Charles Clark, was the means of giving her vision after vision of the country she adored. That car, indeed, brought ploughed lands and wheat fields and trees and skies and seas flowing to her eyes, who could never see enough.

November, 1920   *Flax Bourton*

"My darling Wilfrid, – All goes well here. Last night we dined with the Hares. Mr. Hare tried to make me understand Relativity. But as you want, for that, metaphysics *and* mathematics, and I am incapable of both, it was rather a monologue. I saw Hare's magnificent Patmore collection, including the last book I gave to Coventry, with an inscription, and many other things I am glad to see in the possession of one who really cares for his poetry, and not merely for rarities. Yesterday there was a nice afternoon here. There was 'good talk,' as Dr. Johnson said. On Wednesday evening the Wollastons dined here. Lobbie sighs for the metropolis – I wish it supplied such neighbours! O darling if you could come here! I have seldom wished for anything more, much as I always wish for you. Your JOHNSON."

March, 1921   *Granville Place*

"My darling Viola, – Your father has done a review of Shane Leslie's *Life of Cardinal Manning* – a fine *Observer* article which delighted Garvin. We had a nice luncheon – Garvin, Lord ffrench, Violet Brindley, Madeleine Raoul-Duval and Maurice Healy. Garvin was very dear and affectionate. Otherwise your father and I are rather lonely. We are working hard at the *Dublin Review* for Shane, and I am going through my re-collected essays with Williams and Page and your father for the University Press. Very different counsels prevail. Do you imagine us with the smoke puffing out in the drawing-room? That is what it is doing. Alfred Noyes has paid us a long and pleasant call, and that is about all. How glad we shall be to see you back! Ever, my own Viola, your devoted mother, A. M."

The American nun who was her friend in her latest years wrote a life of Coventry Patmore's daughter Emily, who had been a nun in the same order; and to her my mother wrote:

"My dear Mother Saint Ignatius, – Thank you very cordially for your two most interesting letters. Let me say, first of all, that I should be very sorry if you left out the Ceremonial of the Clothing. Remember how new it is to lay readers, and how beautiful! But indeed I think there is nothing trivial, nothing tedious, in this second volume, except two or three of Emily's letters to Bertha; and perhaps there is too much of Henry and his going up to London. This does not annoy *me*, because I greatly admire Henry's peculiar Patmorian genius, and all connected with Coventry Patmore is important to me. But I do think these letters are too much for the book. One other complaint I have to make, but here I am wrong, no doubt. The description of Emily's spiritual suffering before her death is almost intolerable to me, though I know it ought not to be. I wonder whether it could be recorded with less emphasis? Otherwise I can have nothing but very profound and fervent admiration for this most wise and beautiful Life of a great saint. I think all the interpretation of the Psyche Odes, and all the appreciation of Patmore throughout most admirable. I have read every word with the closest interest. Surely the book cannot spare any of this, nor anything connecting Emily's soul with her Father's genius! Everything, every detail of her religious life must remain. It seemed to me that it was the first volume that needed omissions far more than this.

"The Mayfield part reminds me of what my grandfather (my mother's father) told me of his childhood at Mayfield. He used to play cricket in 'the old arches,' as the boys called the ruin. In after years he visited his old village and went into the church – 'and where I used to pitch my wicket I found an altar of God!' He was not a Catholic, but a very emotional man, and he wept so much, he said, that a nun came to comfort him. He lived to see five of my

children, his great-grand-children. Will some of those
dear Mothers of yours pray for the old man who wept
in their church? I would write at greater length, but
that I am rather ill again. My thanks and my love,
dear Mother. Most sincerely yours, Alice Meynell."

The gradually accumulating disquiet in regard to
Everard's health was a shadow on these post-war years.
One of the most charming little old shops in London, in
East Chapel Street, had become his new Serendipity
Shop, and the journalism had all been resumed. But in
1921 his unwellness was suddenly given the name of consumption. An even darker shutter than in 1914 fell now
on his plans, and, having to make a quick dispersal of his
infinite treasure, he packed up all the things that taste
and knowledge and research and discovery had made a
part of his very self. With his wife and four small children
he sailed for America in July 1921.

July 1921   *Greatham*
"My dearest Everard, – Your first American letter
reached us yesterday, giving I cannot tell you how
much joy, for it sounded so happy. I confess that –
Celia's kindness apart – I am glad your cure is to be
in the East, or rather well about the middle of the
continent, rather than near an ocean. American air
is 'dry' because it is as far inland as you can well get
on this globe. . . .
"We are beginning to gather for the holidays. . . .
Francis and Hilda held their house-warming on
Sunday. Games and bathing in the morning, music

in the afternoon and an evening banquet. I was not quite well enough for the latter, but greatly enjoyed John Goss's singing of the songs I had so much admired at Mrs. Craies': Ben Jonson's 'Charis' Triumph,' which I believe (on technical grounds of metre) he wrote to the music – that is, the music was first. There were also several old English songs, and one Russian, very exciting. A pretty cheapish Irish thing they told me was Danish, to cheat my prejudices.

"I must not forget to tell you of Francis's blue paint. On the floor it is curiously inappropriate. The floors of human dwellings are four – marble, stone, brick, wood. All the very antithesis of blue. Give my love to Grazia and the little ones. Ever, my darling, your devoted mother, A. M."

Sept. 1921   *Greatham*

"My dearest Everard, – Your letters are read and re-read. I wish I had as interesting things to write to you. You know what the holidays are here – very joyful and more so than ever this year with its perpetual sunshine, and bathing for everyone. Cameron Rogers has paid us a long and delightful visit. And for part of the time we had his equally nice cousin Shan Sedgwick. Now these two would really do a great deal to serve me, and they promise me all kinds of things if I should go to America. I need hardly say that the desire to see you, and to belie the fear I had, when you left Greatham, that my weak health and other disabilities might make our reunion very uncertain, has had a great part in my desire to accept an invitation to give a lecturing tour. Your father thinks the idea is mad. But I may be heard exercising my voice in the garden. It is as strong as ever. I will let you know what is finally decided. When the agents first asked me, I thought I was too old and ill, and now they are asking me again I don't think so, – which I suppose proves that I *am*.

"My little book (*The Second Person Singular*) is in the printers' hands at last. I have made many changes. When Viola tells me that an essay is confused or obscure, I know it *is*. Ten of the twenty essays, as they now stand, are up to my little high-water mark, and the other ten are not contemptible second-class. Could you, I wonder, go with me on my lecture-tour? Would it not tend to further your book-interests in America? I made a decent sum when I was much less known than I am now. I would have a good lecture – just one, to be given in each town. Well, if I could *look* better – for that is important in the States – I think I should not hesitate. Your devoted mother, A. M."

Sept. 1921   *Greatham*
". . . I don't grumble for letters during your cure. I should say that irresponsibility was almost as salutary as sunshine. All the families have now left Greatham, more or less in tears; and we are indeed elderly and lonely, except for interesting visitors who have rather abounded."

Oct. 1921
". . . I have to-day at last decided against my dear lecture-tour and visit to you. I am really not well

enough for unusual exertion. (Nothing to be alarmed at.) I have sent Squire a *Mercury* poem; he says 'how strange and lovely a poem!' . . ."

Oct. 1921

"You must not again write a letter when you should be lying flat in the sun. I don't expect it. But what the deuce becomes of the papers we regularly send? By a quite recent letter of yours I find you still in receipt of a solitary *Punch*! Regular *New Statesmen, Nations,* and *Times Lit. Sups.* went to you. It is delightful to get your letters, and as they go round the family, one letter does duty; and you must not tire yourself.

"The cold has arrived at last, and I think another week will see us in town. Your Aunt Mimi has come to town for a month, bringing the MS. of her *Reminiscences*. Everyone is writing such. I know hers will be very well done. It cannot be possible for her to tell the whole truth about her immense *national* success with her first battle-pictures. It would sound exaggerated. But it could not be exaggerated. Viola is just arriving in with a friend, one of the Levanto group, and I must stop a letter so dull that you cannot wish it longer. So you think of sticking to the East. You know best, on the spot. Oh get well, my ever dearest, and let me cherish the hope of your not too indefinite return."

Nov. 1921   *Granville Place*

"Here we are in deep frost – but nothing like yours. I wonder what you have decided to do for the real winter. I cannot tell you how happy I was to hear the good news about the behaviour of your temperature.

"We came up the day before yesterday in the car, starting in bright sunshine, and drawing by degrees into mist, white fog, yellow fog, brown fog, almost impenetrable. Your father was rather depressed by the climate, but was cheered later by the sudden arrival of William Andrew Mackenzie, who has been administering Save the Children funds in Moscow and Vienna and other unhappy places. He had a thousand things to say and said them nearly all in an hour before he left for Rome. But I had still a thousand questions to ask.

"Our little Sylvia is making fair progress from a new operation. Her leg is being straightened, which does not mean that it will be a good bendable knee, of course, but her walk will be quite different, we hope. She lies in a splendid house in Park Lane, through E. V.'s kindness, and is thoroughly enjoying her luxuries and her post. E. V. writes daily, and Murray and Lobbie send her constant packets. I played chess with her yesterday, which she loves.

"I am sending you a copy of my little book. It will probably be published in ten days or so. Squire has dedicated to me his Anthology of poems by women, and they wired to ask me to review it in the *Observer*, which I did."

December 1921   *Granville Place*
". . . Lady Clementine Waring brought us a young man, Oliver Baldwin, who wanted to meet

Francis, so I got them to make acquaintance at dinner. Baldwin was in Russia, and then fighting against the Turks, with the Armenian Army, imprisoned and condemned to be shot, then released. He is only twenty-two, and beautiful to look at. He is connected with Burne Jones's family, and is wonderfully like, not Burne Jones, but Burne Jones's Madonna! – the one in Wilfrid Blunt's Hall.

"We are to go to Greatham for the great Christmas gathering. Garvin asked me for a Christmas poem, which I sent him, for the *Observer*. I was so happy to hear of dear Grazia's singing. How my heart is with you!"

Jan. 12, 1922   *Greatham*

"It is long since I wrote to you, though I have wished Grazia a tardy happy New Year, in thanking her for her dear sweet present. The account of her happiness, and the children's, and of little Wilfrid and Vivian 'on the alter' (I quote from little Alice's letter to Viola) goes far to reconcile me to the parting that I found so hard. . . . Did you get my little book? The binders struck work, and the book-shops – Bumpus's at any rate – sold all their copies, so I lost all the further benefit of the Christmas sales.

"An excitement here has been a great New Year children's party at the Leconfields'. It was a wonderful affair in the great suites of galleries, and the guests were three hundred. Olivia's two in their patchwork frocks were the greatest success. Violet Leconfield has been to see us since.

"Paper-chases are the great game at Greatham now. They career for miles over the country."

With the constantly new-coming young people at Greatham she might have been supposed, in her quietness, to have little to do; but that the impression she made on them was their chief impression is shown in one of their letters:

January, 1922   *Hurlingham*

"My dearest Mrs. Meynell, – In this letter I can only send you my love. I am unable to express or think of anything else, except perhaps the individual parts of which it is composed. It was so perfect to be with you; I can never quite recover from the wonder of coming into a room and finding you there. Do you remember how Donald Goring wrote to Monica telling her how perfectly he had enjoyed his time there, and describing as an instance of it one day when he and some others were gathered on the grass outside the library door, and suddenly you came and said 'Come along in, all of you!'? We laughed a little when it was read out, but to Donald that was his climax; and it is that sense of climax which I feel, though neither he nor I are able to express it. But it is always connected with you.

"I can envy no one. Only myself at Greatham is inexpressibly envied by myself elsewhere. Your loving Anne."

Other letters at this time were written by my mother to her friend Aubone Hare at Flax Bourton. "I have received charming letters as usual from Mr. Hare and his sister," she wrote to Olivia. "To you I owe a very happy friendship." That same literary ardour which, in her, made her the exciting friend of a much younger man, in him, made him an authority she could appeal to. She admired his own verses. "I want to say to you," she wrote, "that I hate to seem to dispose, approve or adjudge, when I am really keeping my own lowly place in regard to what you write and think." They exchanged their opinions: "Middleton Murry is *fine!*" she wrote. "He might with advantage be shorter and simpler over the excellent thought he has, but how masterly, for instance, is his defence of realistic fiction as a really creative work! But he should, when necessary, be stronger and angrier than he ever is. He lets off Swinburne's pocket vocabulary as a 'half-automatic' use of a great thing, not perceiving how deep down in that man's soul lay the ready-made. It was not only verbal. – I don't want any man to stand between me and Cleopatra. I even blame myself for presuming to stand between my reader and Antony, as I have done." (She had written once on this subject: "Thoughts about Shakespeare cannot pretend to be new. Therefore it is enough that the thoughts of us all about him should be practised rather than spoken.") "As to Dante I should tremble to say what I really think. Dante in passages, all right! But Dante as a thinker?" They cleared up doubtful technicalities. "On second thoughts," she wrote, "I do think that *rhythms* (the plural) is hardly possible as a monosyllable. But I still think it is impossible as a dissyllable. Therefore I must conclude that it is not for verse. I am sorry. In the singular it is for verse, requiring great care and due rank and place as a monosyllable. A very full monosyllable duly placed, duly accompanied, is delightful to my ear." After reading some verses of his, she wrote: "I admire the imagination, though before the metaphysics I am respectfully ignorant. You know my limitations. If I were younger I think I should set to work and find my way in."

To another friend, Professor Albert Cock, in letters of this time, she had to make and remake the same disclaimers: "I think I have told you how incapable I am of philosophy – indeed of theology in any philosophical sense. The great things you suggest in your letter are abysses into which I fear to look. I read the words, but the thoughts terrify me. You must have patience with my inabilities. I am doing my trivial work – editing and correcting re-collected essays, suggested by the Oxford University Press. I find I am quite pleased to have some of them dug up by such diligent and judicious searchers. One on Gibbon may, I think, amuse you." "I have read and re-read your letter and thought over it. But you have never realised how incapable I am of philosophy. I really cannot answer your questions. I can only say that when I find a thought worthy of poetry I immediately give thanks for it, and also for such expression as I may have achieved. But this is not at all subtle, and not very conscious. I am afraid that I don't refer (as you do) all beauty to the 'First and only Fair.' I merely refer what I may either write or read to the relative beauty of literature. A Jesuit long ago told me that I alighted and settled on mere 'participations.' No doubt I disappoint you."

But politics and the practice of right and wrong were

things of which she was not afraid to speak. "As far as I know Bolshevism," she said in a letter to Olivia, "it is heretical in the practice of right and wrong. I don't at all allow that we have 'liberty' to think what we happen to choose as to right and wrong. I saw, when I was very young, that a guide in morals was even more necessary than a guide in faith. It was for this I joined the Church. Other Christian societies may legislate, but the Church *administers* legislation. Thus she is practically indispensable. I may say that I hold the administration of morals to be of such vital importance that for its sake I accepted, and now accept, dogma in matters of faith – to the last letter. To make my preachment clearer: Right and Wrong (morals) are the most important, or the only important, things men know or can know. Everything depends on them. Christian morality is infinitely the greatest of moralities. This we know by our own sense and intellect, without other guidance. The Church administers that morality, as no other sect does or can do, by means of moral theology. The world is far from living up to that ideal, but it is the only ideal worth living up to. . . . As to the 'divine' teachings of the Genesis allegory, I cannot withdraw that word. I have to remember that all the morality worth having – the morality that led on to Christianity – had its origin in that parable."

From Flax Bourton she wrote, in February 1922: "My darling Viola, – I am stupidly in two minds whether to go home on Thursday so as to have a little more time with you, or by the early train on Saturday. I always find it difficult to say No to pleading such as Lobbie's. She thinks I shall always be less with her than with you, even when you are married. That is true. You are at any rate in my heart of hearts now and while I live. Ever my own darling. Your mother, A. M."

February 1922   *Flax Bourton*

"My darling Viola, – Get all your business done so that we may gather together all Saturday and Sunday and Monday.

"I whistled before I was out of the wood when I said my cold was better. It is all back, with three recurrences of that trouble which sent your father out in London in the small hours of the morning looking for a doctor's doorplate. But these three together hardly equalled that one.

"If I wanted 'appreciation' I got *too* much yesterday when Green-Armytage came. He was, however, delightful and wise about Chesterton and other writers. To-morrow we are to meet his friend, Dr. Edridge, who is to lecture on me to Bristol University students. I would prefer, in the case of such enthusiasts as these, to remain unseen, for fear they should say (mentally) 'Oh!' – or words to that effect!

"My Viola, I am fortunate in having had so much of you all your life. Your devoted mother, A. M."

March 1922   *Granville Place*

"My dearest Everard, – You had not been quite so well when you last wrote to one of us, but were better. That, I trust, continues? You must never write when you ought to be resting completely, eager as I am for news.

"I met Jack Squire for a few minutes at Lady Astor's, and he gave me accounts of your progress, and had been much impressed by the excellence and beauty of your cure-place. My meeting with him was at a great party 'to meet Mr. Arthur Balfour,' and we took Lobbie to it. 'Miss Meynell,' was on the invitation, and, as it was the evening of Viola's marriage, Lobbie was as much Miss Meynell as she, and really enjoyed the evening and the celebrities, from the Prime Minister to Lytton Strachey. I liked Lady Astor very much; she is frank, sweet, friendly, talkative, and charming to look at. She told me of her principle in public life – to keep self out of it, and hope in God only. Arthur Balfour did not, I think, remember me or perhaps catch my name. My evening was made very happy by Mrs. Alfred Lyttelton who brought up friend after friend to introduce to me and quoted from my little book with great sweetness. Your devoted mother, A. M."

May 1922   *Flax Bourton*

"My darling Viola, – I prize your little letters, and I don't expect more because I know you are very busy. But I do enjoy anything – even a postcard.

"It is a joy that you and Francis and Green-Armytage and Dr. Edridge care for my three last poems. Francis wired 'Marvellous poems the best of your best.' I tell you this because I want you to share my pleasure, or rather my consolations which I need.

"I have had a noble time with dear Lobbie and Murray and the most gloriously beautiful country in the world. Yes, but for the Mediterranean not being about, I think the very most beautiful. I wish the leaves were not in such a deuce of a hurry to come out. But the steep rocks, the ravines full of slender trees! We nearly fell off a neighbour's garden into the view yesterday.

"I do so long to see you, dearest. Hare is coming to talk commas, so I must stop. Lobbie is looking splendid. Wearing – oh, lots of things. Your devoted mother, A. M."

The arrival of Everard's tidings from America, now from hospital, always brought her momentary happiness in an unhappy parting:

June 1922   *Perrysburg, U.S.A.*

"Dearest Mother, – It is a radiant evening, almost Roman or of Greatham. It makes me wonder if you are playing croquet, and if you are still the slim champion of the tufty lawn. I play chess nearly every evening with a German clerk, Bill Huebsch. I make him ashamed, much as I did you, about picking off my pieces, and have almost got him trained not to. He beats me, however, in almost the same way as you did, about three times in four. I look at him across the board and wonder if it means that your mind and his are alike. I have not yet found poems in him! . . .

"I was interested to hear your news and views of the R.A. I agree without going, which suits me admirably. I have been reading – almost nothing! I would like an occasional book. What a pleasant human document is Bernard Barton's *Life and Letters* which I bought lately from a catalogue in imitation of a life-long habit of Father's, who buys it whenever he sees it on a bookstall. B. B. was quite a rare old bird.

"I still enjoy the sun, and it does me good even if it has not performed the miracle I had expected and arranged for. I am one of the exhibition brown men now: visiting doctors are brought up to me and told I was once white. . . .

"Here, in hospital, where my daily and intimate companions are moulders, barbers, professional base-ball players, taxi-drivers, lawyers and mechanical draftsmen, I find that profession and what we in England would call standing, count for nothing. My best friend, a man with a heart of gold and the soul of a gentleman, is an ex-bar-tender (as they call public-house attendants) with the typical flat-footed walk of a waiter. He satisfies all the demands I can make on a friend. I love him; his name is George Kraft. He has a lame wife, also consumptive and in hospital. Amongst these people I cannot keep a sense of the value of class. It has no existence in an institution like this, and I am so far from feeling the lack of it that I may say I have never before been possessed with such peace of mind. To get health of mind is, I suppose, the compensation for losing health of body. . . .

"I set down the things I see here in a sort of diary, which I think might get into print some day, save for the difficulty of its being too personal and intimate. Have you a repulsion for all diaries, or would you

334

sanction one that was craftily edited so as to camou-
flage the egoism?

"Your exquisite poem in *The Mercury* arrived to-
day. Those last two of yours have been absolutely
tip-top. Your devoted son, EVERARD."

August 1922   *Greatham*

"My dearest Everard, – . . . Hard work has
stopped my letter-writing lately – also some unwellness. We went to town that I might see a doctor, and
I am gaining by his treatment. He did not take a
gloomy view of me.

"The work is an Anthology for Children. There are
at least a dozen going round, but Collins, a school-
publisher, seemed to think one from me was wanted,
so I am doing it. It cheers me to think that it will
enable me to make you a little present.

"Miss Tuell, a Wellesley (New England) professor
who has actually come to England on purpose to
study my various works for the thesis for her degree,
we have asked to stay with us here.

"I want details of your progress, my dearest.

"I enclose a cheque for £300, with my great love.
This includes the whole earnings of my *Second Person
Singular* so far – and £75 that I am to receive for my
Child's Anthology by Christmas. Dearest, I wish my
love could have a richer expression. Your devoted
mother, A. M."

Among those newly written poems of hers which she
speaks of with so much intensity, and into which, one

might think, the strength passed that was leaving her otherwise, was one of which she said: "It was written in compassion for someone who has had a duller life than anyone ought to have." It is called "A comparison in a seaside field," and in it a woman whom nothing could deprive of her youth, yet whose youth had been without joy, is compared with a poor, seaside field which has its June, but only negligible flowers. Another poem is suggested by her realisation of having passed her own father's age. ("The mystery of Time," said Mr. Squire, writing of her, "governed much of her meditations":)

> A wilder prank and plot
>   Time soon will promise, threaten, offering me
> Impossible things that Nature suffers not –
>   A daughter's riper mind, a child's seniority.
>
> O, by my filial tears
>   Mourned all too young, Father! On this my head
> Time yet will force at last the longer years,
>   Claiming some strange respect for me from you,
>   the dead.
>
> Nay, nay! Too new to know
>   Time's conjuring is, too great to understand,
> Memory has not died; it leaves me so –
>   Leaning a fading brow on your unfaded hand.

Another is of rivers, travelling, always unknown and but just arrived, "young in their ancient beds":

> For they are new, they are fresh; there's no surprise
>   Like theirs on earth. O strange for evermore!
> This moment's Tiber with his shining eyes
>   Never saw Rome before.

A poem about "A Certain Rich Man" of the gospel story links the two facts of his being first unwilling to share his riches, but secondly unwilling to share his torments with his five brethren:

> Thou wouldst not part thy spoil
> Gained from the beggar's want, the weakling's toil,
> Nor spare a jot of sumptuousness or state
> For Lazarus at the gate.

> And in the appalling night
> Of expiation, as in day's delight,
> Thou heldst thy niggard hand; it would not share
> One hour of thy despair.

> Those five – thy prayer for them!
> O generous! Who, condemned, wouldst not condemn,
> Whose ultimate human greatness proved thee so
> A miser of thy woe.

Another poem, quoting De Quincey's "Everlasting farewells! and again, and yet again, everlasting farewells!" finds that word "farewells" too mild for so impassioned and despairing a meaning:

> 'Farewells!' O, what a word!
> Denying this agony, denying the affrights,
> Denying all De Quincey spoke or heard
> In the infernal sadness of his nights.

> How mend these strange 'farewells'?
> 'Vale'? 'Addio'? 'Leb' wohl'? Not one but seems
> A tranquil refutation; tolling bells
> That yet withhold the terror of his dreams.

The love of poetry itself, and of nature, and of religion

were chiefly the subjects of those poems – subjects that seemed to have encountered in her not a new lover but a new love. "The spirit of that 'Farewell' that cannot be repeated," wrote Mr. Garvin, "breathes very gently, solemnly, through these poems: they are poems of adieu – more implied than expressed, and without a tremor of self-pathos. Only amidst the world and its many things, beloved or grievous, she looks and listens as one who may not again; and in this final mood, with every glance, at every accent, the most familiar of her habitual interests and joys awaken in her strange thoughts and suggest singular analogies brought as it were from the furthest confines of the mind. It is a quality of discovering thought; profound remote reverie; infinite delicacy of discernment; with the extraordinary spiritual acumen and moral sureness of a fixed inviolate soul. Inevitably, as with all mortal faculty so long prolonged, there is a change. That only alchemy of poetic genius – the magic ardour of the blood – is gone. There is less beauty of external form, imaginative picture, and controlled emotion. Her colour is changed wholly into light. The arrowy feeling, looking forward, is turned into an acutely sensitive fortitude. . . ."

All these last poems, almost crowded into a little time, form an important part of her whole work, and drew an important mass of criticism. "Her feelings," said the *Times*, "spring from her mind, her thoughts from her heart. There is grief but no melancholy; feeling that owes nothing to a mere 'fineness'; thought never merely curious; an imagination intent not on trying its wings but on reaching its goal." And the *New Statesman* wrote:

"She has a curious intimacy with tremendous things, a touch at once adoring and familiar."

The search suggested, and partly made, by the Oxford University Press through the masses of her industrious prose that had never been reprinted, resulted, after her revision, in a book that may be thought her best. *The Second Person Singular* appeared at the end of 1921, a perfect summary of her thought and style. It has her Italy, and her landscape, in which are "ancient coloured terraces, coloured as a few masterly landscapes are painted, so that a little of the canvas, or a little of the view, might be set in a ring and worn as a jewel; . . . mere walls of rough houses too, of which, in their place in the landscape, pieces might be set as jewels." It is a landscape full of the Alps, and of waterfalls that are "recognised at each return of the traveller, where they drop, hushed by their distance as much as by the noisy train. There is one, for instance, seen for but a moment, that has so long a fall as to grow weak and to swing in all the light winds":

"They are not only the traffic and the mission of their mountains, the coursing of that cold blood and the pulse of the rock, but they carry the mountain Spirit far out. There is no country under mountains but has its quietness awakened by wilder rivers than other lands are watered by. When the range is out of sight, the torrents are still hasty, cataract below cataract, shallow and clear, quick from the impulse of water-falls. . . . Not all waterfalls make the conspicuous show of the cascades that take their leap from the rocks. In early autumn there is nothing fresher or sweeter than the minute, perpetual waterfall that hides in moss and undergrowth, and slips everywhere from the Alps. The air is nowhere silent, and hardly a blade of grass is unstirred by the delicate thrill of water. Without paths it drops minutely and invisibly into the lakes, the gentlest of all the signs of the barren and lofty snow."

Her literary judgments are represented here. Thomas Lovell Beddoes, among others, is approached with a kind of respect which is only to decide, however, as it turns out, the exact way in which he should be forgotten:

"There are some writers whom the judicious reader forgets by name with the express intention of clearing them away. For oblivion is not always a slovenly thing. It is sometimes directed with no slight care, and has regard to all the distinctive characteristics of the one to be forgotten, effacing him with every possible precision, good aim, and attention. Others, again, it is more convenient to forget in little companies, according to their 'school'; and there is no great precision necessary for picking them off. You shoot, as it were, 'into the brown' for they go close-ranked.

"Of Beddoes it must be said that if he is to be virtually forgotten – and there is hardly a doubt as to that – the act has to be a single and separate one. And yet this measure of distinction is not quite fairly come by. He gains it chiefly because he wrote Elizabethan tragedy in the early nineteenth century, and so gained a kind of isolation. But inasmuch as he wrote couplets to be like Keats, and lyrics to be like Shelley, he might disappear with a batch, and need give no trouble."

Leigh Hunt, too, is summoned to judgment in these pages for his excessive literary amiability:

"It is an early nineteenth-century attempt at the favour and prettiness of the Elizabethans, with an absolute rejection of the Elizabethan 'horrors.' Yet without 'horrors,' without a real murder among the dances, without royal madness embowered, and noble distraction wearing flowers, without the wild convention, without the noble spirit, wilder than nature – a barbaric artifice out-facing nature – what were the Elizabethan favour and prettiness worth? Nay, they would never have been there but to adorn frightful deeds. The men of a hundred years ago took one part and left the other, and were delighted in the civilised choice they had the grace – as they held it – to make, in a tolerant rebuke, in a liberal approval, of the great part."

It seems fitting that this last book should contain, too, essays on George Meredith's work, and on Coventry Patmore's. Of Coventry Patmore she would never have said her last word while she still lived; and this that was actually the last is in the height of her proud certainty. She quotes lines of his. "Every true lover of poetry knows that when he cites great lines it is not the poetry but the hearer that is to be judged."

In the essay itself called *The Second Person Singular*, she says: "Why it is that some, at least, of the civilised peoples in the inevitable evolution of things, should tend to become poor, careless, and inexact grammarians it is hard to understand. The fact is, needless to say, well enough known. Some of the French missionaries, students of American-Indian languages, have astonished us with reports of the enormous vocabularies and the scientific order of those tongues. . . . Not only the tactics of Grammar, but an innumerable variety of words is theirs, so that a speaker might hardly name a common thing without a conscious play of choice." It is chiefly among English races that she finds the tendency to make one word run errands and serve many purposes: "None but ourselves have been so impatient as to put out of common use the second person singular." Even the Quakers who restored it had not time for its inflexions. But in this essay that touches on the comparative riches and poverty of Tongues it is in French that she is most conscious of deprivations, and in the last words of this book, the last words of all her published prose, she names one loss to France and our advantage over her:

"It lacks also negatives worth having, making shift with half-hearted particles or the grotesquely insufficient *peu*. *Peu* is the only negative for some of the most energetic adjectives. Meanwhile we have our profound and powerful particle, in our 'undone,' 'unloved,' 'unforgiven,' the 'un' that summons in order that it may banish, and keeps the living word present to hear sentence and denial, showing the word 'unloved' to be no less than archangel ruined."

XX

THE END

THE making of an Anthology for the young reader was a task to enjoy; and, during the making of it, she seldom lacked the young reader, in the shape of a grandchild, to try out a poem on. In the September of 1922 my father and some others of the family were away for a short time. "I have had only one heart-night," she wrote to my father, "quite a mild one in comparison with that one in town, which I shudder to remember. I am, thank God, writing verse." "Two more dreary days and then your coming! My darling Dimpling and her three left Greatham early this morning. I can never tell you what she has been to me. She has indeed made all the difference here."

She made now a list of the lately-written poems which had not yet gone into book form, and gave it to a friend who greatly admired these poems and who was at hand, writing on it: "List of Poems to be published in book form (if occasion occurs posthumously). No others. If I have to add new ones I will place them also in the hands of Professor Albert Cock. I don't leave this to my husband because I don't want to talk to him of my decease." A supplement to the list was written after an interval of time, and enclosed in a note from Madeline which said:

"Mother is not well. She asks me to send you this. You will understand what these additions are for."

She was failing, but she had another life besides this failing one. Her love of charity and truth and honour could be felt closer than ever to the daily words and acts – one life now almost effacing another. To be beside her in church was to be aware of her breathless adoration and her tears. It was in London that she became very ill; and, during week after week of her lying in bed, hope could be concerned only with her spiritual comfort, or with such little good as the alleviation of an hour, or sleep, or some reading enjoyed. Books of humour that in attending on death-beds do greater work than some greater books, attended hers, and her comment was: "We may be proud in England of the quality of popular humour. In what other country could a writer like Jacobs give us the humour of the docks, and the fun all be innocent fun?"

From her children she tried to withdraw before her end, while they could still see only what she wished should be remembered. She was always sensitive about her looks, always revolted against nature's treatment of the aged and the ageing, and now her revolt was for the dying. With her children she had always preserved the privacy and formality of a stranger in her personal things, so that even in all the crowded life of their childhood they had never once seen her unfinished or unprepared. Now, when most consciousness left her, she was still conscious of these defences of her personal dignity. Lying on this bed, she turned away her face from her son, Francis, when he visited her, and, putting out her hand, said:

"He shall have 'my bluest veins to kiss.' O how wonderful of Shakespeare to have thought of making her say that!"

After an illness of seven weeks she died at dawn on November 27th, 1922, while asleep. She had wished to live, when she knew there was danger, as passionately as if she had been a young girl, but she was able to say towards the end: "This is not tragic. I am happy."

INDEX

EDEN, HELEN PARRY, 244
Edridge, Dr., 331, 332
Elder, Mrs., 190, 191
Elgar, Sir Edward, 237
Ellerman, Sir John, and Winifred, 304
Elmslie, Dr., 291
Exaggeration, 63, 113

FARJEON, ELEANOR, 304
ffrench, Lord, 319
Fields, Mrs., 192
Fitzpatrick, Sir Charles, 245
Freeman, John, 258
Fullerton, Lady Georgiana, 49

GARDNER, MAJOR FITZROY, 144
Gardner, Mrs., 192
Garvin, J. L., 88, 229, 251, 281, 319, 326, 338
Gibbon, 162, 164, 329
Gibson, Mrs. Dana, 172
Gill, Eric, 273
Gosse, Sir Edmund, 210, 283
Grahame, Kenneth, 74
Grainger, Percy, 246
Granet, Mrs., 231, 233
Gray's *Elegy*, 151
Green-Armytage, 331, 332

HAMBROUGH, Mrs., 35
Hamilton, Sir Ian and Lady, 245
Hardy, Thomas, 234, 282, 283
Hare, Mr. and Mrs. Aubone, 318, 327
Harland, Henry, 73
Harraden, Beatrice, 156
Hart-Davis, Sibyl, 245
Head, Mrs. Cameron, 227
Head, Sir Henry, 304
Healy, Maurice, 319
Henley, W. E., 72, 113, 140, 183

Herbert of Lea, Lady, 49
Hind, Charles Lewis, 144, 231
Hodgson, Ralph, 310
Holmes, Oliver Wendell, 29, 213
Housman, A. E., 217
Housman, Laurence, 265
Howells, W. D., 170, 236
Hudson, W. H., 68
Hunter, Mrs. Charles, 216, 229, 245
Hyde, William, 159

ITALY, the Thompsons in, 13, 14, 58, 314, 315; revisited by A. M., 225, 226, 235, 238, 276; in her last poems, 339

JACOBS, W. W., 344
James, Henry, 130, 216
Jeune, Lady, 116
Jewish Women's Club, San Francisco, 183
John, Augustus, 218
Johnson, Lionel, 68, 145
Johnson, Samuel, 76, 133, 207, 259, 292-3, 318

KEY, ELLEN, 289
Kipling, Rudyard, 74, 100, 169, 236, 282

LANG, ANDREW, 246
Laureateship, the, 120, 281
Leconfield, Lady, 326
Le Gallienne, Richard, 81, 143
Leighton, Lord, 112, 141
Leslie, Shane, 301, 319
Lipton, Sir Thomas, 172, 177
Lockhart, Father William, 59, 60
Lowell, J. Russell, 75, 76
Lucas, E. V., 270, 311, 325
Lucas, Percy, 243, 249, 270, 276, 289, 302, 306

INDEX